Getting Started with Oracle SOA Suite 11*g* R1 – A Hands-On Tutorial

Fast track your SOA adoption—Build a service-oriented composite application in just hours!

Heidi Buelow

Manas Deb

Jayaram Kasi

Demed L'Her

Prasen Palvankar

BIRMINGHAM - MUMBAI

Getting Started with Oracle SOA Suite 11g R1 – A Hands-On Tutorial

First published: September 2009

Production Reference: 1230909

Published by Packt Publishing Ltd.
32 Lincoln Road
Olton
Birmingham, B27 6PA, UK.

ISBN 978-1-847199-78-2

www.packtpub.com

Cover Image by Parag Kadam (paragvkadam@gmail.com)

Credits

Authors

Heidi Buelow

Manas Deb

Jayaram Kasi

Demed L'Her

Prasen Palvankar

Acquisition Editor

James Lumsden

Technical Editor

Aanchal Kumar

Indexer

Hemangini Bari

Editorial Team Leader

Abhijeet Deobhakta

Proofreader

Chris Smith

Graphics

Nilesh Mohite

Production Coordinator

Dolly Dasilva

Cover Work

Dolly Dasilva

Foreword

On July 1, 2009 Oracle announced the 11gR1 release of Fusion Middleware of which SOA Suite is a key part. Service-oriented architecture (SOA), business process management (BPM), event-driven architecture (EDA), and related technologies are at the heart of modern enterprise software solutions aimed at providing greater business agility and adaptability. So far SOA and BPM enabling tools have focused mainly on modularizing applications and IT functionalities using services encapsulation, leaving a major gap when it comes to composing real-life business applications from them and managing their entire life cycle. SOA Suite 11g fills this gap in the context of services, processes, and events, as does the entire Fusion Middleware platform in a broader middleware context.

With Fusion Middleware 11g release, Oracle continues to extend the guiding principles behind its Fusion products: *complete*, *integrated*, *open*, and *best-of-breed*. Specifically, for SOA Suite 11g this amounts to a unified platform with all the tools that are necessary to work with services, processes, and events, from conception through development and deployment to operational and change management so as to provide very high developer productivity and operational ease. This also means that all SOA Suite components continue to be based on industry standards, remain *hot-pluggable* to provide best-in-the-industry interoperability in heterogeneous technology environments, and while the SOA Suite components are well integrated, each of them continues to lead the market in its features and performance. Keeping the goal of enablement of business excellence in mind, SOA Suite 11g has been designed to help produce business applications quickly and run them efficiently, adapt these applications easily when business changes demand, manage and monitor these applications, and drastically reduce the gaps in business-IT interactions.

BPM, SOA, and integration solutions involve connection to applications, services, system-level automation, human workflows, document-processing workflows, business rules, and B2B. They also involve security policies, exception handling, and mediation of service requests. These applications are often deployed as distributed applications. To get the maximum productivity and value from these integration solution projects, in addition to a good product, you need a good understanding of the applicable software tools. To help you in understanding the tools better, the SOA Suite product management team has put together this getting-started tutorial.

The authors have had first-hand experience in creating, delivering, and rolling-out SOA Suite 11gR1 training programs internally and externally to partners and customers. This book takes a divide-and-conquer approach and builds up a non-trivial service-oriented composite application in a step-by-step fashion so that it is easy for the reader to follow and appreciate the workings of the SOA Suite product. If your goal is to exploit SOA and related paradigms to deliver business value quickly, this book will put you on the right track. SOA Suite 11g is a result of a lot of careful design and hard work by one of the best software product teams in the industry. It is a best-in-class product and I hope that you will enjoy working with it.

Amlan Debnath
Senior Vice President,
Product Development
Oracle Corporation

About the Authors

Heidi Buelow is a product manager with Oracle and is responsible for Oracle SOA Suite programs such as beta and technical previews. Heidi joined Oracle in 2006, after having spent the previous 10 years as Chief Application Architect with a startup developing a Business Process Management engine, developer toolset, and application framework. Heidi started her career as a software developer at Xerox, working on the Xerox Network Services and Star Workstation products where she first learned to appreciate object-oriented and services-oriented technologies. She holds a Bachelor of Science degree in Computer Science from the University of Southern California.

Manas Deb is a senior director in the Fusion Middleware/SOA, BPM, Governance Suites Product Group at Oracle HQ. He currently leads outbound product management and many strategic engagement initiatives for Oracle's SOA, BPM, and Governance solutions, worldwide. He is also responsible for Oracle/HQ-based SOA Methodology initiatives. Manas has worked in the software industry for over twenty years, most of which was spent in software product management/marketing and on architecting; he has also led a wide variety of enterprise-level application development and business integration projects in a wide variety of industries. A graduate of the Indian Institute of Technology (KGP), Manas attended post-graduate studies at the University of Texas at Austin. He received his PhD in an inter-disciplinary program comprising Computer Science, Applied Mathematics, and Engineering. Manas also has an MBA with specialization in international business.

Jayaram Kasi is a product manager with Oracle, and focuses on SOA technologies. Before that, he had been a software architect for 20 years working on relational database kernels at HP, OLTP monitors based on DCE at HP, High Availability at HP, ECommerce Infrastructure at Commerce One, and Enterprise Service Bus at BEA. Jayaram has a Bachelor of Science degree in electrical engineering from the Indian Institute of Technology, and a Master of Science in electrical engineering from the University of Hawaii.

Demed L'Her is Director of Product Management at Oracle, where he is responsible for the Oracle SOA Suite. He has been with Oracle since 2006, focusing on ESB, JMS, and next-generation SOA platforms. Before joining Oracle, Demed spent eight years with TIBCO Software, a pioneer in electronic trading, message-oriented middleware, and enterprise integration. He has been involved in some of the largest messaging and integration projects around the world, from trading floors in Tokyo to semiconductor manufacturing fabs in Arizona. Demed holds an Engineering Degree from the Ecole Nationale Supérieure des Télécommunications de Bretagne, a Bachelor of Science in Electrical Engineering from Université de Bretagne Occidentale and a Master of Science in Computer Science from Université de Rennes I.

Prasen Palvankar is a Director of Product Management at Oracle and is responsible for providing strategic support to Oracle's SOA Suite current and prospective customers. He is also responsible for outbound SOA Suite product-related activities, including field and partner enablement and training. Prasen has over 20 years of experience in software development and has been working for Oracle since 1998. He was a Technical Director in the Advanced Technology Solutions group at Oracle Consulting, delivering large-scale integration projects before taking on his current role four years ago. Before joining Oracle, Prasen worked as a Principal Software Engineer at Digital Equipment Corporation.

Acknowledgment

The authors would like to thank the Oracle SOA Suite 11*g* development and product management teams, and the leadership team of David Shaffer, Amlan Debnath, Hasan Rizvi, and Thomas Kurian for their vision, strategy, and creation of the industry-leading SOA and process-enabling software suite that was used in this book. The work presented here has substantially benefited from the input and feedback of many, including members of the business integration software product management group, nearly a thousand training attendees within and outside of Oracle, and the instructors who delivered the training to them. We would like to mention specifically the direct contributions of Deb Ayers, Jeff Hutchins, Mihai Munteanu, and Lloyd Williams who provided some of the lab content. In addition, we would like to thankfully acknowledge the help received from Sheila Cepero and Todd Adler in handling all the necessary legal steps within Oracle associated with the publishing of this book.

The publishing team at Packt Publishing was wonderful to work with—the enthusiasm, promptness, and guidance of James Lumsden and Aanchal Kumar throughout the evolution of this book are particularly worthy of mention.

And, finally, we would expressly like to thank our families for their love and support as we took on the challenge of putting this book together on top of our already very busy schedules and borrowed heavily from the invaluable family time.

Thank you for purchasing this Oracle SOA Suite 11g R1 tutorial.

New versions of SOA Suite 11g are in the pipeline, and due for release in the foreseeable future.

Accordingly, Packt would like to offer you complimentary eBook upgrades for the R2 and R3 editions of this tutorial. Packt eBooks come in PDF format, can be printed, and are now copy-paste enabled.

To qualify for this offer, please email oracle@packtpub.com quoting the retailer you bought the book from, and the invoice number.

Packt will then contact you and explain the next step. Don't worry, it's all quick and painless.

For those of you who bought this book directly from Packt, you need do nothing. We will automatically contact you when the next version of the book is available, and advise you how to download your free eBook.

Table of Contents

Preface

As the concept of Service-Oriented Architecture has matured, it has triggered the emergence of new, sophisticated, and specialized tools: Enterprise Service Buses (ESB) for service virtualization, BPEL for orchestration, Human Workflow, Business Rules for externalizing key pieces of logic, and so on. As a result, developers now have a rich set of tools to work with. However, this can itself present a challenge: how can one keep up with all these various tools and their capabilities? One of the key goals of Oracle SOA Suite 11*g* is to assemble these tools in a cohesive, simple-to-use, and highly-integrated development environment. This book, organized around a tutorial that is built in an iterative fashion, will guide you through all the components of the suite and how they relate to each other.

The authors are part of the Oracle SOA Suite product management team, and the idea of the book came as we were delivering an earlier version of this material, as an accelerated internal training at Oracle — before the product was even released. These training sessions were very well received and we decided it was worth sharing this material with a larger audience.

This book is not meant to be used as reference material — it is an *accelerated learning path* to the Oracle SOA Suite. The focus is on *breadth* rather than on depth. More specifically, we wanted to highlight the key capabilities and role of each product in the Oracle SOA Suite and explain how they can be put to work *together* to deliver highly capable and flexible applications. Too often we, as developers, tend to stretch the limits of (not to say abuse!) a few technologies, simply to stay within our comfort zone — and because there is always so little time to learn new things. With its streamlined format, we hope this book will give you the confidence to further explore some of these technologies you had never looked at before.

What this book covers

The principal aim of this book is to get you operational with Oracle SOA Suite 11gR1 quickly and easily. In this spirit, the largest part of this book is dedicated towards a set of hands-on step-by-step tutorials that build a non-trivial SOA composite that you can deploy, test, run, monitor, and manage.

Chapter 1 starts the book off with a quick refresher on some of the useful concepts regarding SOA and services and concludes with an introduction to Service Component Architecture (SCA).

Chapter 2 discusses the key challenges in the technical implementation of SOA-based applications and how Oracle SOA Suite 11g leverages SCA principles to address these challenges.

Chapter 3 describes the business and technical requirements for a purchase order (PO) processing composite and gives you an overview of how the complete solution will be built up in a set of discrete steps using a series of tutorials using Oracle SOA Suite 11gR1.

Chapter 4 gives you the necessary instructions for download, installation, and configuration of Oracle SOA Suite 11gR1.

The core functionalities of the PO processing composite that is described in Chapter 3 are built in Chapters 5 through 10. This series of chapters will teach you the basics of working with Oracle SOA Suite 11g and the IDE (JDeveloper).

You start building the composite using a mediator, as well as web services and database adapters. You then add a file adapter and a BPEL (Business Process Execution Language) component to create a process that orchestrates the overall flow, adding human interaction, creating conditional process execution using business rules, and accessing external services via a JMS (Java Message Service) adapter. At the end of each and every chapter, you will have a composite that can be deployed, run, and tested. You are advised to go through these tutorial chapters, 5-10 in a sequential manner.

The tutorials in Chapters 11 through 19 let you add more functionality to the composite and explore some of the operational features of Oracle SOA Suite 11gR1. You will learn service re-use and virtualization using Oracle Service Bus (OSB), explore some of the composite life cycle management features, test the composite using the unit testing framework, incorporate exception handling, add security policies to a service, set up a business activity-level tracking of the composite transactions using Oracle Business Activity Monitoring (BAM), work with events using the unified services and events platform of Oracle SOA Suite 11g, handle data using Service Data Object (SDO) specification, and connect the composite to a Business-to-Business (B2B) gateway using Oracle B2B.

By the end of Chapter 19, you should have a good grasp of all components in Oracle SOA Suite 11gR1, and be able to create modular, full-featured service composites. The concluding remarks in Chapter 20 will briefly discuss some of the ways you could use such composites to provide business benefits.

Who this book is for

This book is intended for any SOA developer or architect, with some basic understanding of Service-Oriented Architectures and web services technologies. No prior knowledge of Oracle middleware is assumed. However, people with experience with SOA Suite 10g will find this material of interest as well because of its focus on how things work *together*, an area that has been greatly enhanced with the 11g release.

Conventions

In this book, you will find a number of styles of text that distinguish between different kinds of information. Here are some examples of these styles, and an explanation of their meaning.

Code words in text are shown as follows: "Each schema can reference definitions in other schemas by making use of the xsd:import directive."

A block of code will be set as follows:

```
<types>
  <schema xmlns="http://www.w3.org/2001/XMLSchema">
    <import namespace="http://xmlns.oracle.com/Echo"
            schemaLocation="Echo.xsd"/>
  </schema>
</types>
```

When we wish to draw your attention to a particular part of a code block, the relevant lines or items will be made bold:

```
<types>
  <schema xmlns="http://www.w3.org/2001/XMLSchema">
    <import namespace="http://xmlns.oracle.com/Echo"
           schemaLocation="Echo.xsd"/>
  </schema>
</types>
```

New terms and **important words** are introduced in a bold-type font. Words that you see on the screen, in menus or dialog boxes for example, appear in our text like this: "Double-click on the **Case** bar and set the name to **USPS**".

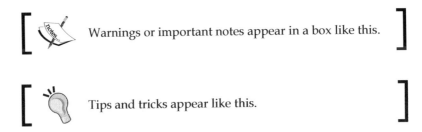

Warnings or important notes appear in a box like this.

Tips and tricks appear like this.

Reader feedback

Feedback from our readers is always welcome. Let us know what you think about this book, what you liked or may have disliked. Reader feedback is important for us to develop titles that you really get the most out of.

To send us general feedback, simply drop an email to feedback@packtpub.com, making sure to mention the book title in the subject of your message.

If there is a book that you need and would like to see us publish, please send us a note in the **SUGGEST A TITLE** form on www.packtpub.com or email suggest@packtpub.com.

If there is a topic that you have expertise in and you are interested in either writing or contributing to a book, see our author guide on www.packtpub.com/authors.

Blog

The authors are contributing to a blog that you might want to consult for updates, additional samples, and information about Oracle SOA Suite. The blog can be found at: http://blogs.oracle.com/soa.

Customer support

Now that you are the proud owner of a Packt book, we have a number of things to help you to get the most from your purchase.

Downloading the example code for the book

Visit http://www.oracle.com/technology/products/soa/ soasuite/11gthebook.html to directly download the example code.

 The downloadable files contain instructions on how to use them.

Errata

Although we have taken every care to ensure the accuracy of our contents, mistakes do happen. If you find a mistake in one of our books—maybe a mistake in text or code—we would be grateful if you would report this to us. By doing this you can save other readers from frustration, and help to improve subsequent versions of this book. If you find any errata, report them by visiting http://www.packtpub. com/support, selecting your book, clicking on the **let us know** link, and entering the details of your errata. Once your errata are verified, your submission will be accepted and the errata added to the list of existing errata. The existing errata can be viewed by selecting your title from http://www.packtpub.com/support.

Piracy

Piracy of copyright material on the Internet is an ongoing problem across all media. At Packt, we take the protection of our copyright and licenses very seriously. If you come across any illegal copies of our works in any form on the Internet, please provide the location address or website name immediately so we can pursue a remedy.

Please contact us at copyright@packtpub.com with a link to the suspected pirated material.

We appreciate your help in protecting our authors, and our ability to bring you valuable content.

Questions

You can contact us at questions@packtpub.com if you are having a problem with some aspect of the book, and we will do our best to address it.

1
SOA and Its Evolution

Service-Oriented Architecture (SOA) is fundamentally a **loosely coupled** computing paradigm and has become a key ingredient of modern business applications and IT infrastructure. Now accepted quite widely by user communities and heavily backed by major software vendors such as Oracle, IBM, SAP, and Microsoft, SOA tools and practices are maturing fast. Since this book is focused on teaching how to use a SOA-enabling tool set, and not on deep exploration of SOA philosophies and methodologies, we will only briefly go over some of the essential aspects of SOA in a refresher style so as to provide you with a reasonable context. Much of the content in this chapter will serve as general background information on SOA and can be useful for overall practice of SOA. In what is to follow, we touch upon what SOA and its essential constituent services are, and why one should one even bother about SOA. We recount how the basics of SOA have evolved and the direction it is headed. We conclude the chapter with an introductory treatise on **Service Component Architecture (SCA)**, as familiarity with SCA concepts is helpful in appreciating the workings of Oracle SOA Suite 11*g* tool set.

SOA and services—what and why

SOA is an architectural framework for software design that works around the concept of **services**. In our day-to-day life, we take the concept of services as a given: if we are sick, we seek the service of a doctor, if a faucet is leaking in our home, we rely on a plumber's service to get that fixed, our children's education depends on the services of teachers, and so on. While services span nearly all the things imaginable, they exhibit a rather simple interaction pattern. When a **consumer** makes a **request** to the **provider** for something to be done, the provider provides a service by executing that request. At a high level, services in SOA would be quite similar to those in our daily lives. Of course, in SOA, the consumers and providers would be some computer applications and the service would be a suitable unit of business or technical functionality that is digitally accomplished. SOA is about working with such services. It is the architectural component of a bigger philosophy, the so-called **service orientation**, and its adoption has a multi-fold impact on an organization in the way it builds and leverages IT assets for ultimate business benefit. SOA impacts, for example:

- **Application architecture**: The way services are used (consumed) by other applications such as business processes or integration processes or portals.

- **Enterprise architecture**: The embellishment of standard enterprise architecture by components specific to handling and management of services, for example, service orchestrator for composition of business processes or composite applications using services, service bus for service request mediation and protocol and format translations, service portfolios, and repositories for service asset management, service repositories, and registries for service look-ups, service security, policy, and quality-of-service management components, and so on. (The following figure shows some of the essential elements of SOA.)

- **Business architecture**: The way a business's activities are to be organized or modified in order to implement and best leverage SOA.

- **Organizational architecture**: The organization roles, responsibilities, and governance as they pertain to SOA-related activities.

For a successful SOA adoption, you need to attend to each of the above aspects, which are not all technology related. This is the reason why you may hear remarks like "SOA is not only technology" or "You cannot buy SOA off-the-shelf". While we acknowledge this comprehensive approach to successful SOA adoption, and Oracle's SOA Methodology delves into details of how SOA may be adopted in a comprehensive manner, in this book, we have chosen to keep our focus on the implementation aspects of SOA solutions.

SOA definitions: Over the years, many definitions have been proposed for SOA. These definitions are similar in many aspects but have some differences. As an example, we offer two such definitions:

Per Gartner, "Service Oriented Architecture (SOA) is a client-server software design approach in which an application consists of *software services* and *software service consumers* (also known as clients or service requesters). SOA differs from the more general client/server model in its definitive emphasis in loose coupling between software components, and in its use of separately standing interfaces."

Per Object Management Group's SOA Special Interest Group, "Service Oriented Architecture is an architecture style for a community of providers and consumers of services to achieve mutual value that (i) allows participants in the communities to work together with minimal co-dependence or technology dependence, (ii) specifies the contracts to which organizations, people and technologies must adhere in order to participate in the community, (iii) provides for business value and business processes to be realized by the community, and (iv) allows for a variety of technology to be used to facilitate interactions within the community."

The following figure shows the key focus areas for a comprehensive and successful SOA adoption:

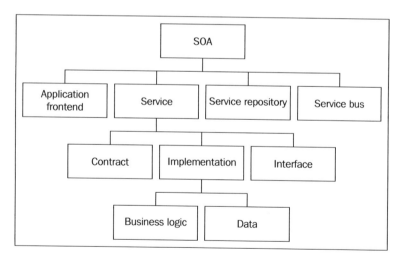

A service in SOA is basically an encapsulation of data and business logic. A service consists of an **interface**, has an **implementation**, and exhibits certain pre-defined **behavior**. The service interface defines a set of **operations**, which portrays its capabilities; operations are the things that a service can do. The provider of the service offers one or more contracts based on the interface and behavior details, and is responsible for creating a service implementation capable of fulfilling such contract(s). The consumer of the service is only concerned with the contract for use of this service. The service functionalities may be derived from diverse sources, for example, databases, legacy applications, packaged enterprise applications, or bespoke applications developed in traditional programming environments like C/C++, Java, or .Net. Mature technologies and tools exist today that can easily package and expose these functionalities as services. A wide variety of service consumers are possible, for example, composite applications, user interaction modules, or business-to-business gateways. Service and IT infrastructures bridge service consumers and the providers and provide mechanisms to apply adequate security and other policies (see the following figure for a high-level SOA Reference Architecture schematic, ref. Oracle SOA Methodology).

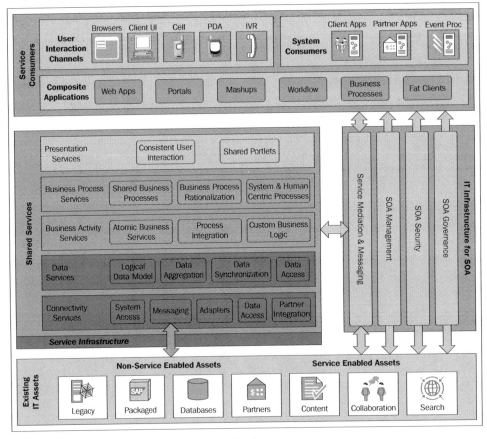

It is worthwhile to point out that the concept of service packaging is quite general. A service can utilize other services along with suitable composition mechanism, for example, using declarative orchestration or some procedural code.

Services are often **classified**, that is, type designations are assigned to services, in order to be able to specify best practices for their implementation and management. There are many strategies for service classification. One classification approach relies on what the service encapsulates, and accordingly we have (adapted from: *SOA Principles of Service Design* by Thomas Erl, Prentice Hall):

- **Entity services**: These services package corporate/business entities such as customer, account, employee, contract, and so on, and provide access to underlying data elements via the basic data access operations like create, read, update, and delete, collectively called the CRUD operations, plus a few others and some logic calculations based on the attributes of the entity. Entity services are generally business process agnostic, for example, data services providing access to data in packaged applications.

- **Task services**: These services perform a portion or all of some business process or activity and in turn may access functionalities of various entity or other task services. A payment update action involving updates to several entities such as customer and account is an example of a task service. Task services often represent sub-processes of higher-level business processes.

- **Utility services**: These are helper services to entity and task services providing connectivity to applications (for example, connector services), access to security infrastructure (for example, directory services), or other generic utilitarian activities like logging.

Utility services are typically technical or infrastructural in nature while entity and task services usually carry business semantics. Utility and entity services are, generally speaking, more reusable than task services.

As a general rule, when scoping capabilities of services, do not mix business process/application specific and agnostic functionalities — doing so is likely to hinder re-use and composability of services.

The key business expectations for service orientation (and SOA), in fact the main reasons why this paradigm has been gaining such increased attention in recent years, can be summarized as:

- Cost reduction for IT application development via service reuse, and for IT operations via well-defined services-based operations layers

- Increased business agility, that is, reduction in time-to-market of a company's offering by speeding up creation of new or modification of existing IT applications and business processes by composing and assembling applications from existing assets as opposed to building from scratch

- Change resilience, that is, ability of higher-level applications and processes to remain insulated from changes in lower or backend applications, for example, a customer order management process not being affected by the introduction of a new order fulfillment system

- Continuous improvement of operations via improvements in performance of services and **Service Level Agreements (SLAs)** without disrupting business operations

- Better communication between business and IT using business-oriented service specifications thus reducing the so-called **business-IT gap**

In order to achieve the above business benefits, SOA implementations and services therein must follow certain essential disciplines:

- **Loose coupling**: Consumers refer to service contracts in order to use services and not their implementations thus reducing the level of dependency between consumers and providers.

- **Discoverability**: Services should be self described and be published into services registries and repositories so as to facilitate design-time searches and runtime look-ups.

- **Location transparency**: This refers to the ability of a service consumer to be able to invoke a service regardless of its actual location in the network; this also assumes the discoverability property (described above) and that the consumer has the right to access the service. Often, the idea of service **virtualization**, where the consumer simply calls a **logical** service while a suitable SOA-enabling runtime infrastructure component, commonly a service bus, maps this logical service call to a **physical** service, also relates to location transparency.

- **Autonomy**: Services, within the bounds of their contracts that they make with their resource providers and contracts that they offer to their consumers, need to be self-contained as far as their execution is concerned; this implies that services must manage their own dependencies on other services or contributing applications.

- **State management**: Services need to handle their own state management per their contract. While it is highly desirable that services be **stateless**, **stateful** implementations may be unavoidable in certain cases.

- **Reusability**: A service should package information and business logic in a manner that, where and when applicable, multiple consumers should be able to use it as a shared resource either directly or via composition.

- **Composability**: Services should be easily composable from other services and technical functionalities, and should be able to participate easily in other higher-level functionalities, such as a composite service or a composite business application.

Some of the statements above have been influenced by a recent multi-part discussion series, *Evolution of principles of Service Orientation* by Michael Poulin (see: `http://www.ebizq.net/blogs/service_oriented/2009/02/evolution_of_principles_of_service_orientation_part_1.php`) on SOA principles described in Thomas Erl's books on SOA.

It should be pointed out that the above properties, while quite distinct in their own right, are not always mutually exclusive. Also, when making design considerations for a service, business requirement-driven pragmatic trade-offs that prioritize importance of these properties can be expected. Note also that if a composite application is built out of component services and other functionalities like business rules, and so on, with the intention of packaging and exposing this application as a service, then this composite application becomes subject to the above set of disciplines.

 The ability of an organization to follow SOA disciplines routinely depends on the SOA maturity of the organization. Based on its business needs, and by following a suitable SOA maturity model, an organization can create an SOA adoption roadmap to attain higher SOA maturity over a period of time.

Services are like mini applications and have distinct life cycle stages and corresponding owners. Usually triggered by some business or operational requirement, **candidate services** are put forth, some of which then, via an appropriate governance process, may be selected for implementation. A candidate service that is targeted for implementation will go through the usual life cycle stages of analysis and design before building, testing, and deployment. However, services, much like applications, are versioned. Versioning can be quite a useful strategy in managing evolution of services and in limiting the unwanted impact of changes introduced in the services. New service versions are released as additional capabilities are added in order to accommodate the needs of newer service consumers. SOA providers would support multiple service versions simultaneously, just like commercial packaged applications, and existing consumers using older versions of the services would be able to continue operating without being forced to change over to the latest version.

SOA—past, present, and future

There is no doubt that businesses have benefited from information technologies and have moved into the so-called *digital age*. Still, there are some commonly prevailing complaints: "IT is too complex", "IT is too expensive", and "IT is too slow". The main reason for increased attention to SOA these days is the expectation that by exposing and leveraging the existing IT assets as services, SOA will help simplify IT applications development and operations, and will help businesses gain significant cost advantages and agility. Interestingly, SOA is not the first time that the industry tried to enhance the business benefit of IT.

Alexander Pasik of Gartrner coined the term "SOA" in 1994.
Yefim B. Natis and Roy W. Schulte of Gartner published the first report on SOA in 1996.

Elements of the SOA paradigm have been in the making for nearly three decades. The present day service-oriented computing has its roots in computing models like modular programming, client-server computing, object-oriented programming, component-based and model-based developments, and in distributed computing technologies like Distributed Computing Environment with remote procedure calls and **Distributed File Systems (DCE/RPC/DFS)**, **Message-Oriented Middleware (MOM)**, **Object Request Brokers (ORBs)**. Contemporary SOA also leverages tremendous advancements of the last decade in LAN- and WAN-based computing and in the Internet technologies.

Unlike many of the technologies of the past, modern SOA utilizes technology and vendor neutral standards like XML, HTTP, and Web Services (WS-*) that are heavily backed by all leading software vendors. This has now led to a much stronger acceptance of SOA as compared to similar technologies and styles that preceded it. With the introduction of **Enterprise Service Bus (ESB)** products, it has become much easier to **mediate** service requests and to build shared services infrastructure layers on top of IT assets. These service infrastructure layers can effectively support higher-level composite applications like business processes and portals while insulating them from changes below the service layer, and thus facilitating application rationalization and legacy modernization.

 Simple Object Access Protocol (SOAP) based **Web Services (WS)** have gained major popularity in SOA implementation, and this book follows this trend. However, it is possible to use other technologies to implement SOA as long as the basic principles of SOA are adhered to.

With essential philosophies and practices demystified, SOA is now becoming the foundation of many mission-critical applications—this drastically increases the performance, scalability, reliability, and policy enforcement requirements of SOA solutions. Services layers are often the building blocks on which agile business processes rest. Many real-life applications require handling of **events** and it is becoming important for SOA-enabling infrastructures to be able to accommodate event handling and processing alongside services. Services are also being seen as key ingredients in shared computing environments such **Software-as-a-Service (SaaS)** or cloud computing. Does this level of industry acceptance of SOA mean that we have attained *SOA nirvana*? The answer, of course, is No, or at least, Not Yet! Part of the reason is the increase in complexity as the SOA solutions are aimed at non-trivial and mission-critical applications. The complexity, at least as it relates to implementation of the solutions, mainly arises from the fact that to build such applications, you not only have to access and orchestrate services, but also, as in tiered compositions, orchestrate the orchestration of services, or include human workflow features like approvals and manual exception handling, or use business rules to add flexible decision making. In such cases, multiple development environments with corresponding technologies, metadata, and runtime engines would be necessary.

The developers would have to deal with these different development environments and would have to integrate the individual components themselves. The operations people would have to deal with the nuances of such custom integration of integration components for deployment, monitoring, and management. This complexity eats into the potential SOA benefits by significantly increasing the activity costs for SOA solutions.

Therefore, what is needed is a **service platform** where the design-time elements of all the necessary tools are available in one **Integrated Development Environment (IDE)**, where such complex solutions can be composed easily out of the necessary components with *drag-and-drop* type simplicity, and from where the composed solution can be deployed and managed as one unit. From a technical perspective, emergence of such service platforms is the key to the next generation of SOA-enabling infrastructures. Of course, some guiding disciplines would be required to create such a platform. The recently proposed technology and vendor neutral **Service Component Architecture (SCA)** specification, that is backed by most of the leading software vendors concerned with SOA, is an important step in that direction. As we will see throughout this book, Oracle SOA Suite 11*g* leverages SCA in order to deliver such a service platform.

Composition, SCA, and service platform

One of the definitions of **composition**, as per the Merriam-Webster dictionary, is *a product of mixing or combining various elements or ingredients*. Services are often put together by combining functionalities from a variety of sources. Services are also combined together, in the spirit of service reuse, to create higher-level services termed **composite services**. Of course, composition in SOA does not only involve leveraging services or other functionalities from applications, but also could include conditional executions, message or payload format transformations, embedding human tasks, or business rules. Standard programming languages or scripts like Java, C++, C#, PHP, and so on could be used to accomplish such compositions. However, beyond trivial use cases, this strategy often renders the composition too rigid and difficult to understand, to maintain, and to change. Declarative composition tools, in particular the ones based on open standards, for example, a **Business Process Execution Language (BPEL)** orchestrator, have helped alleviate this composition problem to some extent. However, for more general compositions, there existed a strong need for a more powerful discipline that could handle a wider variety of contributing elements, such as disparate metadata and implementation technologies, yet would be relatively simple to work with.

In the following figures, you can see schematics of an SCA "Composite" and "Component", respectively (ref. www.osoa.org):

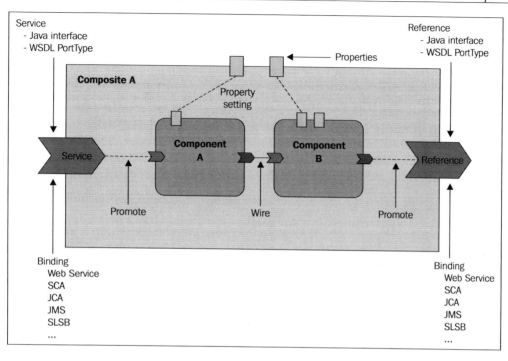

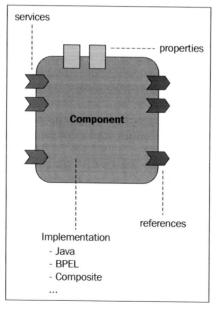

In recent years, as a result of collaboration among the leading software vendors involved in SOA enabling tools, the **Service Component Architecture (SCA)** specification set has emerged as a suitable discipline that is capable of handling very general composition tasks and can facilitate easy deployment and monitoring of the end result of the composition, also known as a **composite** (see: www.osoa.org). SCA specifications allow creation of composite services using a variety of technologies such as Java, C/C++, PHP, XML, and BPEL, offer extensions for platform-specific technologies, facilitate various communication technologies such as JMS, HTTP, SOAP, and REST, and provide for ways to attach policies and to make the composite easily configurable. This mix-and-match of technologies and functionalities is kept track of using the SCA **Assembly** specification, and is accomplished by creating a sort of *global deployment descriptor* that is rendered in XML and describes all of the artifacts that are used to build a composite service and how they are related to each other. The key features of the SCA Assembly model (see preceding figures) are:

- **Composite**: A composite is the highest-level description of a composite service, and is expressed using XML. The rest of the SCA assembly artifacts are included within a composite description. A composite encapsulates a set of business functions, which can be exposed through **services** (see below). Also, a composite can leverage functionalities offered by others via **references** (see below).

- **Component**: Components are the basic units of construction for a composite. Similar to composites, component functionalities can be exposed through services (see below), and components could leverage functionalities offered by others via references (see below). Some of the component-level services and references can be pushed out (or **promoted** in SCA terminology) to the composite level, of which the component is a part. Component configurations refer to some specific **implementation**, for example, a BPEL process or a Java class file. Components also have configurable properties, some of which can be made available at the composite level as well.

- **Services** and **References**: These are the SCA mechanisms for communications into and out of components and composites (see earlier). For a composite, these are essentially a combination of **interfaces** (for example, Java interface or WSDL PortType) and **bindings** (for example, JMS, Web Services, JCA, and so on).

- **Wire**: Wires in SCA are connections that link together services, components, and references. Wires are used to indicate to the runtime platform how to route messages between the network layer and the pieces of business logic that are used to implement the composite service.

The preceding description was meant for you to get a quick idea of SCA and the concept of composites. These and the other features will be further touched upon in this book as they come up in connection with the use of Oracle SOA Suite 11*g* tools. Should you be interested in all the published details of the various aspects of SCA, you can download them for free from www.osoa.org. Note also that there are other specifications within the SCA body of specifications besides the Assembly Model described here—these are focused on aspects of components and composites other than their assembly. For example, non-functional or operational requirements for SCA composites and components are handled by the SCA Policy Framework.

SCA 1.0 specifications completed incubation in February 2007 and were published on www.osoa.org. The authors that included Oracle announced their intent to submit the specification to OASIS for advancement through its open standards process. Additionally, a new member section, the Open Composite Services Architecture (oasis-opencsa.org) was created in OASIS to coordinate several Technical Committees (for example, Assembly, Bindings, Policy, Java, C-C++, BPEL, and so on) to process these specifications.

Design-time and run-time tools for SOA-based applications could utilize these SCA specifications and concepts to create what we have called a *service platform* that would facilitate the whole life cycle of such applications. With such a platform, a developer would not have to go in and out of multiple development environments in order to design the various components of a service-oriented business application, and would not have to then create custom integrations of these disparate technology components. There would be common metadata pertaining to all the elements of the composed solution and it would minimize the effort and errors during deployment and migrations, and for editing the solution to introduce changes. Such a platform would also allow easy tracing of transactions through the solution composites and would provide for uniform exception handling. Thus, such a platform would afford increased business agility, higher developer productivity and lower operational cost. As you will learn in the remainder of this book and will experience by doing the suggested tutorials in this book, Oracle SOA Suite 11*g* is indeed such a platform based on SCA specifications, and at the time of this writing and to the knowledge of the authors, the most advanced and complete commercial implementation of SCA.

Summary

SOA is a software design paradigm based on the principle of loose coupling. The basic building elements of SOA are services that provide access to and processing of business logic and data. XML and Web Services have become a popular choice for implementing SOA-based solutions. SOA has been receiving a lot of attention in recent years due to its potential for reducing a variety of IT costs as well as for increasing business agility. SCA specifications have emerged as a suitable discipline for creating highly productive SOA development environments. Oracle SOA Suite 11*g*, which you will be working with in rest of this book, leverages SCA heavily to provide a unified service platform for creation, deployment, testing, management, and monitoring of SOA-based composite business applications.

2
Product Architecture

SOA technologies have significantly matured over the past few years and there are a number of very capable SOA offerings on the market today. Many could argue that the critical factor to successful SOA projects is now mostly the methodology and execution rather than software. While that is true to a large extent, a capable and flexible SOA software stack that can meet your methodology requirements is a key element to success.

Oracle SOA Suite 11*g*: Release drivers

SOA infrastructure tools usually fall into one of two main groups:

1. Former **Enterprise Applications Integration (EAI)** tools that have morphed into SOA infrastructure
2. Collections of best-of-breed individual components

This lineage translates into very significant architectural differences. EAI tools typically offer "all-in-one" cohesive solutions but they come at the cost of flexibility and footprint. Best-of-breed components typically excel at their primary task, but assembling the right combination of tools to meet your end-to-end requirements can be a daunting task, sometimes dubbed as the challenge of "integrating your integration".

It is the idea of combining the best of both worlds that is behind the architectural changes in Oracle SOA Suite 11*g*: combine the simplicity of a black-box all-in-one integration tool with the power and flexibility of a modular best-of-breed suite.

Challenges solved by Oracle SOA Suite 11*g*

Let's have a look at the key product architectural aspects of Oracle SOA Suite 11*g* and what type of problems they help solve.

Simplifying the design-time environment

The evolution and refinement of highly specialized SOA tools has led to very capable products. However, this has also introduced a new challenge: the ability for a single developer to master all the individual design-time environments and keep track of their different requirements in terms of methodology and life cycle. In its 11*g* release, Oracle SOA Suite 11*g* is taking control of this proliferation of technologies.

Composite Editor to assemble heterogeneous technologies

A typical SOA development environment requires the developer to learn different tools and switch contexts and development environments frequently. Let's take a typical example of an SOA application used to process purchase orders:

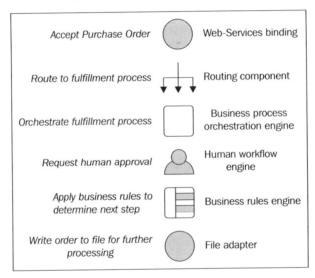

Using best-of-breed discrete tools for each task is the right thing to do as it preserves the flexibility that is key to SOA and ensures that the developer has the right tool for each task. However, in the simple example depicted above, this would also mean working with a handful of development tools: an ESB editor for routing and connectivity, a BPEL editor for orchestration, a human workflow tool to involve people, and a business rules engine to externalize certain decision logic. This is a lot for a single person to master!

In Oracle SOA Suite 11*g*, all design tasks are performed in a single environment: **JDeveloper**. JDeveloper is Oracle's primary **Integrated Development Environment (IDE)** and provides all the required tools for creating composite applications. The consolidation to JDeveloper of formerly standalone best-of-breed design tools started with the 10*g* release but was extended in 11*g* to some of the more recent SOA Suite additions such as Business Rules and Web Services Manager. More significantly, the 11*g* release introduces the SOA **Composite Editor** that lets you assemble, in a drag-and-drop fashion, a variety of components and technologies that eventually make up your composite application. This new editor is used extensively throughout our tutorial later in the book. It is worth mentioning that the composite editor leverages an emerging set of standards called **Service Component Architecture (SCA)**—you can further explore this by looking at the underlying XML composite descriptors that the environment generates.

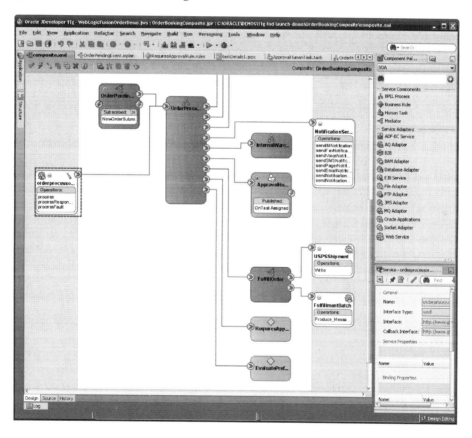

Service Component Architecture (SCA)

Refer to the *Composition, SCA, and service platform* section in Chapter 1 for background information on SCA.

Streamlining life cycle management

Another challenge facing developers working with a multitude of tools is life cycle management. As you can imagine, developing a composite application using disparate technologies also introduces challenges downstream, during deployment and management phases. Even though all these separate components are *logically* a single composite application, the disparate nature of underlying technologies makes it harder to manage them as a single entity. Typically this means that each component within your end-to-end applications ends up being deployed, versioned, and monitored independently. And certain things that used to be fairly simple in traditional mono-technology development end up being fairly complex. Indeed, what is the exact version number of a composite application made up of heterogeneous technologies and deployed over a distributed set of servers?

In SOA Suite 11*g*, a comprehensive composite application containing a variety of technologies, from BPEL to XSLT transformations, from JCA adapters to Business Rules and human workflows, is now expressed using a single XML descriptor and can be deployed as a single entity, in a single click. Convenience of deployment is not the only benefit of this model. This also means that versioning suddenly becomes much simpler: the composite application that used to be a purely virtual concept is now concrete and can be easily versioned.

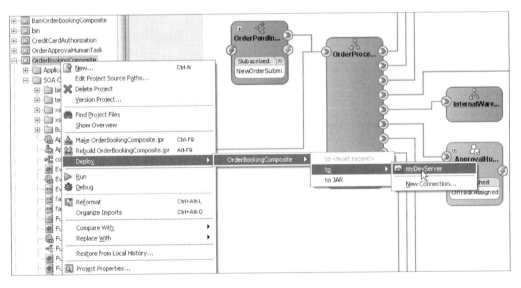

Metadata Storage (MDS) for tighter control and governance

Another very important implication of multiple, disparate SOA tools is that each one ends up maintaining design-time and runtime artifacts and associated information in its own format and in its own repositories. Going back to the order-processing example earlier, a BPEL designer would store artifacts like the BPEL definition, associated WSDLs, and XML schemas in a local store during design time. Likewise, the service bus would store routing tables, associated WSDL, schemas, and transformation maps in its own server-side repository.

Similarly, at runtime, each of these engines stores these artifacts in its own deployment formats. This fragmentation of metadata (the data that describes your project) makes it difficult to get a unified design-time or runtime view. Fragmentation of metadata also means that it is almost impossible to provide end-to-end tracking easily and to enforce effective governance without complex and heavy tools.

In Oracle SOA Suite 11*g*, all design-time artifacts are consolidated in the **Metadata Store (MDS)**, a repository that holds all artifacts, from BPEL definitions to security policies. Each developer has a local MDS repository underneath JDeveloper but can deploy to a central global repository when the assets are ready to be shared.

This consolidation of locations and formats greatly simplifies the task of the governance tools—no need to crawl and decrypt hundreds of locations and formats. Governance capabilities have greatly improved in Oracle SOA Suite 11*g*, partly because of the adoption of MDS but also due to the incorporation of key technologies from the BEA AquaLogic product line. While a fascinating topic in itself, Governance is not covered in this book because of space and scope constraints.

Event-Delivery Network (EDN) to reconcile Event-Driven and Service-Oriented Architectures

Message-Oriented Middleware (MOM) is a critical integration technology that provides unique features and has a long track record of reliability and robustness. Such features as publish and subscribe or first-in-first-out (FIFO) queuing models are equally useful to an SOA application as they are in traditional application integration. However, prevalent MOM technologies predate most SOA and XML tools. As such they tend to offer much more technical, low-level tools, and very rudimentary constructs with which to work.

For instance, a JMS developer would deal with queues, topics, connection factories, and a handful of raw message types, while a SOAP developer would work with WSDL and XML schemas. If a service needs to publish an event when a new purchase order with value of over a million dollar is received, it can't just specify that it publishes an event called "NewHighValuePO" of a certain format. It also has to define which topic or queue the message will be published to and the appropriate naming and look-up mechanism the consumer of the event should use and so on, depending on the messaging system the queue or topic is created in.

The **Event Delivery Network (EDN)** in Oracle SOA Suite 11*g* brings the power of publish and subscribe semantics to developers without them having to worry about low-level messaging considerations. Using EDN, developers can graphically, right from JDeveloper:

- Browse for and subscribe to events they are interested in
- Generate their own events
- Describe events using the richness of XML Schemas (XSD)
- Filter events using XPath expressions, for instance to restrict their consumption of events to the specific instances containing data they care about

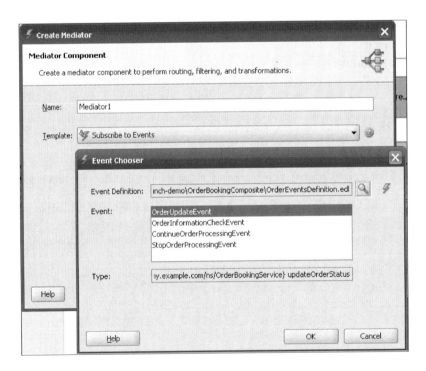

Unifying runtimes for performance and simplified deployment

In the same manner that having to work with a multitude of very capable tools can get in the way of productivity, distributing the processing of an application across loosely-coupled, distinct runtimes can introduce performance and monitoring overheads. Of course, this also greatly complicates the life of IT administrators having to manage a fragmented infrastructure. Oracle SOA Suite 11g addresses this concern through a consolidated runtime infrastructure.

Removing inefficiencies through the Service Infrastructure

One of the key requirements of a service in an SOA is that the consumer of the service should not care or know about the implementation. This generally adds a layer of abstraction to the application architecture. From a performance perspective, every layer that gets added to the application architecture has the potential to increase the cost of doing any operation since more resources are required to handle the activities in these layers. Add to this the rich data representation of XML, core to any SOA-based application, and the fact that many invocations go over the wire and this results in more demands on network and memory resources.

In addition, any interaction between heterogeneous components introduces the costly overhead of *marshalling* and *un-marshalling* of messages flowing between them. For example, if a component with a web-service binding needs to invoke an operation on a Java component that uses RMI or a simple method call, the underlying infrastructure needs to translate the SOAP message to corresponding RMI or Java method calls and vice-versa on the response. This adds to the runtime overhead of the composite application.

To optimize these interactions, Oracle SOA Suite 11g has introduced a unified runtime infrastructure called **Service Infrastructure** (also sometimes referred to as SOA Infrastructure). The Service Infrastructure is a single J2EE application that provides the runtime environment to execute SCA composites and all components (BPEL, Rules, Mediator, and so on) they can contain. The core service engines—BPEL, Mediator, Business Rules, and Human Workflow, all run within the service infrastructure as pluggable engines.

To reduce the amount of costly marshalling and un-marshalling of messages, all service engines use a common normalized message format. Incoming messages are normalized on the way in, passed around in this normalized form that all engines can work with, and de-normalized as they leave the infrastructure.

There are many other benefits to this runtime consolidation as we will see in the subsequent sections. It is to be noted that while the Oracle Service Bus shares components (such as the JCA framework) with the Service Infrastructure, it is an independent runtime (that is, its own J2EE application). This reflects the typical production deployments where the service bus sits in a different tier from the applications it virtualizes.

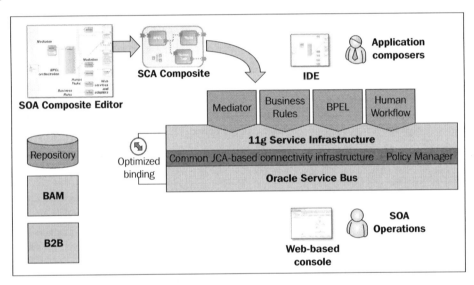

Eliminating redundancies by sharing components

The runtime consolidation in this modular service infrastructure yields many other benefits such as the ability to eliminate many of the redundant functions and features in the various service engines—and a side effect of this is that several features that used to be available in only one engine are now elevated to the composite level and available across engines. Such examples are adapters: the same JCA adapters are shared across engines, but also unit testing, a feature that used to be available only in BPEL in 10g but that can now encompass any service engine.

Simplifying installation and deployment

Having to manage a heterogeneous runtime environment might not be such a problem in simple topologies consisting of one instance of each server engine. However, in a typical production environment tailored for high-availability, having to install, cluster, and tune highly different engines can quickly become a complex endeavor. Oracle SOA Suite 11*g* drastically simplifies things in that regard. As mentioned earlier, all that is needed to execute these composite applications is a single J2EE application. Deploying and clustering this application is radically simplified and can be easily automated to ensure that scaling up becomes a very simple operation. In addition, the adoption of WebLogic Server as the default container allows for the use of WLST and domain templates to deploy new nodes and clusters quickly. Note that these advanced administration concepts are not covered in this book to which is focussed on getting developers started, but hopefully this is just enough information to make you want to learn more.

Increasing visibility and streamlining management

Another challenge of working with heterogeneous and distributed technologies is end-to-end monitoring. It's not until something goes wrong because of some transient exception that one realizes the complexity of finding what exactly went wrong—and where.

Enterprise Manager for end-to-end monitoring

Ordinarily speaking, in the case of the order-processing example, you would have to use a management console to query the state of your process and another management console to diagnose any routing issues. This operational challenge becomes exponentially more complex as you introduce more technology and tools.

A direct benefit of the unified runtime infrastructure in Oracle SOA Suite 11*g* is the consolidation of all management and monitoring consoles in **Oracle Enterprise Manager Fusion Middleware Control (EM)**. EM is a web-based management console that provides the functions necessary to manage and monitor all aspects of a composite application. Some of Enterprise Manager's core functions are:

- **J2EE application management** and monitoring, which includes deploying and un-deploying applications
- **Administration** of the SOA infrastructure and the service engines

- **Management of composites**, which includes deploying, redeploying, and un-deploying composites as well as starting and stopping composites

- **Performance tuning and monitoring** of the SOA infrastructure

- **End-to-end instance tracking** providing a graphical view of the complete chain of execution of composites as well as the ability to drill down into individual component instances

Global, policy-driven security

Security requirements are increased in the context of SOA where assets are shared and where data travels back and forth over the network. But the distributed nature of SOA can make the enforcement of end-to-end security a challenging task, even more, though, when these distributed services are also implemented using a variety of different technologies. While the use of security standards might help to ensure interoperability, it does not solve the problem of management and visibility. If components embed authentication and authorization logic within their implementation, how can security administrators quickly update end-to-end security (for instance, to enforce new encryption requirements within the company)? And how can they have a global view of security violations?

Global and policy-driven security management is another task taken upon itself by Enterprise Manager 11g in conjunction with Oracle Web Services Manager (OWSM), which provides the underlying policy framework. The primary benefit of using policy-driven security is that this model clearly separates security concerns from application logic—no more hardcoded security entangled in your code. Developers can focus on building an application that meet the business requirements and delegate the security concerns (What level of encryption? What standard to use? and so on) to the experts. Policies can be created, attached, and detached in JDeveloper at design-time. Or this can be done after deployment in the global policy manager in Enterprise Manager. This environment is also where the security-related configuration (credentials store, roles, and policies), as well as monitoring of security will take place. While the policy-driven security was available in earlier versions of the SOA Suite and OWSM, the main changes in 11g are that the enforcement agents are now built into the SOA composites, without the developer having to do any configuration, and that the global policy manager is fully integrated in Enterprise Manager.

Exception handling

In a heterogeneous environment, such as the one SOA typically implies, consistent and centralized exception handling becomes critical. Without a common exception management solution, triaging runtime errors and exceptions can take significant effort, each technology/tool-set providing its own error handling solution.

Exception management is another feature that was consolidated across all products of the Oracle SOA Suite in 11*g* and controlled through Enterprise Manager. Operators can drill down into failed composites and retry, abort, replay, re-throw, or continue the processing—generally after trying to remediate the initial cause of the exception. You will see during the tutorial how exception management is also enhanced in SOA Suite 11*g* via the use of fault policies.

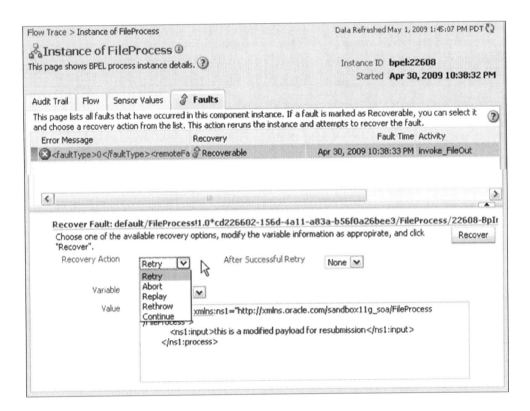

Summary of the Oracle SOA Suite 11*g* components

In this chapter, we explored the key architectural aspects of Oracle SOA Suite 11*g* and what problems they were meant to solve. Let's summarize the various components that make up the Oracle SOA Suite and that you will be working with in the rest of this book:

- **SOA Infrastructure**: The common runtime environment for executing composites and in which the service engines plugin.

- **Service Engines**:
  - ° **BPEL**: The service engine in charge of orchestration.
  - ° **Mediator**: The service engine that provides filtering, routing, and transformation capabilities.
  - ° **Business Rules**: An inference-based rules engine responsible for providing decision services.
  - ° **Human Workflow**: A workflow engine that provides human workflow services.

- **Metadata Store (MDS)**: A central metadata repository that holds all runtime artifacts of all deployed applications and composites, as well as generic artifacts like security and management policies.

- **Oracle Service Bus (OSB)**: A high-performance service bus that provides· service virtualization, protocol translation, request routing, traffic shaping, and so on.

- **Enterprise Manager**: A web-based console that provides a single, integrated management console for all Fusion Middleware components.

- **Web Service Manager**: An integrated policy management and enforcement service, which is part of the Oracle Portability Layer on which the SOA Infrastructure runs.

- **B2B**: A multi-protocol engine that provides business-to-business communication services over a variety of protocols and formats, such as EDI, RosettaNet, ebXML, HL7, and so on.

- **Adapter Framework**: A **Java Component Architecture (JCA)**-based adapter framework that provides standards-based access to non-service-oriented enterprise information systems. Database adapter, FTP adapter, JMS adapter, and eBusiness Suite adapter are some examples of adapters leveraging the adapter framework.

- **JDeveloper** and the composite editor provide a single, integrated development environment.

- **Oracle Business Activity Monitoring (BAM)** is an activity monitoring tool that, unlike Enterprise Manager, is geared towards business users. It uses push techniques to offer real-time business dashboards, leveraging data captured as part of a composite's execution flow.

3

The Tutorial Project: Purchase Order Processing

Using this tutorial, you will build a complex composite application, exploring all of the major components in the Oracle SOA Suite, and learn how they can be used together. The methodology is iterative and the overall application is built incrementally, component by component, chapter by chapter. In each chapter, you add a new feature to the application and at the end of each chapter, you have a working application that you can deploy and test before moving on to the following chapter.

Structure of the tutorial

This book is architected around a tutorial: building a purchase order processing application. Each chapter starts with an overview of the concepts to enhance the application with new capabilities and components, and then goes through the steps to exercise them in the context of the tutorial application.

The chapters in the book fall in two main categories:

- "Sequential" chapters (Chapters 4 to 10) need to be followed in order, each new chapter enriching the application from where the previous chapter left it.

- "Independent" chapters (Chapters 11 to 19) can be done in any order. These chapters are independent of each other and simply assume that the core tutorial application (built up to Chapter 10) is in place.

The following diagram depicts this structure:

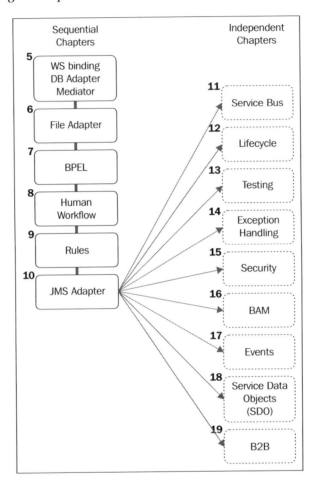

 Chapters 5 to 10 need to be implemented sequentially as they have dependencies on each previous chapter. On the other hand, Chapters 11 to 19 are independent of each other and can be done in any order—they only require Chapter 10 to be implemented first.

Note that in case you want to skip one or more of the sequential chapters, we are providing the solution for each chapter. These pre-built solutions allow you to start the tutorial at any point, for instance, to skip basic components with which you might already be familiar.

In addition, the instructions for each chapter are written at two levels of complexity:

1. Detailed **step-by-step instructions** make up the bulk of each chapter and guide you through each click required to build the lab.

2. **Quick-Build instructions**, found at the end of each chapter provide a summary of the objects to build, along with names and specific properties. This is intended for more advanced users who do not need or want the step-by-step, click-by-click details provided earlier in the chapter.

This modular structure of the tutorial application means that it can be used in a variety of ways:

-   **Complete tutorial for new users**: If you are new to the Oracle SOA Suite, or want a complete tour of the 11*g* capabilities, then follow the exact book structure, executing in sequence the step-by-step instructions. When you are finished, you will have gone through the basic usage of the Oracle SOA Suite 11*g* components and gained an understanding of how they relate to one another.

-   **Complete tutorial for advanced users**: If you have prior experience with SOA 10*g* and are looking for a quick introduction to 11*g*, you may choose to design the tutorial using only the introduction and quick-build instructions available at the end of each chapter.

-   **Targeted tutorial**: If you are already familiar with the overall SOA Suite and simply want to explore certain specific 11*g* components, you can use the provided solutions as a starting point and dive in the book at the relevant chapter.

-   **Demo or extensive end-to-end sample**: If you are looking for an advanced SOA composite application illustrating the core capabilities of the SOA Suite 11*g*, simply deploy the solution for Chapter 10.

Tutorial scenario

The application implements the backend of a purchase order-processing application that could be used in a variety of industries. The requirements for the application are as follows:

1. All of the orders need to be persisted to disk for bookkeeping and auditing purposes.

2. Small orders (defined as those under $1,000) are to be approved automatically.

3. Large orders (those greater than or equal to $1,000) should go through a validation and approval process:
   ○ The customer's credit card must be validated.
   ○ If the order is $5,000 or more, a customer service representative must manually approve the order.

4. The status of approved orders will be set to "approved".

5. The status of large orders with an invalid credit card will be set to "invalidCreditCard".

6. The status of large orders rejected by the customer service representative will be set to "rejected".

7. All of the approved orders are sent to the fulfillment service which uses the order value to determine the shipping company to use: orders under $1,000 go through USPS, orders greater than or equal to $1,000 and less than $5,000 go to UPS, and orders greater than $5,000 go to FedEx.

The following diagram summarizes this business process logic:

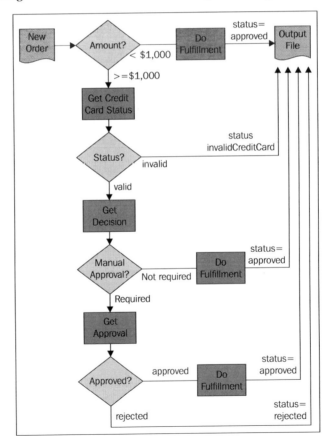

Overview of the tutorial chapters

The following table gives an overview of the tutorial chapters:

Installation and config	Chapter 4, you install and configure the software required to implement the tutorial, namely Oracle SOA Suite 11*g*, WebLogic Server, and Oracle JDeveloper 11*g*.
5 WS binding DB Adapter Mediator	In Chapter 5, you build the first composite in our tutorial. This composite simulates a credit card validation service invoked as a *web service* and uses a *database adapter* to look up the credit card status in a database. The logic is implemented in a *Mediator* component.
6 File Adapter	In Chapter 6, you start laying the foundations of the other composite in our tutorial: the POProcessing application. It takes a purchase order as input and writes it out to a file using a Mediator component and a *File Adapter*.
7 BPEL	In Chapter 7, you enhance the POProcessing composite by adding a *BPEL process*, to process large orders and invoke the credit card validation service.
8 Human Workflow	In Chapter 8, you add to PO Processing a *Human Workflow* component that will be used to get certain orders manually approved.
9 Rules	In Chapter 9, you augment the application with a *Business Rule* component to decide if human approval is required. You will also create the fulfillment BPEL process and add a Business Rule decision table to decide which fulfillment carrier to use.
10 JMS Adapter	Chapter 10 you use the *JMS Adapter* to put the order on a message queue for fulfillment.
11 Service Bus	Chapter 11 you learnt about Enterprise Service Buses and how it is used to provide service virtualization and operational agility. You decouple the composites making up our tutorial by inserting the *Oracle Service Bus* in the architecture.
12 Lifecycle	In Chapter 12, you explore the *life cycle* of a SOA composite application and learn how to customize your composite for the environment you are deploying to, using a configuration plan.
13 Testing	Chapter 13 explains the basics of *unit testing* and how it can be used to improve the quality of your applications. You build a unit test for PO Processing.

14 Exception Handling		In Chapter 14, you learn about *exception handling* by creating fault policies in BPEL and Mediator.
15 Security		Chapter 15 you use the security tools to perform end-to-end application *security* using policies.
16 BAM		Chapter 16 you see how to gain real-time business visibility into your applications. You collect events from the mediator and BPEL and create a *Business Activity Monitoring (BAM)* dashboard to display *Key Performance Indicators* (KPI).
17 Events		Chapter 17 yu learn about the new *Event Delivery Network (EDN)* in Oracle SOA Suite 11g. You use EDN to build a new channel to submit orders to the PO Processing composite application.
18 Service Data Objects (SDO)		In Chapter 18, you learn how to use *Service Data Objects (SDO)* through entity variables in BPEL to manipulate remote data.
19 B2B		Finally, Chapter 19 you see how you can extend this PO Processing application beyond the boundaries of your enterprise. You use the *B2B* gateway to receive orders from a trading partner and route them to the PO Processing application.

Tutorial files

To build this tutorial, you need a few files. These files can be downloaded as a single compressed archive from the Oracle Technology Network at:
`http://www.oracle.com/technology/products/soa/soasuite/11gthebook.html`

Unzip the `Getting Started With Oracle SOA Suite 11g` archive file to `c:\stageSOA`. You will see a top-level directory named `po`.

Inside the `c:\stageSOA\po` directory, you have the following directories:

- `bin` — executable files
- `input` — sample input data files
- `lib` — JAR library file
- `schemas` — XSD files used throughout when defining services
- `solutions/ch#` — a solution project for each chapter
- `sql` — database scripts used during setup

After unzipping, copy the po directory to c:\po. This will be your working area for the tutorial.

The instructions in this book assume that you are working on the Microsoft Windows operating system and that you are using this default path of c:\po for the files used by the tutorial. If you are using the Linux operating system or another location for the tutorial files, you will need to remember to adjust instructions accordingly when operating system specific instructions are specified or c:\po is referenced.

Documentation

All of the documentation for this tutorial is in this book. Occasionally, other resources are noted. In addition, you can find the complete documentation library for SOA Suite 11g at this location: http://download.oracle.com/docs/cd/E12839_01/soa.htm. To confirm that you have the correct version of the library, refer to the version number on the top right. It should be *11g Release 1(11.1.1)* to match the SOA Suite 11gR1 version used in this tutorial.

4
Product Installation

This chapter provides the instructions for installing and configuring the Oracle SOA Suite server and the Oracle JDeveloper development tool needed to run the tutorial. These instructions are for the GA version of 11*g* Release 1 (11.1.1.1.0), dated July 2009.

In addition, this chapter includes the instructions for installing Oracle Service Bus used for Chapter 11 of the tutorial. You do not need to install Oracle Service Bus until you are ready to do Chapter 11.

These instructions are Windows based but Linux users should have no difficulty adjusting them for their environment.

Checking your installation

If you already have SOA Suite and JDeveloper installed, confirm that you have the correct version and configuration by following the steps in the section below called *Testing your installation*. In addition, you may want to complete the items in the section called *Additional actions*. Finally, you must complete the section called *Configuration* to do the tutorial.

What you will need and where to get it

Before you can begin, you need to check your machine, download installation files, and check your database, browser, and JDK versions. Follow the instructions in this section carefully for a successful install.

Memory and Disk Space requirements

This installation requires 3 GB or more available memory. If you have less memory, try separating the installation of the database, the servers, and JDeveloper onto different machines.

The installation process requires about 12 GB of disk space. After installation, you can delete the files used by installation to save about 4 GB.

As you can see, you are installing a lot of software with a large memory and disk footprint. Running your disk defragmentation program now, before you start downloading and installing, can significantly improve install time as well as performance and disk space usage later on.

Downloading files

Download all the software to get started.

1. In the following steps, save all downloaded files to c:\stageSOA. This document assumes that path. If you save them somewhere else then make sure there are no spaces in your path and adjust accordingly when c:\stageSOA is referenced in this document.

2. Go to: http://www.oracle.com/technology/products/soa/soasuite/ index.html, and download the following from *SOA Suite 11g Release 1 (11.1.1.1.0)* to c:\stageSOA:

   ○ WebLogic Server:
     wls1031_win32.exe

   ○ Repository Creation Utility:
     ofm_rcu_win32_11.1.1.1.0_disk1_1of1.zip

   ○ SOA Suite:
     ofm_soa_generic_11.1.1.1.0_disk1_1of1.zip

   ○ JDeveloper Studio, base install:
     jdevstudio11111install.jar

3. Unzip the SOA Suite ZIP file to c:\stageSOA.

4. Unzip the RCU ZIP file to c:\stageSOA.

5. Additional Files needed:

   ○ *Tutorial Files*: In Chapter 3, you were directed to download the files needed for this tutorial. Do that now as some are used during installation. You can download the files from here: http://www.oracle.com/technology/products/soa/ soasuite/11gthebook.html. Unzip the tutorial ZIP file to c:\stageSOA.

   ○ *SOA Extension for JDeveloper*: You will get this later using the JDeveloper update option.

   ○ *Oracle Service Bus*: When you are ready to do the Oracle Service Bus (OSB) lab, you will download the install file to install OSB.

Checking your database

Having your database up and running is the most important pre-requisite for installing SOA Suite.

1. Read the following bulleted requirements carefully to be sure you are ready to begin the SOA Suite installation:

    °   You need one of:

        i.   Oracle XE Universal database version 10.2.0.1

        ii. Oracle 10*g* database version 10.2.0.4+

        iii. Oracle 11*g* database version 11.1.0.7+

    °   You cannot use any other database version in 11*g*R1 (certification of additional databases is on the roadmap). Specifically, you cannot use XE Standard, it must be Universal.

    °   We have seen problems with installing XE when a full 10*g* database is already installed in the environment. The Windows registry sometimes gets the database file location confused. It is recommended to pick one or the other to avoid such issues.

    °   If you need to uninstall XE, make sure that you follow the instructions in *Oracle Database Express Edition Installation Guide 10g Release 2 (10.2) for Microsoft Windows Part Number B25143-03, Section 7, Deinstalling Oracle Database XE* (`http://download.oracle.com/docs/cd/B25329_01/doc/install.102/b25143/toc.htm`).

    °   If you need to uninstall 10.2, be sure to follow the instructions in *Oracle Database Installation Guide 10g Release 2 (10.2) for Microsoft Windows (32-Bit) Part Number B14316-04, Section 6, Removing Oracle Database Software* (`http://download.oracle.com/docs/cd/B19306_01/install.102/b14316/deinstall.htm`).

2. Optional: Install *OracleXEUniv.exe* — recommended for a small footprint database. Make sure that you read step 1 above before installing. You can get XE from here: `http://www.oracle.com/technology/products/database/xe/index.html`.

 When you are using XE, you will see a warning when you install the database schema that this database version is too old. You can safely ignore this warning as it applies only to production environments.

3. If needed, configure *Oracle XE Universal*.

   When you are using Oracle XE, you must update database parameters if you have never done this for your database installation. You only have to do this once after installing. Set the processes parameter to >=200 using the following instructions.

```
sqlplus sys/welcome1@XE as sysdba
SQL> show parameter session
SQL> show parameter processes
SQL> alter system reset sessions scope=spfile sid='*';
SQL> alter system set processes=200 scope=spfile;
SQL> shutdown immediate
SQL> startup
SQL> show parameter session
SQL> show parameter processes
```

 The shutdown command can take a few minutes and sometimes the shutdown/startup command fails. In that case, simply restart the XE service in the **Control Panel | Administrative Tools | Services** dialog after setting up your parameters.

Checking your browser

Oracle SOA Suite 11gR1 has specific browser version requirements.

1. Enterprise Manager requires Firefox 3 or IE 7.

   ◦ Firefox 3—get a portable version, such as the one available from http://portableapps.com, if you want it to co-exist peacefully with your Firefox 2 installation.

   ◦ Firefox 2 and IE 6 are not supported and will not work.

2. BAM requires IE 7.

   ◦ Beware of certain IE 7 plugins that can create conflicts (a few search plugins have proved to be incompatible with BAM).

   ◦ IE 8 is not supported with 11gR1 (but is on the roadmap). IE 6 has a few issues and Firefox will not work with BAM Studio.

Checking your JDK

If you are going to install WebLogic server and JDeveloper on the same machine, you will use the JDK from WebLogic for JDeveloper too. However, if you are going to install on two machines, you need Java 1.6 update 11 JDK for JDeveloper.

1. JDK 1.6 update 11—from the Sun downloads page: `http://java.sun.com/products/archive/`
   ° You must use Java 1.6 update 11. Update 12 does not work.

Installing Admin Server and Managed Servers

Now that you have verified that everything is ready, you can begin installation.

Installing WebLogic Server

First, you install Oracle WebLogic Server.

1. To install WebLogic Server, open a command window and enter:
   ```
   cd c:\stageSOA
   wls1031_win32.exe
   ```
2. When the **Welcome** screen for the install wizard comes up, click on **Next**.
3. Select **Create a new Middleware Home** and enter: `C:\Oracle\Middleware\home_11gR1`.
4. This document assumes that path. If you use a different middleware home then adjust accordingly when `C:\Oracle\Middleware\home_11gR1` is referenced throughout this document.

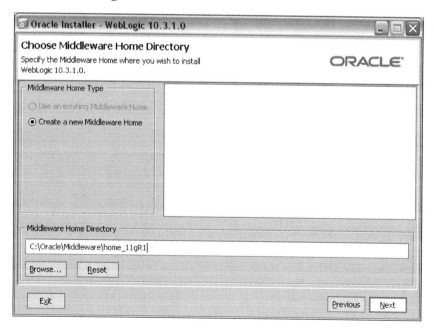

5. Click on **Next**.

6. Enter email address to register for security alerts or deselect the checkbox and decline—whichever you prefer—and click on **Next**.

7. Select **Typical**, and click on **Next**.

8. Review installation directories.

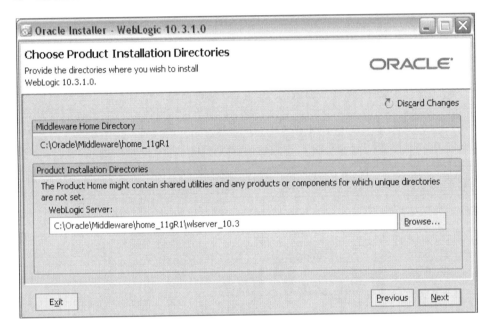

9. Click on **Next**.

10. Select **"All Users" Start Menu** folder and click on **Next**.

11. Review **Summary**.

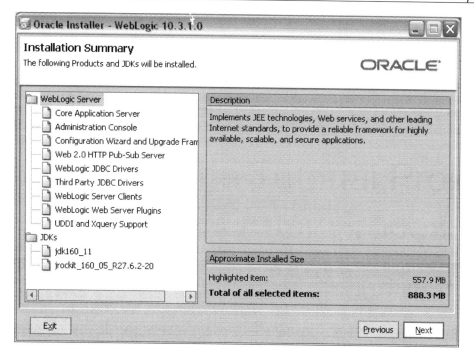

12. Click on **Next** to start the installation process. Installation takes about three minutes.

13. When the installation is complete, deselect the **Run Quickstart** checkbox and click on **Done**.

Dropping the existing schema

If this is the first time you are installing, you do not need to go through this step and you should jump ahead to the *Configuring schema* step. Otherwise, if you are reinstalling, continue with these steps to drop your existing schema first. If you would like to keep your existing schema, jump ahead to the *Configuring schema* step and use a new schema prefix when prompted.

1. To drop your existing schema, copy the following into a command window:

    ```
    cd c:\stageSOA\rcuHome\bin
    rcu.bat
    ```

2. The `bat` command returns to the prompt immediately and after a few seconds, the **Repository Creation Utility** opens.

3. On the **Welcome** screen, click on **Next**.

4. Select **Drop**.

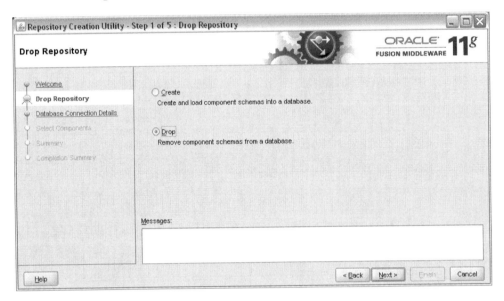

5. Click on **Next**.

6. Complete the database information.

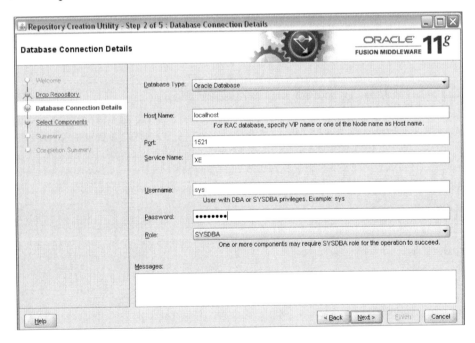

7. Click on **Next**.

8. The pre-requisites are reviewed. When completed, click on **OK**. The utility moves to the next page—with a slight delay, just wait for it.

9. The utility finds the existing schema and offers the drop-down list of all prefixes. Check that the prefix is correct and review the schema.

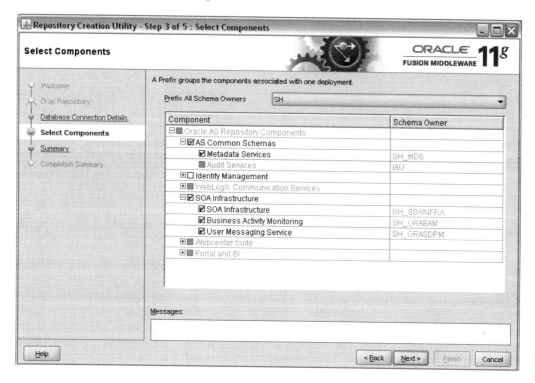

10. In this example, we are dropping the schema with the *SH* prefix. Click on **Next**.

11. On the drop schema warning, click on **OK**.

12. The pre-requisites for this step are reviewed. When completed, click on **OK** to move to the next page—with a slight delay, just wait for it.

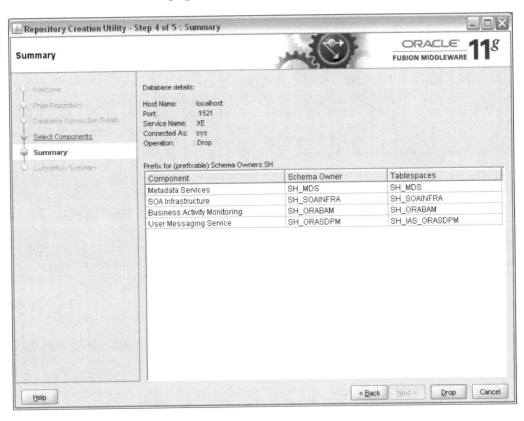

13. Click on **Drop** to drop the schema. This takes a few minutes.

14. When it is finished, click on **Close**.

Configuring schema

Now, create the database schema for the BAM and SOA servers.

1. To create the new schema, open a command window and enter the following:

```
cd c:\stageSOA\rcuHome\bin
rcu.bat
```

2. The `bat` command returns to the prompt immediately and, after a few seconds, the **Repository Creation Utility** opens (if you just ran the utility to drop the schema, it opens the second time much more quickly).

3. On the **Welcome** screen, click on **Next**.

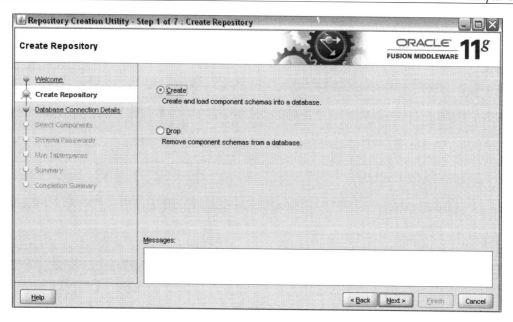

4. Select **Create** and click on **Next**.

5. Enter the database information.

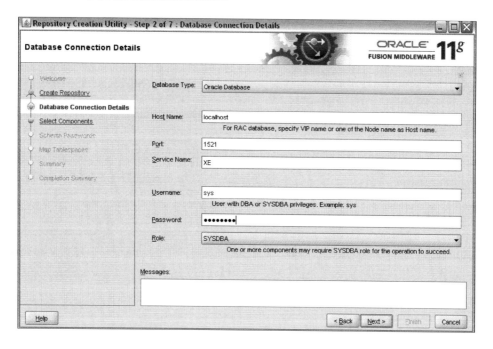

6. Click on **Next.**

7. If you are using XE, you will see a warning at this point that this version is too old. You can safely ignore this warning as it applies only to production environments.

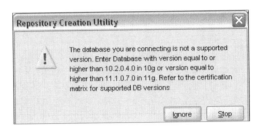

8. The pre-requisites are reviewed. When complete, click on **OK**. The utility moves to the next page—with a slight delay, just wait for it.

9. On the **Select Components** screen, enter **DEV** in the field for creating a new prefix.

10. Select the component **SOA Infrastructure**. Dependent schemas are selected automatically.

11. If you choose to select other components, these install instructions may not match your install experience. Also, you may have to increase processes in XE (you will get a message telling you what is required).

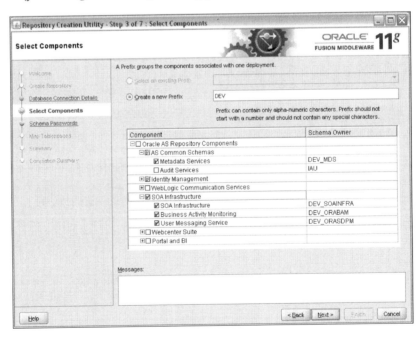

12. Click on **Next**.

13. The pre-requisites for this step are checked. When completed, click on **OK**.

14. Select the radio button to **Use the same password for all schemas**. Enter a schema password. The password **welcome1** is assumed in this document but you should choose your own secure password or a different one for each schema and be sure to record your passwords as you will need them later.

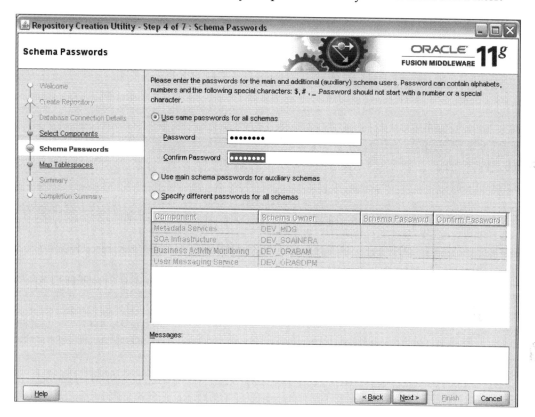

15. Click on **Next**.

16. Review the tablespaces and schema owners for the components.

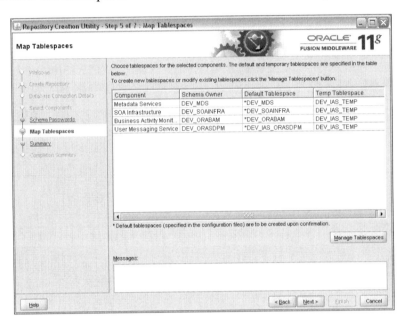

17. Accepting the defaults, click on **Next**, and then click on **OK** to create the tablespaces.

18. When the pre-requisites for this step are completed, click on **OK**.

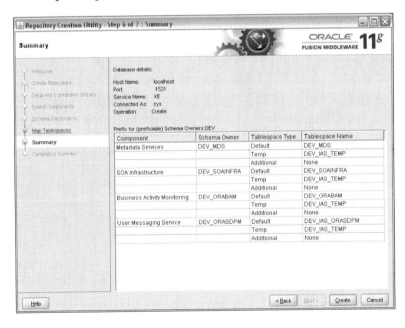

19. Click on **Create** to create the tablespaces. This takes about two minutes.

20. When completed, click on **Close**.

Installing SOA

Once the database is configured, you can install the SOA server into the **Oracle Home** on the WebLogic server.

1. In a command window, enter:

```
cd c:\stageSOA\soa\Disk1
setup -jreLoc C:\Oracle\Middleware\home_11gR1\jdk160_11
```

2. When the install wizard **Welcome** screen comes up, click on **Next**.

3. Wait for the pre-requisite check to complete (it's quick!).

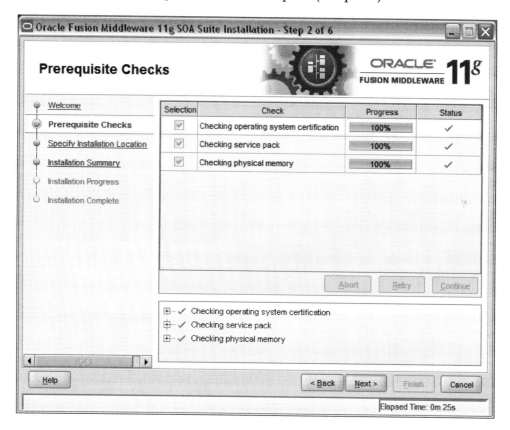

4. Click on **Next**.

5. On the **Specify Installation Location** screen, select the middleware home:
   C:\Oracle\Middleware\home_11gR1.

6. Enter Oracle home: **Oracle_SOA1.** If you use a different Oracle home, then adjust accordingly when **Oracle_SOA1** is referenced throughout this document.

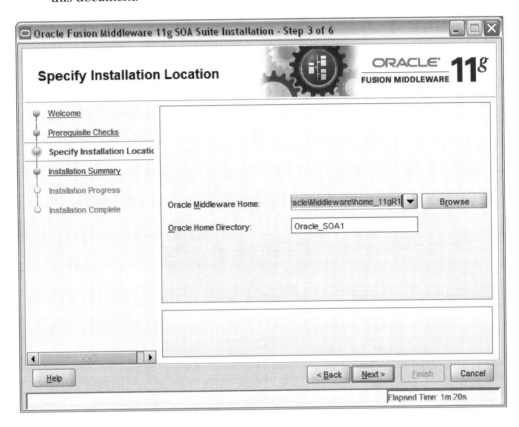

7. Click on **Next**.
8. Review **Summary**.

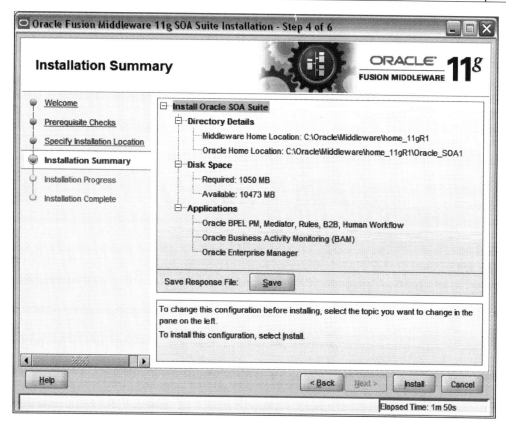

9. Click on **Install**.

10. Wait for the installation to complete—it takes a few minutes.

11. Click on **Finish**.

Creating Domain

From the Oracle Home location, you configure the WebLogic server domain for the SOA and BAM servers.

1. In a command window, enter:

```
cd C:\Oracle\Middleware\home_11gR1\Oracle_SOA1\common\bin
config.cmd
```

2. When the configuration wizard's **Welcome** screen comes up, select **Create a new WebLogic domain**, and then click on **Next**.

3. Select **Generate a domain** and select **SOA Suite, Enterprise Manager**, and **Business Activity Monitoring**. Dependent products are selected automatically.

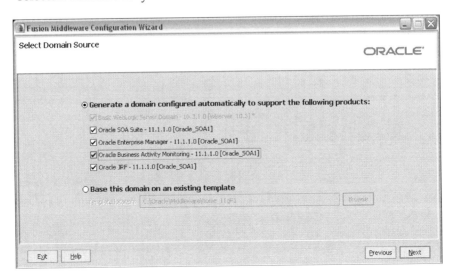

4. Click on **Next**.

5. Enter the domain name: **domain1**.

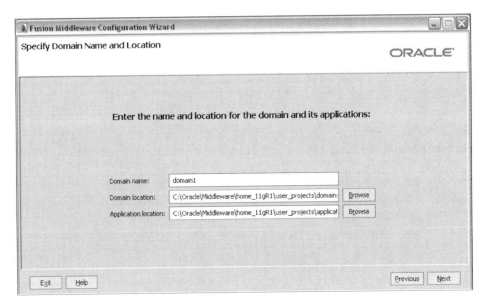

6. Click on **Next**.

7. Enter the user name as **weblogic** and a password. The password **welcome1** is assumed in this document but you should choose your own secure password and remember it for later in the document when the password is referenced.

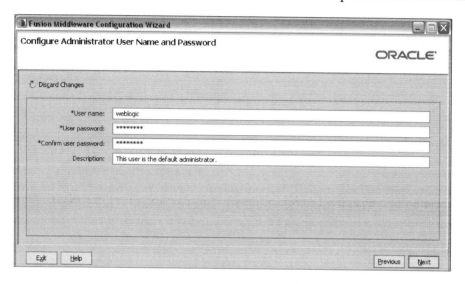

8. Click on **Next**.
9. Select the **Sun SDK 1.6_11** and leave **Development Mode** checked.

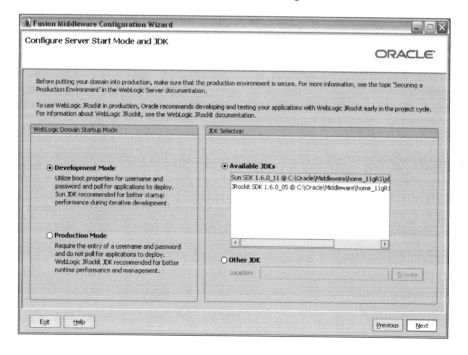

10. Click on **Next**.

11. On the **Configure JDBC Component Schema** screen, you select the components that you want to change, and then enter the property value for those components. First, select all of the components and enter **welcome1** for the password in the **Schema Password** field.

12. With all of the checkboxes selected, enter the **Service**, **Host**, and **Port** values.

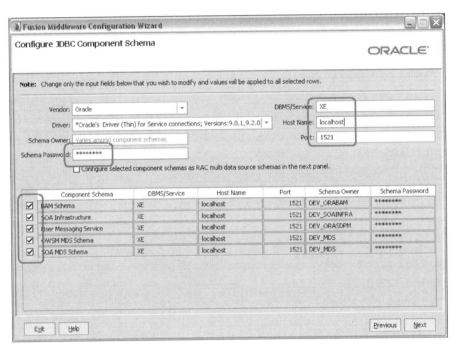

13. Now, look at the table. Review the **Schema Owner** column and confirm that the values are the same as what you configured in the **Configure Schema** section when you ran the **RCU**. Go back and review the screenshots in that section of this document for the schema owners if you do not remember them.

14. Complete the following if the schema owners need to be updated:

    i.   Deselect all the component checkboxes.

    ii. Select **BAM Schema** only.

    iii. Enter the **Schema Owner** for BAM.

    iv. Next, deselect **BAM Schema** and select the next one.

    v. Enter the schema owners one-by-one.

    vi. Continue until all schema owners are entered.

15. Click on **Next**.

16. The data source connections are all tested.

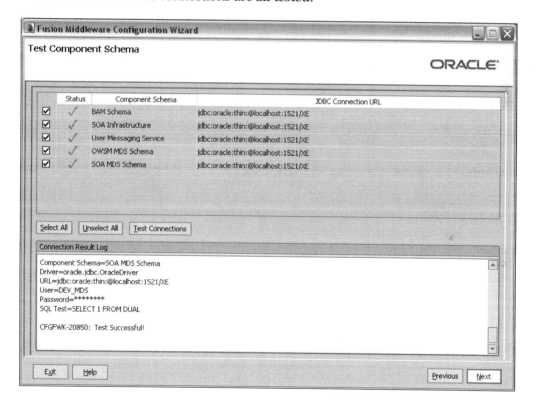

17. If all are successful, click on **Next**, otherwise click on **Previous** and correct any errors.

18. Click on **Next** once more, accepting defaults (no optional configurations), and you reach the **Configuration Summary** screen.

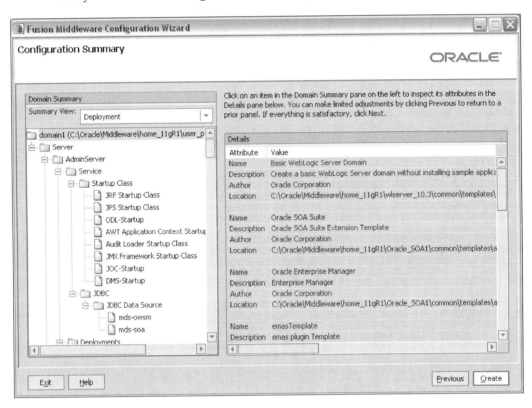

19. Click on **Create**.

20. Wait for the creation to finish—it takes just a minute.

21. Click on **Done**.

Installing JDeveloper and SOA Composite Editor

Now that your servers are install JDeveloper and the JDeveloper extension for SOA Composite Editor.

Installing JDeveloper

After installing the servers, you can install the JDeveloper IDE.

 If you are installing JDeveloper on a machine that is not the same as your WebLogic server installation, you must have installed the JDK 6 update 11 first. See the pre-requisites section for download location.

1. Open a command window and enter (if you copy/paste, make sure there is no space after the = sign and eliminate trailing spaces):

```
set JAVA_HOME=C:\Oracle\Middleware\home_11gR1\jdk160_11
cd c:\stageSOA
%JAVA_HOME%\bin\java.exe -jar jdevstudio11111install.jar
```

You will see a message that the JAR is extracting:

```
%JAVA_HOME%\bin\java.exe -jar jdevstudio11111install.jar
Extracting 0%.........................
```

When it reaches 100%, the installation wizard will open. This takes a few minutes.

 If you see the splash screen briefly but then you do not see the extracting message and the installation wizard does not open, it's probably because the Java is the wrong version. Enter `%JAVA_HOME%\bin\java.exe -version` to see the version. It must be version 1.6_11.

Complete the installation wizard as follows.

 Installing JDeveloper also installs an embedded WebLogic Server that you can use for testing Java applications. You will use this in one of the labs.

2. Welcome Screen—click on **Next**.

3. Choose Middleware Home Directory: select **Create a new Middleware Home** and enter **C:\Oracle\Middleware\jdev_11gR1**. This document assumes that path. If you enter something else, then adjust accordingly when **C:\Oracle\Middleware\jdev_11gR1** is referenced.

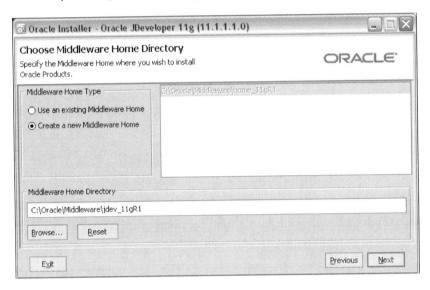

4. Click on **Next**.
5. Choose **Install Type** as **Complete**, and then click on **Next**.
6. **JDK Selection**: you will see your JAVA_HOME.

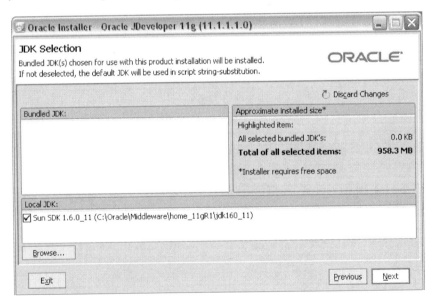

7. Click on **Next**.

8. Confirm **Product Installation Directories**. You should see:

    ° Middleware Home Directory: `C:\Oracle\Middleware\jdev_11gR1`

    ° JDeveloper and ADF: `C:\Oracle\Middleware\jdev_11gR1\jdeveloper`

    ° WebLogic Server: `C:\Oracle\Middleware\jdev_11gR1\wlserver_10.3`

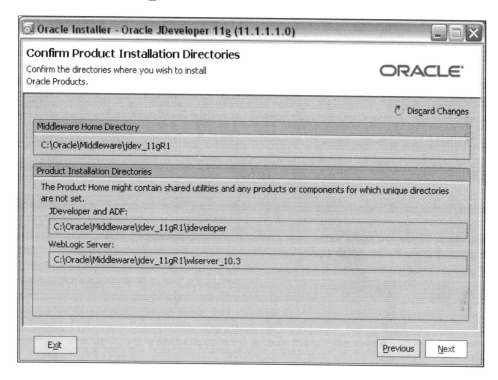

9. Click on **Next**.

10. Choose **Shortcut** location: **"All Users"**, and then click on **Next**.

11. Review **Installation Summary**.

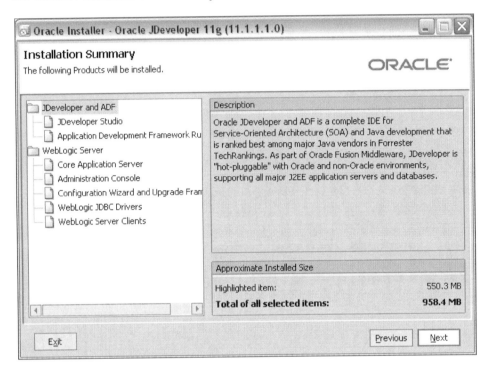

12. Click on **Next** and the installation starts.

13. Wait for the installation to complete—a few minutes.

14. When installation completes, deselect **Run Quickstart** and click on **Done**.

Updating JDeveloper with latest SOA

SOA design time in JDeveloper requires a JDeveloper extension called SOA Composite Editor. While this is normally updated over the network when using release-level software, you can also perform the update manually if you have the extension file. JDeveloper periodically prompts you to accept an automatic network update. Since this is released software, you have the option to click on **OK** to update to a newer version. The SOA extension is about 230 MB and may take some time to download.

1. Start **JDeveloper Studio 11.1.1.1.0** from the Windows Programs menu: **Oracle Fusion Middleware 11.1.1.1.0** or run C:\Oracle\Middleware\ jdev_11gR1\jdeveloper\jdeveloper.exe.

During startup, select the following when prompted:

2. Select **Default Role**, deselect **Show this dialog every time**, and click on **OK**.

3. Click on **No** to "**Migrate from previous release**"

4. If you are prompted to select file extensions to associate with JDeveloper, deselect everything or select the ones you would like for your machine and continue.

5. After starting JDeveloper, wait for the *Integrated Weblogic Domain* to be created. This domain is created the first time you run JDeveloper after installation. It is not used by SOA. Watch for the completion message for setting up the domain in the JDeveloper Messages log window at the bottom of the JDeveloper IDE:

```
[12:37:11 PM] Creating Integrated Weblogic domain...
[12:38:05 PM] Extending Integrated Weblogic domain...
[12:38:14 PM] Integrated Weblogic domain processing completed
successfully.
```

Now you can update the SOA Composite Editor extension. These instructions show you how to update the extension over the network.

1. Select **Help | Check For Updates**; click on **Next**.

2. Select **Search Update Centers** and select **Oracle Fusion Middleware Products**.

3. Click on **Next**. The system will search the update center for extensions.

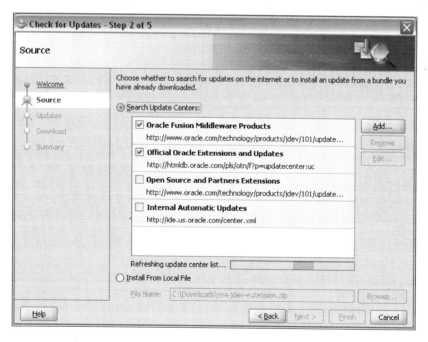

4. From the list of extensions, select **Oracle SOA Composite Editor** and click on **Next** to begin downloading. The extension is about 230 MB and takes a few minutes to download.

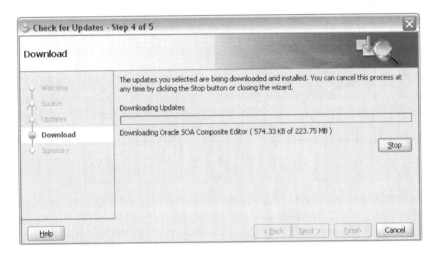

5. When the extension has finished downloading, it is listed with the version number detail.

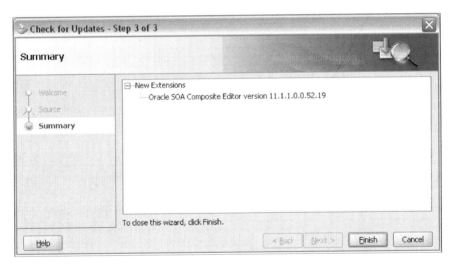

6. Confirm that the **SOA Composite Editor** version matches the version number detail as shown: **11.1.1.0.0.52.19**.

 The Update Center provides the most recent version of the SOA Composite Editor that is compatible with your version of JDeveloper and you may have a newer version than the one listed here. The last two numbers, 52.19, refer to the version that was released in July 2009. If the Update Center gives you a newer version, take note of the version number for verification in the step below.

7. Click on **Finish**.

8. Restart JDeveloper when prompted. You will say **No** again to **Migrate from previous release** question as JDeveloper starts up.

9. When JDeveloper is running again, go to **Help | About** and confirm the JDeveloper version is as shown: JDEVADF_11.1.1.1.0_ GENERIC_090615.0017.5407.

10. Select the **Version** tab, and confirm the SOA Composite Editor was installed properly by confirming the version: 11.1.1.0.0.52.19, or the version you noted above.

Additional actions

In the following section, you will be performing additional configuration that is optional but will greatly improve performance and usability in the context of the development work you are about to start with the tutorial.

Setting memory limits

Review the memory settings. This value is dependent on your machine resources and may need to be adjusted for your machine. Allocating less memory for startup will give you better performance on a machine with less memory available. This value is appropriate for a 3 GB memory machine or less.

1. Edit the SOA domain environment file found here (make sure you have the SOA Domain environment file):

   ```
   C:\Oracle\Middleware\home_11gR1\user_projects\domains\ domain1\
   bin\setSOADomainEnv.cmd
   ```

2. Set memory values:

   ```
   set DEFAULT_MEM_ARGS=-Xms512m -Xmx512m
   ```

Starting and stopping

Now it's time to start your servers. You can start them using the provided script or you can start them separately. Instructions for both methods are included.

Starting

First set `boot.properties` and then start the servers.

1. Before you start, set the boot properties so you are not prompted to log in during server startup. Copy `C:\po\bin\boot.properties` to `C:\Oracle\Middleware\home_11gR1\user_projects\domains\domain1`.

2. Edit the copied file to reflect the password for your configuration (entered during domain configuration). The first time the server is started this file is encrypted and copied to the server locations.

   You can start the servers one at a time or you can use the `start_all` script to start the admin and SOA managed servers (not BAM). To start them one at a time instead, skip to step 6.

3. Copy the startup script to the Oracle directory:

   ```
   C:\po\bin\start_all.cmd to
   C:\Oracle\Middleware
   ```

4. Edit the copied file to reflect your environment.

5. Open a command window and start your servers as shown. You must specify how many seconds to wait after starting the admin server before starting the managed server. The admin server must be in the **RUNNING** state before the managed server starts (see the following screenshot). Try `180` seconds and adjust as necessary. You will need more time the first time you start after a machine reboot than for subsequent restarts:

   ```
   cd C:\Oracle\Middleware
   start_all.cmd 180
   ```

   Your servers are now starting automatically so you can skip steps 6-10. Jump to step 12 to continue.

   To start the servers manually, continue with the following steps.

6. Open three command windows, one for the WebLogic admin server, one for the SOA managed server, and one for the BAM managed server (only start BAM when you need it for a BAM lab).

7. Start the Admin Server first:

   ```
   cd C:\Oracle\Middleware\home_11gR1\user_projects\domains\domain1
   startWebLogic.cmd
   ```

8. Wait for the Admin Server to finish starting up. It takes a few minutes—watch for status **RUNNING** in the log console window:

```
<Mar 5, 2009 11:40:24 AM PST> <Notice> <Server> <BEA-002613> <Channel "Default[2
]" is now listening on 144.25.142.205:7001 for protocols iiop, t3, ldap, snmp, h
ttp.>
<Mar 5, 2009 11:40:24 AM PST> <Notice> <Server> <BEA-002613> <Channel "Default[4
]" is now listening on 127.0.0.1:7001 for protocols iiop, t3, ldap, snmp, http.>
<Mar 5, 2009 11:40:24 AM PST> <Notice> <WebLogicServer> <BEA-000331> <Started We
bLogic Admin Server "AdminServer" for domain "domain1" running in Development Mo
de>
<Mar 5, 2009 11:40:24 AM PST> <Notice> <WebLogicServer> <BEA-000365> <Server sta
te changed to RUNNING>
<Mar 5, 2009 11:40:24 AM PST> <Notice> <WebLogicServer> <BEA-000360> <Server sta
rted in RUNNING mode>
```

9. Start the SOA managed server in the second command window. This start script is in the `bin` directory. You can also run it directly from the `bin` directory:

```
cd C:\Oracle\Middleware\home_11gR1\user_projects\domains\domain1
bin\startManagedWebLogic.cmd soa_server1
```

10. When prompted, enter the username **weblogic** and password **welcome1**. If you did step 1 and set `boot.properties`, you will not be prompted. The server is started when you see the message, **INFO: FabricProviderServlet.stateChanged SOA Platform is running and accepting requests**.

```
INFO: Deferred locker started successfully !!!
Mar 5, 2009 12:00:51 PM oracle.tip.mediator.serviceEngine.MediatorServiceEngine
startListeners
INFO: ****** MediatorServiceEngine:: Deferred Listeners initialized ******
Mar 5, 2009 12:00:51 PM oracle.integration.platform.blocks.scheduler.FabricSched
ulerFactory stateChanged
INFO: FabricSchedulerFactory: Fabric starting scheduler
INFO: FabricProviderServlet.stateChanged SOA Platform is running and accepting r
equests
Mar 5, 2009 12:00:53 PM oracle.bpel.services.common.ServicesLogger __log
WARNING: <.> Notification via email, voice, SMS or IM will not be sent. If you w
ould like to enable them, please configure corresponding sdpmessaging driver. Th
en modify the accounts and set NotificationMode attribute to either NONE, EMAIL
or ALL in workflow-notification-config.xml
```

11. Start the BAM managed server in the third command window—do this only when needed for the BAM lab:

```
cd C:\Oracle\Middleware\home_11gR1\user_projects\domains\domain1
bin\startManagedWebLogic.cmd bam_server1
```

12. When prompted, enter the user name **weblogic** and password **welcome1**. If you did step 1 and set `boot.properties`, you will not be prompted. Watch for the **RUNNING** status.

Console URLs

Log in with **weblogic/welcome1** for all consoles:

- Weblogic console: `http://localhost:7001/console`
- Enterprise Manager console: `http://localhost:7001/em`
- SOA worklist: `http://localhost:8001/integration/worklistapp`
- B2B console: `http://localhost:8001/b2b`
- BAM (must use IE browser): `http://localhost:9001/OracleBAM`

Stopping servers

Whenever you need to stop the servers complete the following:

1. Stop the managed servers first by entering *Ctrl+C* in the command window. Wait until stopped.
2. Stop the admin server by entering *Ctrl+C* in the command window.

WebLogic Server console settings

There are two suggested changes to make in the WebLogic Server console.

First, you will be viewing application deployments often using the WebLogic server console. This is a lot more convenient if you change the settings not to show libraries as this makes the list a lot shorter and you can find what you need more quickly.

1. Start the WebLogic Admin Server (WLS) if it is not already running.
2. Log in to the WLS console `http://localhost:7001/console`.
3. Click on **Deployments** in the left navigation bar.
4. Click on **Customize this table** at the top of the **Deployments** table.
5. Change the number of rows per page to **100** (there are only about 30).
6. Select the checkbox to exclude libraries and click on **Apply**.

Second, when the server is started, internal applications like the WLS console are not deployed completely and you see a slight delay when you first access the console. You saw this delay just now when you first accessed the console URL. You can change this behavior to deploy internal applications at startup instead and then you don't get the delay when you access the console. This is convenient for demos (if you want to show the console) and also if you tend to use the console each time you start up the server.

1. Click on **domain1** in the left navigation bar in the WLS console.
2. Click on **Configuration | General** tab.
3. Deselect **Enable on-demand deployment of internal applications** checkbox.
4. Click on the **Save** button.

EM settings for development

The Enterprise Manager can provide different levels of information about composite runtime instances based on a property setting. During development, it is helpful to have a higher setting. These settings are not used on production machines except when specifically needed for debugging purposes as there is a performance cost.

1. Start your servers if they are not already running.
2. Log in to the EM console at `http://localhost:7001/em`.
3. Right-click on the **soa-infra (soa_server1)** in the left navigation bar to open the SOA menu and select **SOA Administration | Common Properties**.

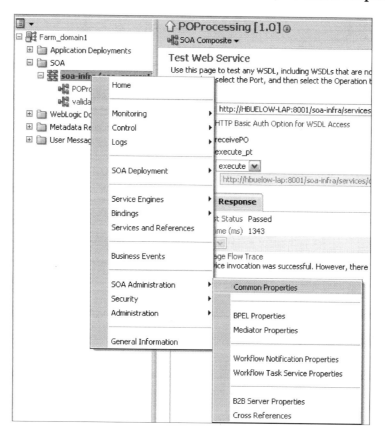

4. Select **Audit Level**: **Development** and select the checkbox for **Capture Composite Instance State**.

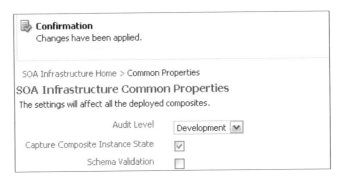

5. Click on **Apply** and click on **Yes**.

If you need to uninstall JDeveloper and servers

If you need to uninstall everything, complete the following:

1. First save anything from `C:\Oracle\Middleware\jdev_11gR1\jdeveloper\mywork` that you want to keep as this directory will be deleted.

2. Run **Uninstall** from the program menu to completion for both JDeveloper and WLS.

3. Delete `C:\Oracle\Middleware\jdev_11gR1` and `C:\Oracle\Middleware\home_11gR1`. If you get an error message about not being able to delete because a name or path is too long, change the names of the composite directories within `home_ 11gR1\user_projects\domains\domain1\deployed-composites` to `a\b\c\d` and try deleting again.

4. Delete program groups from `C:\Documents and Settings\All Users\Start Menu\Programs\`:
   - Oracle Fusion Middleware 11.1.1.1.0
   - Oracle SOA 11*g* - Home1
   - Oracle WebLogic

5. Complete the *Dropping existing schema* section earlier in this chapter to clean up the database.

Configuration

This section provides the instructions for creating database and JMS resources that are required by the tutorial. Start your database and WebLogic admin servers and complete the following configuration steps.

Installing the database schema

First, create a table in the database owned by the `soademo` user:

1. Make sure your database is running.

2. Create the `soademo` user using the following script. It is OK to run this script even if the `soademo` user already exists. From a command line, `cd` to the `c:\po\sql` directory and run the following replacing `pw` with your own system user's password:

    ```
    cd c:\po\sql
    sqlplus system/pw @create_soademo_user.sql
    ```

3. Now, create the credit card info table. It is OK to run this script again even if the table already exists. Make sure that you run it with the `soademo` user for proper ownership:

    ```
    cd c:\po\sql
    sqlplus soademo/soademo @create_creditrating_table.sql
    ```

Creating the JMS resources

Next you must create a JMS resource. You create this by using the WebLogic Server console. First you create the JMS queue and connection factory and then a connection pool for that connection factory.

1. Make sure thatyour server has started using the instructions above. If it is not already open, open `http://localhost:7001/console` to start the **Web Logic Server (WLS)** console and log in using **weblogic/welcome1**. Replace the host and port and username/password to match your own configuration if necessary.

First add the *JMS Queue*:

1. In the WLS console, on the left navigation bar, expand **Services | Messaging** and click on **JMS Modules**.

2. Click on **SOAJMSModule** (click on the name, not the checkbox).

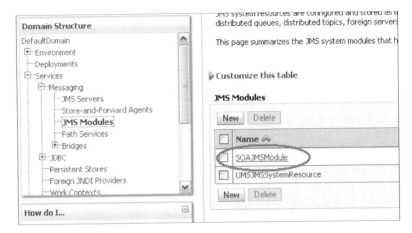

3. In the **Summary of Resources** table, click on **New**.

4. Select the resource type: **Queue** and click on **Next**.

5. Enter **Name** as **demoFulfillmentQueue** and **JNDI** Name as **jms/demoFulfillmentQueue**.

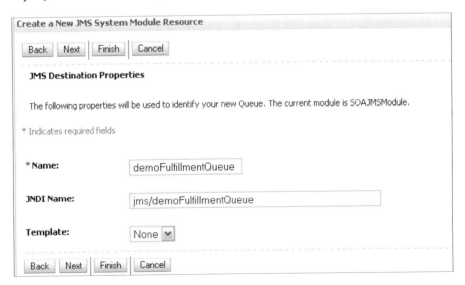

6. Click on **Next**.

7. From the **Subdeployments** list, select **SOASubDeployment**.

8. From the **JMS Servers** list, select **SOAJMSServer**.

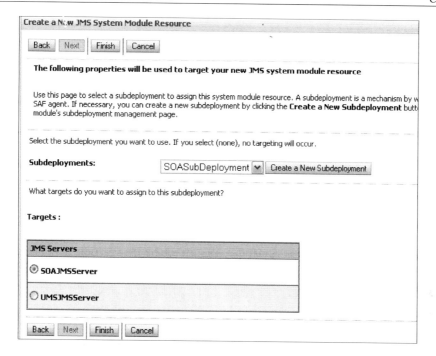

9. Click on **Finish**.

Now add the **Connection Factory**.

1. In the **Summary of Resources** table, click on **New**.
2. Select the resource type: **Connection Factory** and click on **Next**.
3. Enter **Name as demoCF** and **JNDI name** as **jms/demoCF**.

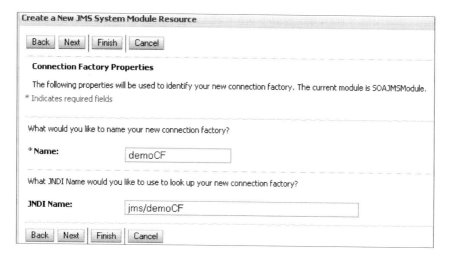

4. Click on **Next**.

5. Click on **Finish**.

You should see both the queue and the connection factory listed in the **Summary of Resources** as shown here:

| | demoCF | Connection Factory | jms/demoCF | Default Targetting | DefaultServer |
| | demoFulfillmentQueue | Queue | jms/demoFulfillmentQueue | SOASubDeployment | SOAJMSServer |

Now add the connection pool. The connection pool is configured in the JMSAdapter application and uses a Deployment Plan. First, create a directory to contain that plan.

1. Create a directory here: `C:\Oracle\Middleware\home_11gR1\Oracle_SOA1\soa\JMSPlan` (adjust the path according to your installation).

2. In the left navigation bar of the WLS console, click on **Deployments**.

3. Click on **JMSAdapter** (click on the name, not the checkbox).

4. Click the **Configuration** tab and then the **Outbound Connection Pools** tab.

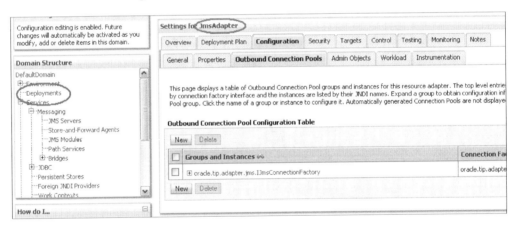

5. Click on **New**.

6. Select the **oracle.tip.adapter.jms.IJmsConnectionFactory** factory.

7. Click on **Next**.

8. Enter **eis/Queue/demo**.

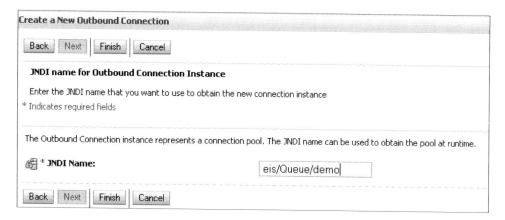

9. Click on **Finish**.

10. At this point, you are asked for the deployment plan location. Click on the path to the directory you created earlier and enter **Plan.xml** for the plan name.

 If you are not asked for the plan location at this time, it means you already have a plan for the JMS adapter from an existing configuration. That plan file will be used for this configuration. You can skip ahead to the next step to hook up the connection factory.

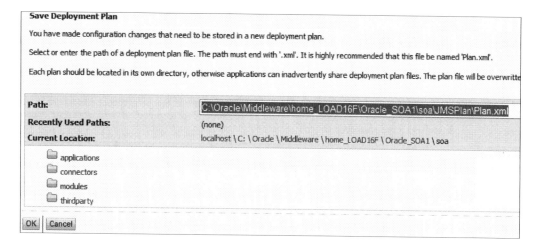

11. Click on **OK**.

12. Verify the plan name is set to **Plan.xml** in the **JMSPlan** directory.

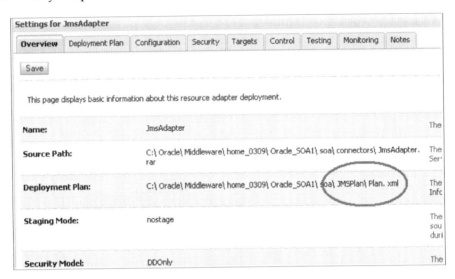

Go back to the new connection pool to hook up the connection factory:

1. Click on the **Configuration** tab.
2. Expand the group: **oracle.tip.adapter.jms.IJmsConnectionFactory**.
3. Click on **eis/Queue/demo**.

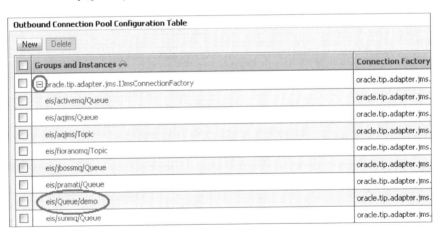

4. To change a property value you must enter the value and then press the *Enter* key and then click on the **Save** button. Do not use the *Tab* key after entering the value. Follow these instructions exactly:

   i. Select the cell on the far right for the property **ConnectionFactoryLocation**.

ii. An edit box appears. Type in the value **jms/demoCF** and press the *Enter* key.

iii. You must use the *Enter* key for the value to be entered in the field.

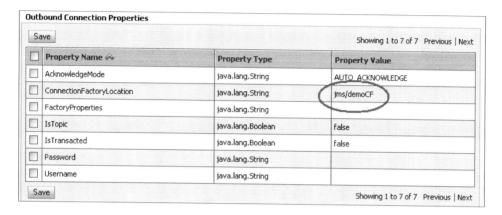

5. Click on **Save**. You must use the **Save** button to save the value.

6. Now the adapter must be redeployed. Click on **Deployments** in the left navigation bar.

7. Select the checkbox next to **JMSAdapter**.

8. Click on **Update** at the top of the **Deployment** table.

9. Verify that the correct deployment plan is selected.

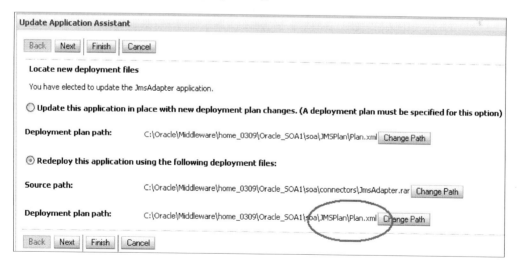

10. Click on **Next**.

11. Click on **Finish**.

Creating the database resource

The tutorial application requires a database data source. You create this using the WebLogic Server console. First you create the data source and then you create a connection pool for that data source.

1. Make sure that your admin server is started using the instructions provided earlier. If it is not already open, open `http://localhost:7001/console` to open the Web Logic Server (WLS) console and log in using **weblogic/welcome1**. Replace the host and port and username/password to match your own configuration.

2. On the left navigation bar, click on **Services | JDBC | Data Sources**.

3. In the data source table, click on **New**.

4. Enter the data source information:

   ○ **Name: soademoDatabase**

   ○ JNDI Name: **jdbc/soademoDatabase**

   ○ Database Type: **Oracle**

   ○ The Database driver defaults to the correct driver: **Oracle's Driver (Thin XA) for Instance connections**

5. Click on **Next**, click on **Next** again.

6. Enter the database information:

   ○ **Database Name: XE** (your database SID)

   ○ **Host name: localhost** (host where your database is running)

   ○ **Port: 1521** (set according to your configuration)

   ○ **Database user name: soademo** (created in previous section)

   ○ **Database user password: soademo**

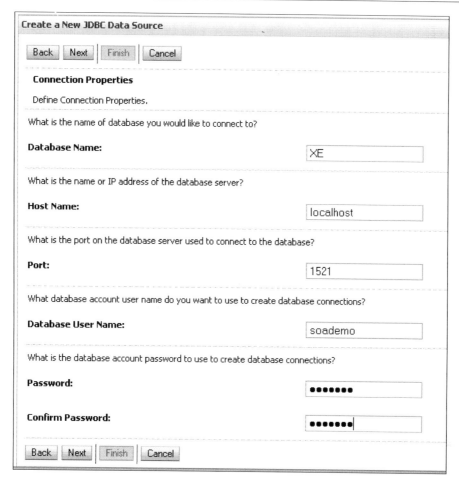

7. Click on **Next**.

8. Click on **Test Configuration**. Confirm success message at the top of the page.

9. Click on **Next**.

10. Select the **Target server** where your SOA component is running: **soa_server1**.

11. Click on **Finish**.

Now create the connection pool. You have to edit the database adapter application and it uses a Deployment Plan. First, create a directory to contain that plan.

1. Create a directory here: `C:\Oracle\Middleware\home_11gR1\Oracle_ SOA1\soa\DBPlan` (adjust the path according to your installation).

2. In the left navigation bar, click on **Deployments**.

3. Click on the **DbAdapter** application (click on the name, not the checkbox).

4. Click on the **Configuration** tab, and then click on the **Outbound Connection Pools** tab.

5. Click on **New**.

6. Select the radio button for **javax.resource.cci.ConnectionFactory** and click on **Next**.

7. Enter the **JNDI Name** as: **eis/DB/soademoDatabase**.

8. This is not the same value as in the previous step. It matches the value you enter in your database connection you create later when building your application using JDeveloper. Click on **Finish**.

9. At this point, you are asked for the deployment plan location. Click on the path to the directory you created earlier and enter the deployment plan name **Plan.xml**.

If you are not asked for the plan location at this time, it means you already have a plan for the DB adapter from an existing configuration. That plan file will be used for this configuration. You can skip ahead to the next step to hook up the connection factory.

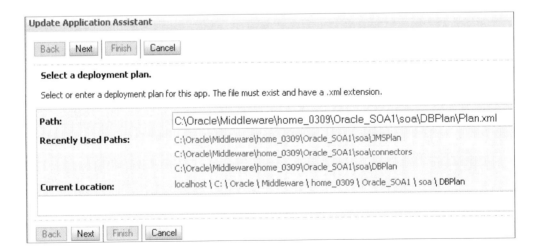

10. Click on **OK**.

11. Confirm the name of the deployment plan.

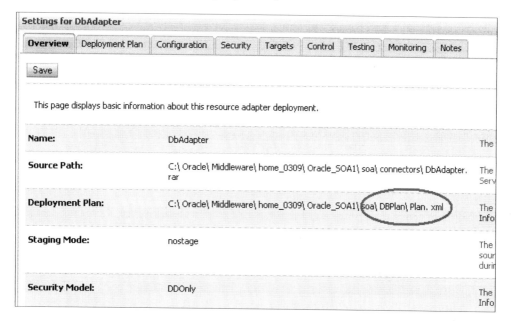

12. Now, edit the connection pool to reference the data source. Click on the **Configuration** tab, expand the connection factory and click on your new connection pool, **eis/DB/soademoDatabase** (click on the name, not the checkbox).

13. To change a property value you must enter the value and then press the *Enter* key and then click on the **Save** button. Do not use the *Tab* key after entering the value. Follow these instructions exactly:

    i.   In the **Properties** table, select the box to the far right of **xADataSource**.

    ii. The edit box appears. Type in your data source name that you created above: **jdbc/soademoDatabase**.

    iii. Press the *Enter* key to apply the value. You must use the *Enter* key for the value to be entered in the field.

14. Select **Save**. You must use the **Save** button to save the value.

15. Go back to the main **Deployments** page to update the **DbAdapter** as follows. Click on **Deployments** in the left navigation bar.

16. Select the checkbox next to **DbAdapter**.

17. Click on **Update**.

18. Select **Redeploy this application** and confirm the deployment plan location.

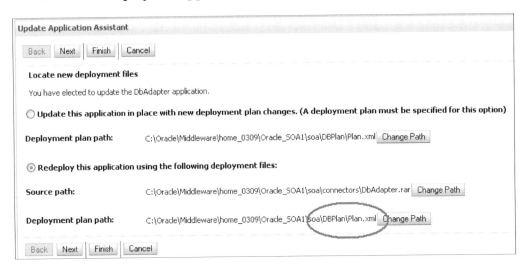

19. Click on **Finish**.

20. Confirm that the connection pool is added by going back to the **DbAdapter | Configuration | Outbound Connection Pools** and expanding the connection factory listed there.

21. Confirm the value of the **xADataSource** property that you entered previously. It should be **jdbc/soademoDatabase**. Look closely! This is the most common place where the configuration is in error.

22. Go back to the **JMSAdapter Outbound Connection Pools** tab and review the connection factory property value for the **eis/Queue/demo** connection pool that you entered previously. It should be **jms/demoCF**. Look closely! This is the most common place where the configuration is in error.

When the two resources are added and confirmed, you are ready to start building the SOA composites. Continue with the next step to test your installation.

Testing your installation

This section shows you how to verify your installation and configuration.

After installing SOA Suite and JDeveloper, confirm that you have the correct 11.1.1.1.0 version.

You have three things to check:

1. *JDeveloper*: Start J Developer and select from the toolbar, **Help | About**. You should see this build: JDEVADF_11.1.1.1.0_GENERIC_090615.0017.5407.

2. *SOA Composite Editor*: Select the **Version** tab on the JDeveloper **Help | About** dialog. You should see this value: 11.1.1.0.0.52.19. It is OK that this includes 11.1.1.0.0 instead of 11.1.1.1.0.

3. *SOA Server*: Run soaversion.cmd from C:\Oracle\Middleware\ home_11gR1\Oracle_SOA1\bin and you should see this build: PCBPEL_11.1.1.1.0_GENERIC_090618.1440.5219.

Now verify the database table you created for the credit card information. This table was created in the *Configuration* section earlier.

1. Use SQLPlus to show the table. Be sure to connect using the soademo user.

   ```
   sqlplus soademo/soademo
   select * from creditcardinfo;
   ```

   Next, verify your database and JMS resources. These resources were created in the *Configuration* section earlier.

2. In the WLS console, on the left navigation bar, expand **Services | JDBC | Data Sources**. It is OK if you have a newer version that matches the version from the Update Center.

3. Confirm that you see the resource **soademoDatabase**.

4. On the left navigation bar, expand **Services | Messaging** and click on **JMS Modules**.

5. Click on **SOAJMSModule** (click on the name, not the checkbox).

6. In the **Summary of Resources**, confirm you see the queue and the connection factory, **demoFulfillmentQueue** and **demoCF**.

7. Confirm that the database connection pool is added by going to **Deployments** in the left navigation bar and clicking on **DbAdapter | Configuration | Outbound Connection Pools** and expanding the **eis/DB/ soademoDatabase** connection factory listed there.

8. Confirm the value of the **xADataSource** property that you entered previously. It should be **jdbc/soademoDatabase**.

9. From **Deployments**, click on **JMSAdapter**, then click the **Outbound Connection Pools** tab and review the connection factory property value for the **eis/Queue/demo** connection pool. It should be **jms/demoCF**.

Oracle Service Bus installation

Chapter 11 is a lab in the tutorial that uses Oracle Service Bus (OSB). This is one of the independent labs (see Chapter 3 for the lab descriptions). When you are ready to do this lab, come back here and install OSB. You do not need to install OSB until you are ready to do the OSB lab.

1. Go to `http://www.oracle.com/technology/products/integration/service-bus/index.html` and download `osb1031_wls103_win32.exe`.

2. Execute the program `osb1031_wls103_win32.exe` to start the installer.

3. On the **Welcome** screen, click on **Next**.

4. Select **Create a new BEA Home**.

5. Enter the location where you would like to install the product.

 Make sure you do not specify the Middleware home of the SOA Suite Install. OSB will run on a different WebLogic domain than SOA Suite.

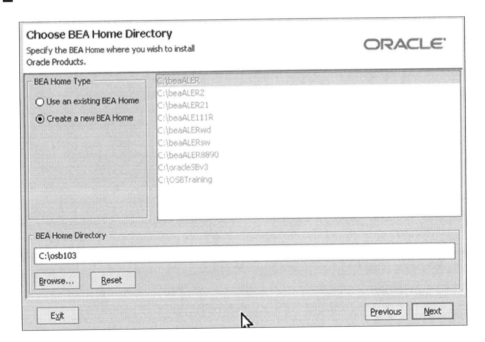

6. Click on **Next**.

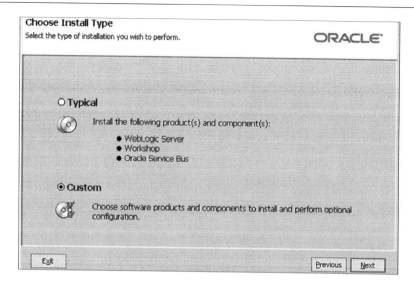

7. Choose **Custom** and click on **Next**.

8. There are two components unchecked, namely **Server Examples** and **Service Bus Examples**. Scroll down and check the **Service Bus Examples**. The lab requires the **Service Bus Example** server to be installed.

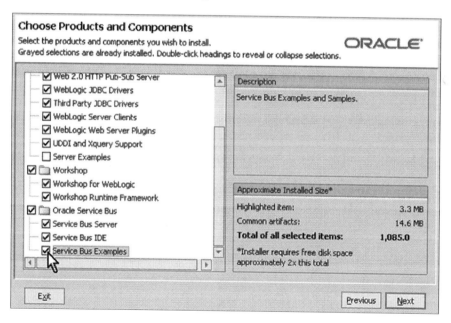

9. Click on **Next**.

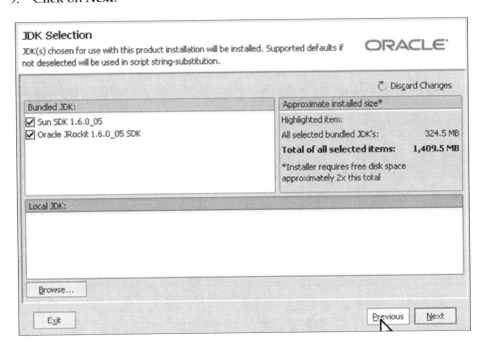

10. Accept the default selections for the **JDK** and click on **Next**.

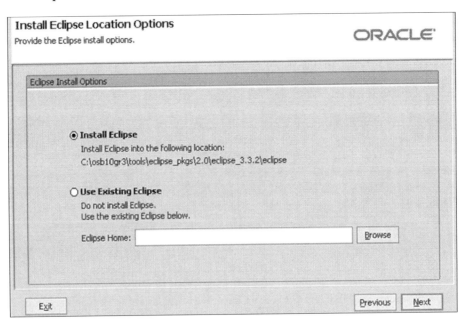

11. Accept the default to **Install Eclipse** and click on **Next**.

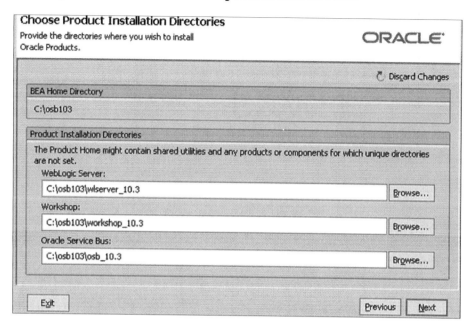

12. Accept the default directories for the installation and click on **Next**.

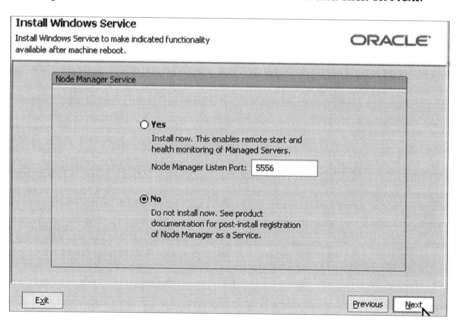

13. Accept the default to skip the Windows Service installation and click on **Next**.

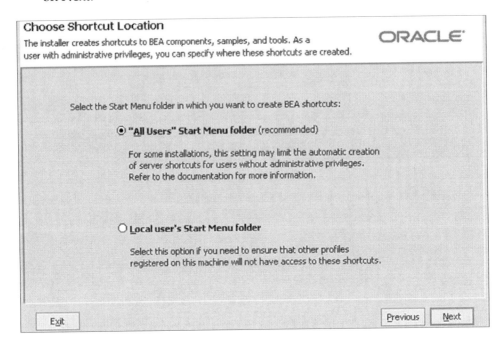

14. Choose **All Users** to give all accounts access to the product shortcuts, then click on **Next**.

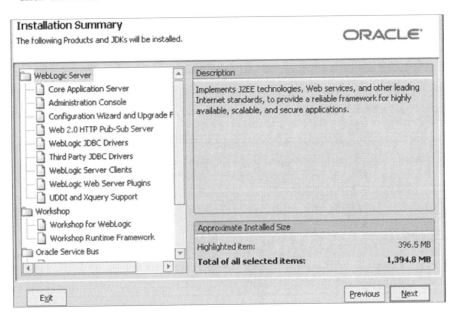

15. The **Installation Summary** page is displayed. Click on **Next**. Installation begins.

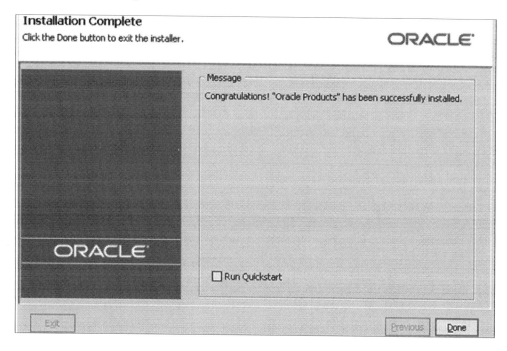

16. When installation is complete, uncheck **Run Quickstart** and click on **Done**.

Testing your OSB installation

Now verify that the installation was successful. You use the Example Server created during installation. This example server is the only server in an OSB Weblogic domain and serves the function of both an admin server and an OSB managed server.

1. Launch the **Oracle Service Bus Examples Server** using the start menu that was created when you installed the product.

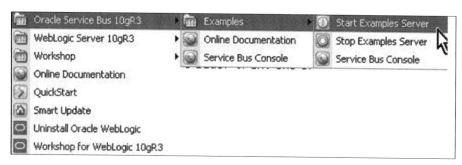

2. The OSB web application automatically loads and displays a page similar to the one shown here. Load the examples by clicking on the **Load the Examples** button.

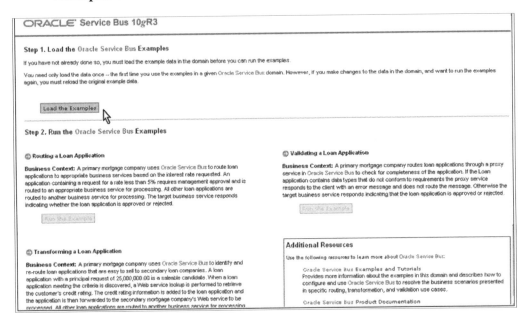

3. Test the example code by executing any one of the use scenarios shown on the page. If any one of them is successful, the system has passed the smoke test.

Removing samples (optional)

The lab uses the Examples Server but not the examples themselves. You can remove the examples if desired.

1. If the OSB examples server is not running, start it up by selecting the Start Examples Server menu choice.

2. Log in to theOSB web console using this URL: `http://localhost:7021/ sbconsole`. The username/password is **weblogic/weblogic**.

3. In the **Change Center** on the top left, click on the **Create** button to start a change session.

4. Scroll down and on the left navigation panel click on **Project Explorer**.

5. Delete the **Mortgage Broker** project by clicking the trash can.

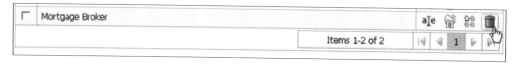

6. Click on the **Activate** button to commit the OSB configuration change.

7. Then click on the **Submit** button.

Uninstalling OSB

To uninstall the Oracle Service Bus, select **Uninstall Oracle WebLogic** from the start menu. Make sure that you are uninstalling WebLogic for OSB and not WebLogic for SOA Suite. Move your mouse over a file in the group menu to see the directories where the files are located to be sure you have the correct one.

Summary

At this point in time, you should have installed and configured all the software required to go through the tutorial. We have tried to condense all installation steps in one single chapter so do not worry if you have lost track of what exactly you have installed! By the end of this tutorial you will have a good understanding of the very extensive and capable set of tools that you now have at your disposal. Open the next chapter and begin.

5

Basic components: Web Services Binding, Mediator, and Database Adapter

Web Services binding

Mediator

Database Adapter

There are two main philosophies when it comes to building service-oriented applications (SOA) or solutions: top-down and bottom-up. A top-down approach usually involves some master plan driven from a central architecture group and that all development teams have to adopt. On the other hand, a bottom-up approach is more organic in nature, with individual development teams publicizing the services they are offering for re-use. No matter what application architecture approach you decide to take, the basic integration tools are required to expose existing services over standard interfaces.

The basic integration tools, or basic components, that will allow you to start building your services layer are:

- **Bindings** and **adapters**, to connect to technologies (such as messaging, databases, and so on) or commercial off-the-shelf software (SAP, Oracle E-Business Suite, and so on), respectively

- **Some mediation** capability to interconnect endpoints, map varying interfaces, and perform routing and filtering

Introducing the basic components

In this chapter, you will be working with the most common representatives of the above categories of components:

- **Web Services binding**: The Web Services binding can be used either inbound, to expose your SOA composite applications over SOAP, or outbound, to consume external SOAP services. For instance, the WS binding is the perfect tool to integrate with existing .Net services exposed over SOAP.

- **Database Adapter**: The Database Adapter's role is basically to service-enable databases without having to write a single line of SQL (note that sometimes you want to write SQL, and the adapter will let you do that too). The number of SOA projects that require database integration is typically very high and the Database Adapter is likely to become the workhorse in your SOA toolbox.

- **Mediator**: The Mediator is in charge of interconnecting, within an SOA composite application, components that expose different interfaces. In addition, the Mediator can perform duties such as filtering and making routing decisions.

Mediator and Service Bus — Disambiguation

Another component that performs mediation duties in Oracle SOA Suite is the **Oracle Service Bus**. While both the **Mediator** and the **Service Bus** can perform such tasks as interface and data mapping, routing, and filtering, their scopes are very different: the Mediator is a component that performs *intra-composite mediation*, to connect components within a given composite. The Service Bus on the other hand is in charge of *inter-composite mediation*, that is to say that it connects different composites together — and while doing that, it can also carry out other fundamental tasks of a service bus such as service virtualization, protocol translation, service pooling, and so on. You will explore the capabilities of the service bus in Chapter 11.

Tutorial: Building the credit card validation service

In order to follow the tutorial in this chapter, you must have set up the environment as described in Chapter 4.

Overview

To explore the basic usage of the Database Adapter, Mediator, and Web Services binding, you will build a simple credit card validation service. This service takes for input a credit card number and returns a status: valid or invalid. Obviously you are not building a realistic credit card validation service here—such a service would require much more information such as expiration date, and so on—but this should be enough to illustrate the usage of the basic components.

The implementation of this service uses a Web Service binding that receives a request over SOAP as well as a Mediator to route the request to the Database Adapter. The Database Adapter will then execute a query against the database and return the result. Once done, your project will look like the following screenshot:

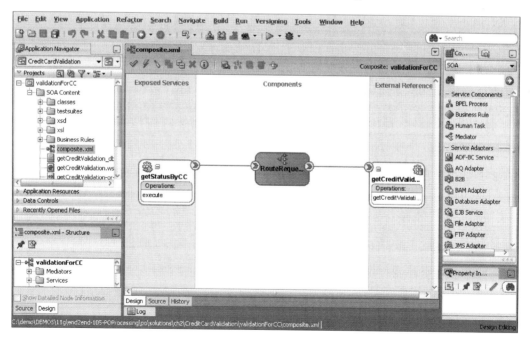

The database table that you will use is **CREDITCARDINFO**—it was created in Chapter 4—and has the following structure:

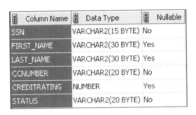

Column Name	Data Type	Nullable
SSN	VARCHAR2(15 BYTE)	No
FIRST_NAME	VARCHAR2(30 BYTE)	Yes
LAST_NAME	VARCHAR2(30 BYTE)	Yes
CCNUMBER	VARCHAR2(20 BYTE)	No
CREDITRATING	NUMBER	Yes
STATUS	VARCHAR2(20 BYTE)	No

and contains the following data:

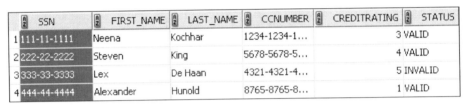

	SSN	FIRST_NAME	LAST_NAME	CCNUMBER	CREDITRATING	STATUS
1	111-11-1111	Neena	Kochhar	1234-1234-1...	3	VALID
2	222-22-2222	Steven	King	5678-5678-5...	4	VALID
3	333-33-3333	Lex	De Haan	4321-4321-4...	5	INVALID
4	444-44-4444	Alexander	Hunold	8765-8765-8...	1	VALID

Database Navigator

Use the **Database Navigator** in **JDeveloper** to look at the structure and the data of a given database table—or even execute SQL commands. To open the navigator, go to **View | Database Navigator**.

Designing the flow

In this section, you create a new synchronous composite application, exposed over SOAP through the Web Services binding. This synchronous composite queries the database for the credit card number and returns the status over the SOAP call.

Relationship of Applications, Projects, and Composites in JDeveloper

A JDeveloper (JDev) application contains one or more JDev projects. When you are developing SOA technologies, a JDev project is equal to a composite application.

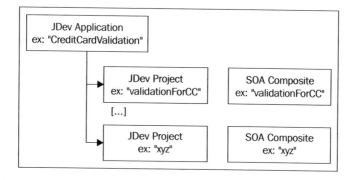

Creating a new application and project

1. Start JDeveloper 11*g*.

2. Create a new application: there are various ways and shortcuts to do this but in this case choose **File | New...** from the top menu bar.

3. Select **All Technologies** in the top tab, if present.

4. From the **Categories** tree, click on **Applications**.

5. Select **SOA Application** from the **Items** field.

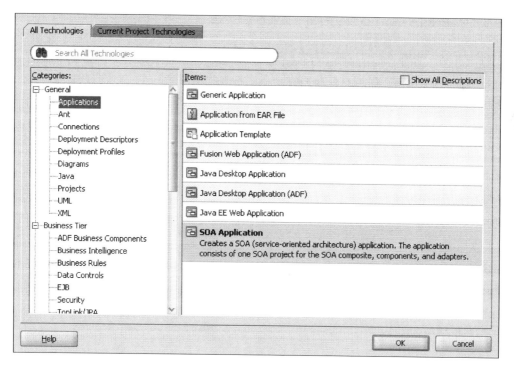

6. Click on **OK**.

7. In the subsequent **Create SOA Application** dialog, set the following fields, leaving the others with their default values:

   ○ **Application Name**: **CreditCardValidation**

   ○ **Directory**: **C:\po\CreditCardValidation**

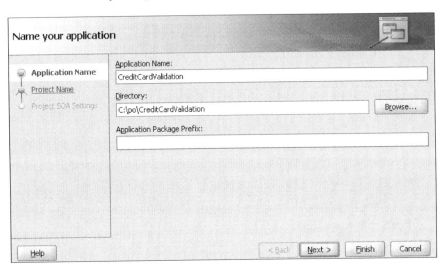

8. Click on **Next**.

9. The next screen prompts you to create a new project—this is because a JDeveloper application needs to contain at least one project. In the realm of SOA, a JDeveloper project corresponds to an SOA composite application.

   Set the following fields for the project:

   ○ **Project Name**: **validationForCC**

   ○ **Directory**: **C:\po\CreditCardValidation\validationForCC**

   Since this project is contained within an SOA application, SOA is already selected as a technology—leave it as-is.

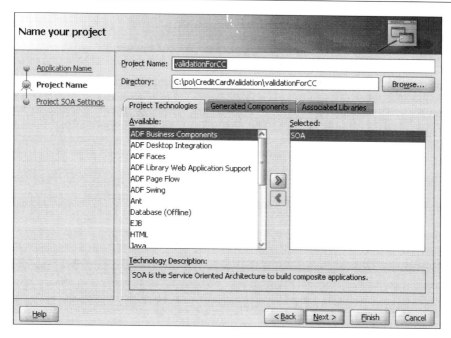

10. Click on **Next**.

The next step offers various options to start your project. In this case, select **Empty Composite**.

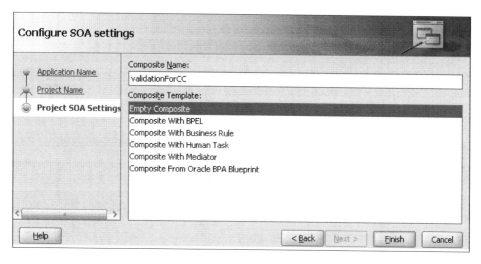

Using Composite Templates

JDeveloper offers various options to jump-start your development when you create a new project: you can start with an empty composite, with a BPEL component, with a Business Rule component, and so on. Note that these options are merely *shortcuts to save you a few clicks*—they will eventually all lead to the SOA composites identical in nature. For instance, if you choose **Composite With BPEL**, upon creating the new project, you will find yourself in the BPEL editor (itself included in a composite). You could have achieved the exact same result by starting with an empty composite and then dragging a BPEL component into it. And of course, even if you start a **Composite With BPEL** nothing prevents you from later adding to it any other component such as a Mediator or Human Task.

11. Click on **Finish**.

12. You should now see an empty canvas displaying three swim lanes: (1) **Exposed Services**, (2) **Components**, and (3) **External References**.

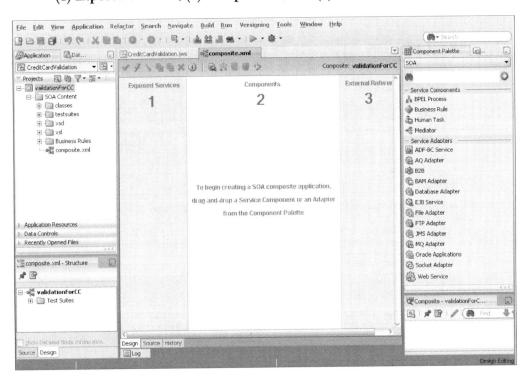

Adding the Database Adapter

Now that you have your application shell, you are ready to start building the application.

1. The first component you need is a Database Adapter that will return from the database the status (valid or invalid) for a given credit card number:

   Drag-and-drop a **Database Adapter** onto the **External References** swim lane.

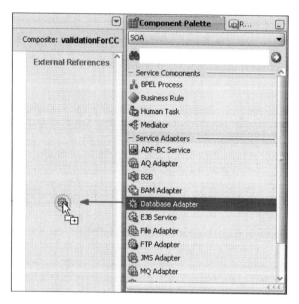

 Not seeing the Component Palette?

If you don't have the Component Palette open, then from the toolbar menu select **View | Component Palette**.

 The palette doesn't show the SOA components?

If the Component Palette is not showing the SOA components, select **SOA** from the drop-down list.

2. This action of dropping an adapter on the references swimlane will start the Database Adapter wizard.

3. Skip the first page of the database wizard by clicking on **Next**.

4. On step 2, enter the **Service Name**: getCreditValidation:

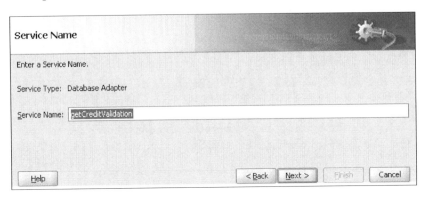

5. Then click on **Next** to go to step 3 and enter the **Service Connection** information:

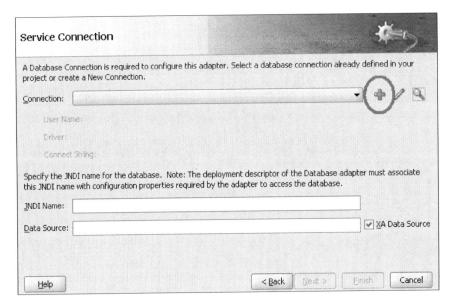

6. In order to configure the Database Adapter, you need to establish a connection to the database. You could use a connection created at the JDeveloper level, or create one on the fly, for the sole use of your current composite application. Since you haven't created any database connection yet, you will create one right here:

    i.   Click on the green colored plus icon to the right of the **Connection** drop-down list to create a new database connection

    ii. In the **Create Database Connection** dialog, enter the following details:

- ° **Connection Name**: soademoDatabase
- ° **Connection Type**: Oracle (JDBC)
- ° **Username**: soademo
- ° **Password**: soademo
- ° **Save Password**: Checked
- ° **Enter Custom JDBC URL**: Unchecked
- ° **Driver: thin**
- ° **Host Name**: **localhost** (or the name of the machine hosting your database)
- ° **JDBC Port**: **1521** (or the port number of your database)
- ° **SID**: **XE** (or the service ID of your database)

iii. Click on the **Test Connection** button and verify that your connection works:

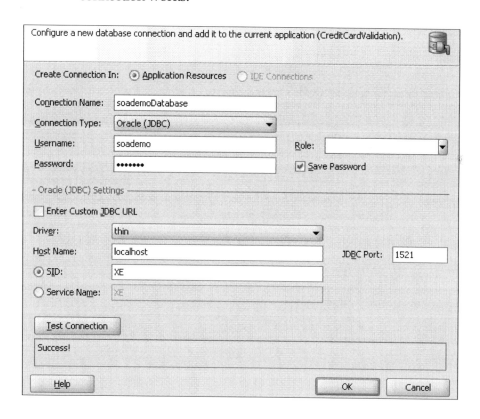

Click on **OK** to return to step 3 of the **Database Adapter Configuration** wizard.

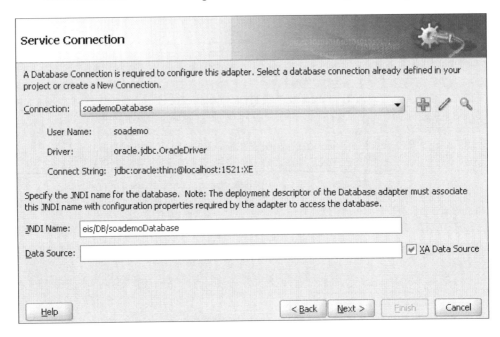

7. Make sure the **JNDI Name** matches the data source connection pool JNDI Name you entered in Chapter 4.

8. You can leave the **Data Source** field empty.

9. Click on **Next** to switch to the next step of the wizard.

10. In this step, you will specify what operation to perform against the database. This operation could be calling a stored procedure or performing various SQL operations such as **Insert**, **Delete**, or **Select**. In this case, the operation is **Select**.

11. Set the following fields:

    ° **Perform an Operation on a Table**: Selected

    ° **Select**: Checked

All other fields should be unchecked.

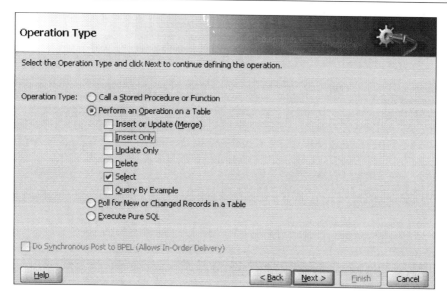

12. Click on **Next**.

13. At this step, you will select the tables you want to work with. Click on the **Import Tables** button. The wizard will connect to your database and present you with a new dialog to search and select tables.

14. Click on the **Query** button to retrieve the list of tables for the *soademo* user from the database. If you do not see any tables, go back to Chapter 4 to make sure the table was created properly.

15. Select the **CREDITCARDINFO** table and move it to the **Selected** field by pressing the **Add** arrow button.

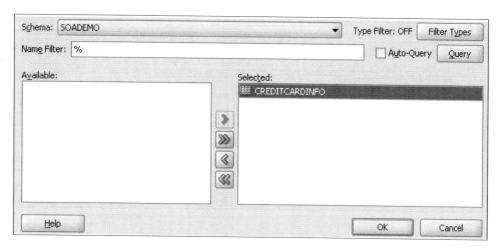

16. Click **OK** to close this dialog.

Back in step 5 of the **Database Adapter Configuration** wizard, click on the **CREDITCARDINFO** table to select it.

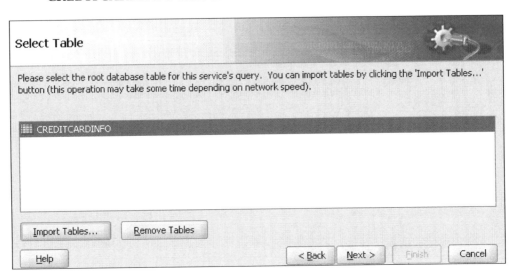

17. Click on **Next**.

18. Step 6 of the wizard lets you override or define the primary key for your table. In this case no primary key is defined in the database, so you'll need to specify it. Check **CCNUMBER** and leave the rest unchecked.

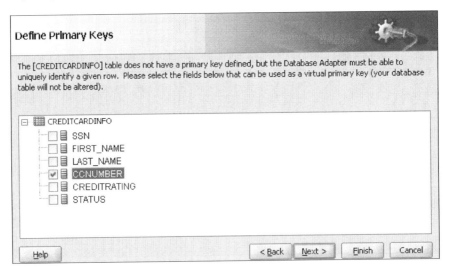

19. Click on Next.

20. Step 7 lets you define parent-child relationships if you are selecting from multiple tables. Since there is only a single table, there is no relationship to define. Click on **Next** to get to the **Attribute Filtering** dialog.

21. At this stage, you can define the data that you want the adapter to fetch. You only care about the status, so uncheck all fields except **status**. That is the only column you want to query from the database.

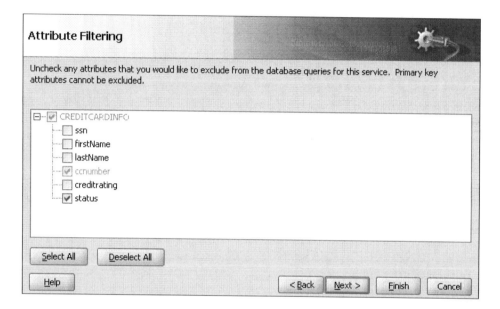

22. Click on **Next**. This gets you to step 9 where you can specify your selection criteria. In this case, you will add a parameter to the query. The parameter will be set at runtime to select the row for the credit card you want.

23. Click on the **Add** button to add a new parameter called **ccnb**. Click on **OK**.

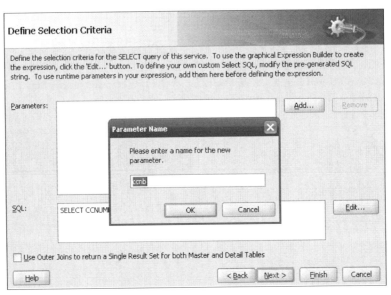

24. Back in step 9, click on the **Edit** button to bring up the **Expression Builder** dialog and click on the **Add** button to add a new condition.

25. Click on the **Edit** button in the **First Argument** section.

In the **Query Key** dialog select **ccnumber**.

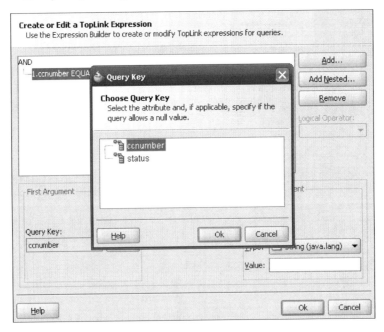

26. Click on **OK**.

27. In the **Second Argument** section, select **Parameter**.

28. Ensure that **ccnb** is selected in the drop-down menu.

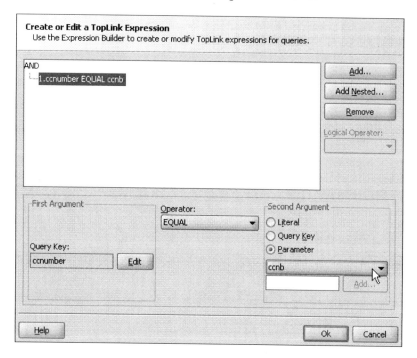

What you have done in this dialog is to instruct the adapter to query the database using the **ccnumber** column, with a value contained in the **ccnb** variable.

29. Click on **OK**.

Back in step 9, you are presented with the SQL query that results from the operations performed in the previous screen:

```
SELECT CCNUMBER, STATUS FROM CREDITCARDINFO WHERE (CCNUMBER =
#ccnb)
```

The parameter **ccnb** will be populated at runtime and the query will select a row based on that parameter.

30. At this point, you could go on to configure some advanced options, or end the wizard by clicking on **Finish**. Click on **Finish**.

31. The Database Adapter will process your choices and generate a service that implements the operation configured—this means that your project will now contain a new WSDL file to represent that service: **getCreditValidation.wsdl**. You should see this new WSDL file in the project navigator:

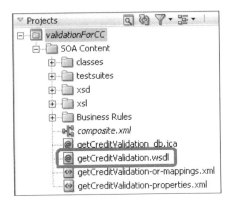

as well as a new component in the composite diagram:

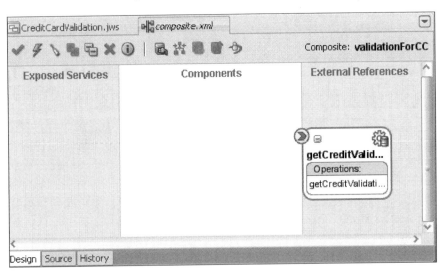

About the Adapter Wizards

Most adapter wizards follow a similar flow to the one you just went through for the Database Adapter. This flow is depicted in the following diagram:

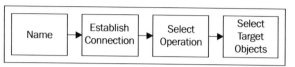

You start by giving a name to the new adapter. Then you establish a connection to the target system: it could be a database, some application—or even just a file system (in which case, it is not really a connection, but simply a path). After this, you select an operation—the operations that are offered by the wizard will of course be different for each target system: a database will offer the expected SQL operations (select, insert, delete, and a few more), a file system will be read or write, and so on. Finally, in the last stage, you specify the objects on which you are going to be operating: database tables, specific files, or directories in the file system, records in an application and so on.

Adding the Mediator component

The Mediator is the component in charge of interconnecting other components within a composite application. You add a Mediator component that you then use to route a SOAP request to the Database Adapter you just configured.

1. Drag a Mediator component onto the composite diagram in the **Components** swim lane:

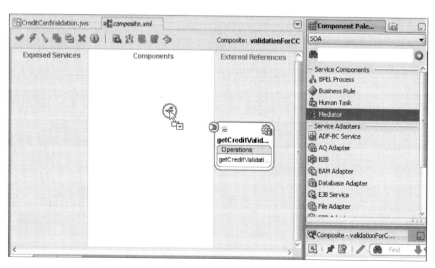

2. In the **Create Mediator** dialog, specify these settings:
    ○ **Name**: **RouteRequest**
    ○ **Template**: **Define Interface Later**

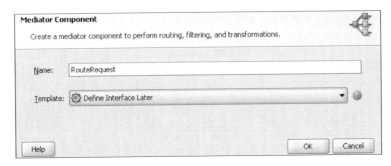

The composite editor in JDeveloper gives you the flexibility to define the interface now, to choose an existing interface, or to define the interface later as you wire components to the Mediator.

3. Click on **OK**.

Adding the Web Service binding

In this section, you will use a Web Service binding to expose this composite application over SOAP.

1. Drag a **Web Service** binding to the **Exposed Services** swim lane:

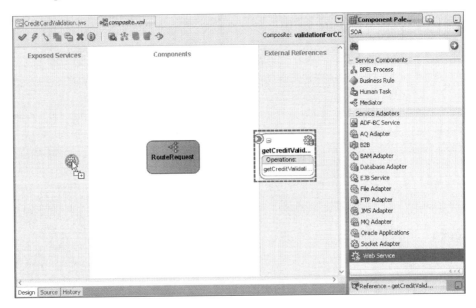

2. In the **Create Web Service** dialog that appears, set the following fields:

   ○ **Name**: **getStatusByCC**

   ○ **Type**: **Service**

3. Click the cog icon next to the **WSDL URL** field to define the interface:

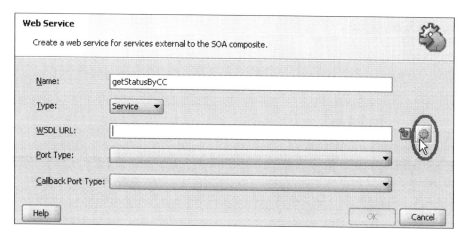

The **Create WSDL** dialog lets you specify the message invocation types for the service. You have been given an existing **XML Schema Definition** (XSD) that specifies the types of the input and output for the service, which you will reuse for this application.

4. Click on the magnifying glass icon to the right of the **URL** field to browse for a schema file:

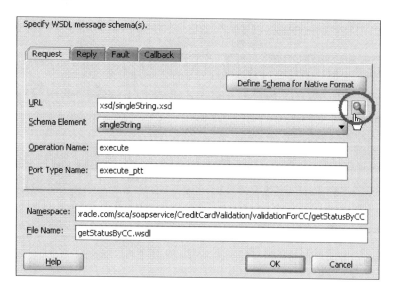

5. In the **Type Chooser** dialog, click on the **Import Schema File** button.

6. In the **Import Schema File** dialog, click on the magnifying glass to browse for the schema file.

7. In the **SCA Resource Lookup**, make sure **File System** is selected.

8. Navigate to and select `c:\po\schemas\creditcheck.xsd`.

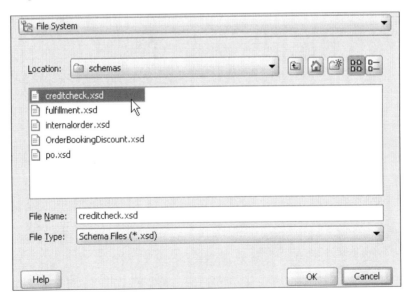

9. Click on **OK**.

10. Back in the **Import Schema File** dialog, make sure **Copy to Project** is selected.

11. Click on **OK**.

12. In the **Localize Files** dialog, deselect **Maintain original directory structure for imported files** and click on **OK**.

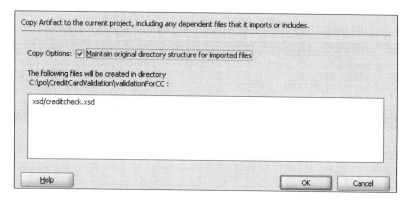

13. Back in the **Type Chooser** dialog, expand the **Project Schema Files | creditcheck.xsd** nodes.

    Select **creditcardStatusRequest**:

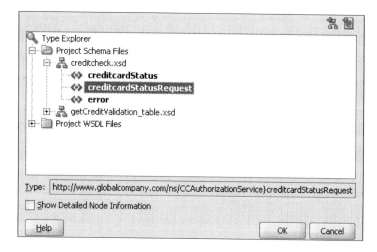

14. Click on **OK**.

    The **Create WSDL** dialog is as shown below. *Do not click OK yet!* You're not quite finished.

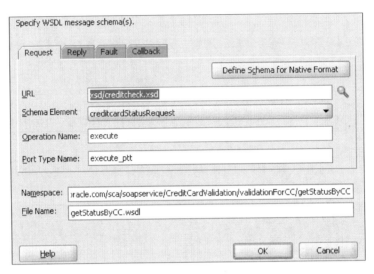

    While you have selected a schema for your *request*, you need to also pick schemas for the *reply* and *fault*.

15. Select the **Reply** tab.

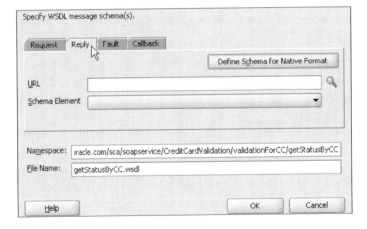

16. Repeat the schema selection process that you did earlier for the request (by clicking on the magnifying glass). Pick up the **creditcardStatus** schema element for the reply. Note that this time around you don't need to browse the file system to import the schema file—indeed, you have already copied the schema in the previous step. You should end up with this:

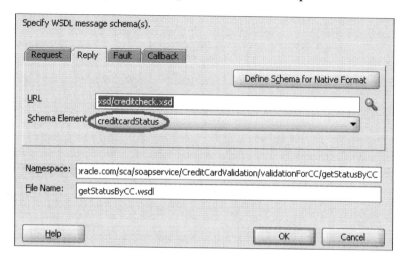

Similarly, choose the schema for the **Fault**. Switch to the **Fault** tab and choose the **error** schema element:

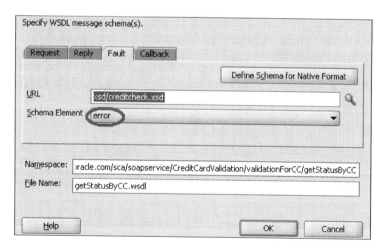

17. You're done with this **Create WSDL** dialog: click on **OK** to close it.

18. The **Create Web Service** dialog should now look like this:

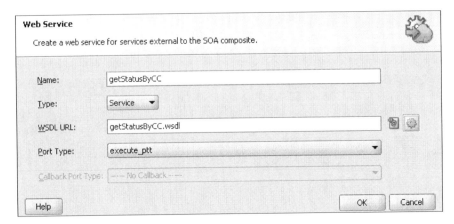

> If you edit one of the schema elements...
>
> If you click the cog icon again and edit any one of the three schema elements (request, reply or fault) for one of the invocation types, you will have to remember to reset the other two invocation types again as well.

19. Click on **OK** to exit the **Web Service** creation wizard and get back to the composite editor.

> **Explore the JDeveloper XSD and WSDL editors**
>
> Now it is time to explore some of the extra tools available in JDeveloper! In the project navigator in the lefthand pane, double-click on creditcheck.xsd (in the xsd folder under your project) or getStatusByCC.wsdl. This should bring up the graphical XSD and WSDL editors. Note how you can switch from the **Design** view (that is, a graphical representation) to the **Source** view, by using the tabs at the bottom left of the editor. These editors are not specific to SOA and can be used on their own or during Java development.

20. Now that you have all the components, *wire* them together to start defining their interactions.

21. First, wire the inbound Web Service to the Mediator. To do this, click on the arrow at the top right of the binding icon, drag to the lefthand side of the Mediator and release. This creates a wire between the two components.

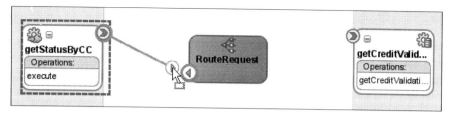

22. Now wire the Mediator to the Database adapter:

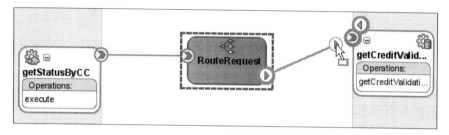

23. If you selected more than one database operation when configuring the Database Adapter, you will be prompted to choose an operation. If so, use these settings:

   ○ **Mediator Operation: execute**

   ○ **Target Operation: getCreditValidationSelect**

24. The composite diagram gives an overview of your application:

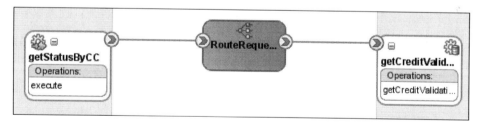

Droppable zones for a wire

Did you notice how certain areas of the composite turned green as you started pulling a wire? These green zones indicate all the valid targets for the wire that you are holding.

Adding a transformation to the Mediator component

In this section, you will modify the **RouteRequest** Mediator component to do an **XSLT** transformation on the message payload. This is required because the incoming message to your publicly exposed service (**getStatusByCC**) is in a different format than the service created by the Database Adapter (**getCreditValidation**). Transforming data from one representation to another is, along with routing, one of the key functions of the Mediator.

To start this you will perform a new gesture: double-click on a component in the composite editor to drill-down into the specific details of that component.

1. Double-click on the **RouteRequest** Mediator component to open the Mediator editor:

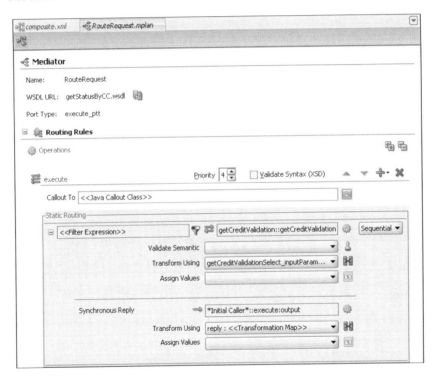

You will explore the other Mediator settings (such as filter expressions) in subsequent sections so only focus on XSLT transformation here.

2. Click on the transformation icon to the right of the **Transform Using** field in the request section (that's the first **Transform Using** field).

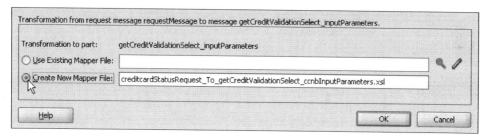

3. Select **Create New Mapper File** and accept the default name.

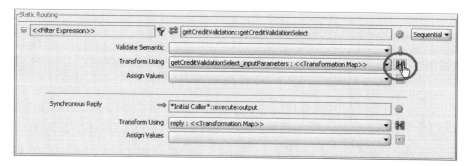

4. Click on **OK** to open the XSLT **mapping editor**.

5. You will be working a lot with this mapping tool so here is a quick tour. On the lefthand side is the source object, on the righthand side the target object, and the middle strip contains the transformations.

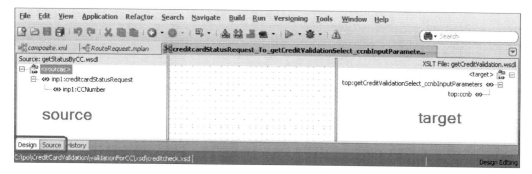

As you must have noticed by now, this editor also has the two tabs, **Design** and **Source**, that allow you to switch from graphical editing to source code editing:

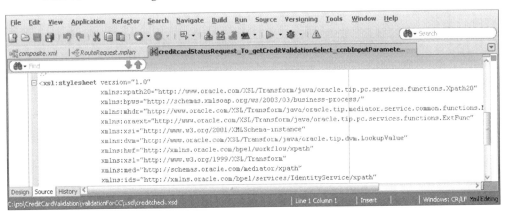

6. Back to the exercise: expand all the nodes on both sides. You can do it manually, or rightclick on **<sources>** and select **Expand All**. Do the same for **<target>** on the right-hand side.

7. Map CCNumber from the source side to ccnb on the target side by dragging a wire from one element to the other.

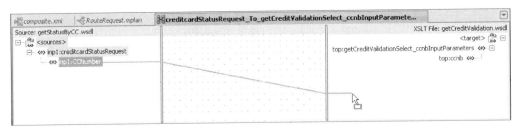

Your mapping now looks like this:

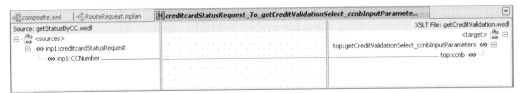

8. Save and close the mapper by selecting the close window icon on the right side of the tab. You may need to use the tab bar scroll buttons to navigate right to get to the close window icon. Alternatively, you can press *Ctrl+S* to save the mapping (and accept the dialog to save all files in the project), then press *Ctrl+W* to close it.

9. Now that you have mapped the *request* going from the Web Service binding to the Database Adapter, it's time to work on the *reply* that goes back in the opposite direction.

10. Back in the Mediator editor, click on the transformation icon to the right of the **Transform Using** field in the reply section (that's the second **Transform Using** field).

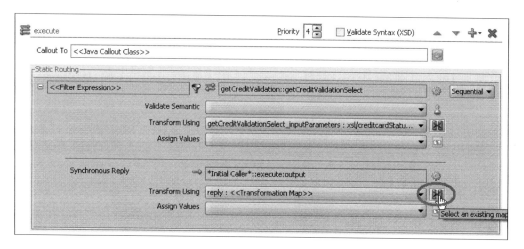

11. In the **Reply Transformation Map** dialog select **Create New Mapper File** and accept the default name.

12. Click on **OK** to open the mapper.

13. Expand all the source and target nodes.

14. Map `status` from the source to `creditcardstatus` from the target.

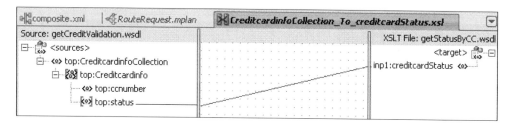

15. Save and close the mapper to return to the Mediator editor.

16. Save and close the Mediator editor to return to the composite diagram. You can use the toolbar buttons or the menu, or simply press *Ctrl+S* to save and *Ctrl+W* to close this tab.

That's it for the design of your first SOA composite application! Pat yourself on the back and celebrate a little before going further.

Deploying and testing the composite application

The first design iteration being complete, it is now time to **deploy** and **test** the composite.

Creating a server connection in JDeveloper

Before you can deploy, you need to instruct JDeveloper where the server you want to deploy to is located. This server could be running locally on the same machine as JDeveloper or on a remote machine. You achieve this in JDeveloper by creating a **server connection**.

You need to create a connection from JDeveloper to the Oracle WebLogic Server configured for Oracle SOA Suite in order to deploy from JDeveloper.

1. From the **Application Menu**, select **New**.

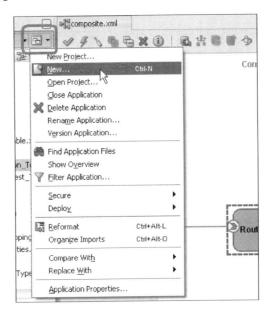

2. In the **New Gallery**, in the **Categories** tree, select **General**, and then **Connections**.

3. Select **Application Server Connection**:

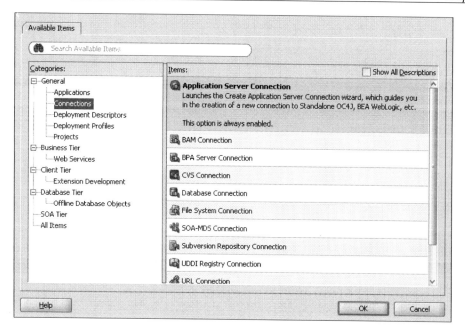

4. Click on **OK**.

5. The **Create Application Server Connection** page is displayed.

6. Enter **MyAppServerConnection** in the **Connection Name** field and select **WebLogic 10.3** from the **Connection Type** list.

7. Click on **Next**.

8. The connection **Authentication** page is displayed:

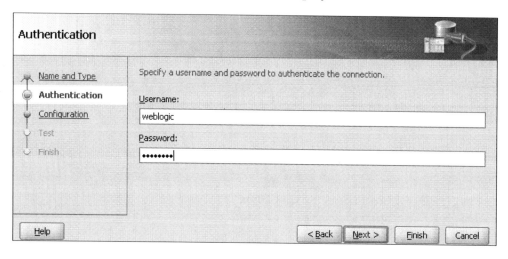

9. Enter **weblogic** as the **Username** and the password for that administrator in the **Password** field.

10. Click on **Next**. The **Configuration** page displays.

11. Enter the following values (or adjust as necessary for your configuration):

    ○   **Weblogic Hostname (Administration Server): localhost**

    ○   **Port: 7001**

    ○   **WLS Domain: domain1**

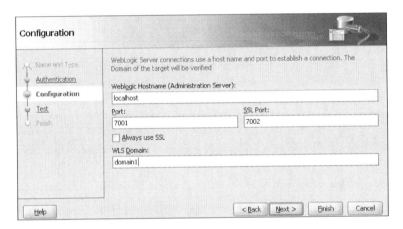

12. Click on **Next**. The **Test** page displays.

13. Click on **Test Connection**.

14. The following status should appear:

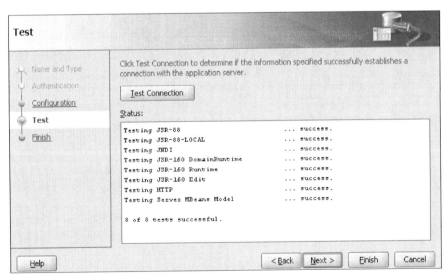

15. Click on **Next**, and in the **Finish** page, click on **Finish**.

Cannot establish a connection to your server?

- Use the **Test Connection** button. If you can connect to the server it will let you know whether you might have a username, password, or domain name issue.
- Ensure that your server is up and in the RUNNING status (you can see this in the command-line window you used to start the server, as well as from the WebLogic Server console).
- Try to ping the server machine.
- Ensure you properly configure or disable any personal firewall you might have on either the JDeveloper machine or the Server machine.

Deploying Composites to the Application Server

Once you have created a server connection, you are ready to compile and deploy your composite to the server.

1. In the project menu, right-click on the *project* name, select **Deploy**, and follow the menu to select **MyAppServerConnection**. Make sure you are in the *project* menu and *not in the application menu* to see this option.

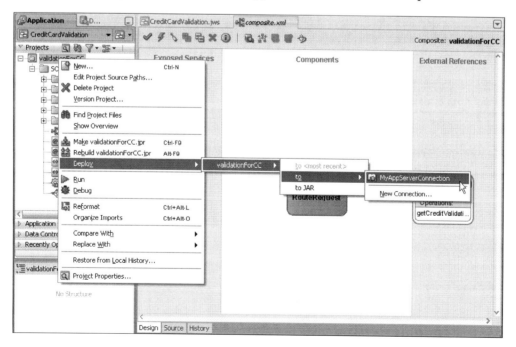

2. The **SOA Deployment Configuration Dialog** opens. If you are redeploying your application, you must either select the checkbox to overwrite the previous version, or you can enter a new version. Otherwise, the deployment will fail.

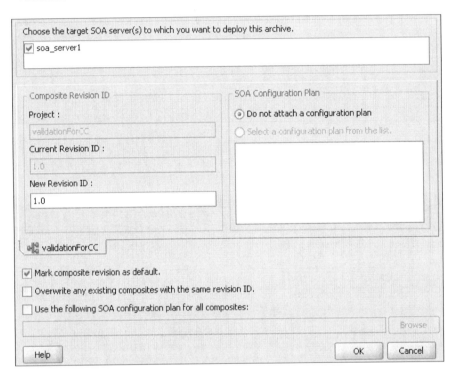

3. Click on **OK**.

4. At this point, JDeveloper will start compiling the project and checking for its validity. If the compiler finds any problem, it will report them in the log window below the project. If the project compiles successfully, you will see **BUILD SUCCESSFUL** in the SOA tab of the log pane, and the deployment will start.

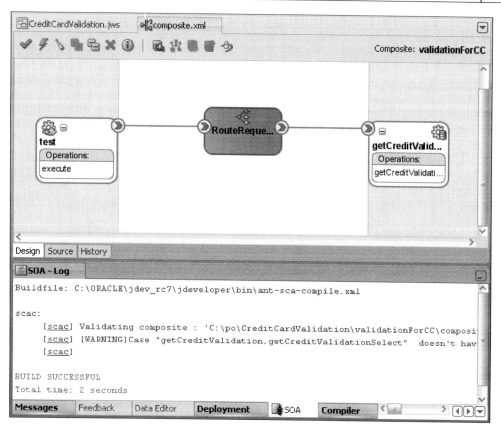

5. If this is the first time you are deploying since server startup or if the connection has timed out, you will be prompted for the admin username and password:

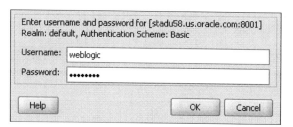

6. Enter the appropriate values and click on **OK**.

7. You can view the details of the deployment in the **Deployment** tab of the log pane:

```
Deployment - Log
[01:28:29 AM] ----  Deployment started.   ----
[01:28:29 AM] Target platform is  (Weblogic 10.3).
[01:28:29 AM] Running dependency analysis...
[01:28:29 AM] Building...
[01:28:33 AM] Deploying profile...
[01:28:34 AM] Wrote SAR file to C:\po\CreditCardValidation\validationForCC\deploy\sca_
[01:28:34 AM] Deploying sca_validationForCC_rev9.9.jar to soa_server1 [stadu58.us.orac
[01:28:34 AM] Processing sar=/C:/po/CreditCardValidation/validationForCC/deploy/sca_va
[01:28:34 AM] Adding sar file - C:\po\CreditCardValidation\validationForCC\deploy\sca_
[01:28:34 AM] Preparing to send HTTP request for deployment
[01:28:34 AM] Creating HTTP connection to host:stadu58.us.oracle.com, port:8001
[01:28:35 AM] Sending internal deployment descriptor
[01:28:35 AM] Sending archive - sca_validationForCC_rev9.9.jar
[01:29:37 AM] Received HTTP response from the server, response code=200
[01:29:37 AM] Successfully deployed archive sca_validationForCC_rev9.9.jar to soa_serv
[01:29:37 AM] Elapsed time for deployment:  1 minute, 8 seconds
[01:29:37 AM] ----  Deployment finished.   ----
```

8. Wait for the deployment to be finished.

Testing your composite using Enterprise Manager

Once the deployment is complete, you can test it.

1. Open Enterprise Manager at the following link: `http://localhost:7001/em`.

2. Log in (if you have used the suggested default during installation, it is weblogic/welcome1).

3. Click on the **validationForCC** link in the **SOA** folder in the lefthand side navigation tree:

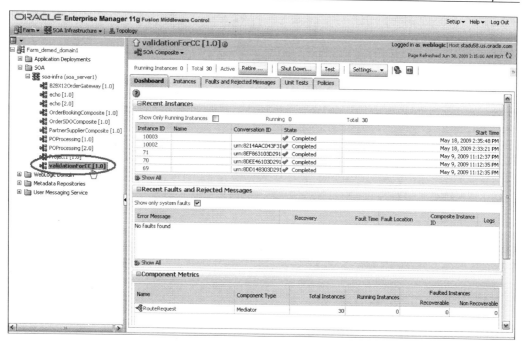

4. Open the Test page by clicking on the **Test** button:

5. This opens the test page that you can use to trigger a new instance of the validationForCC composite application. Scroll to the bottom of the page and the **Input Arguments** section:

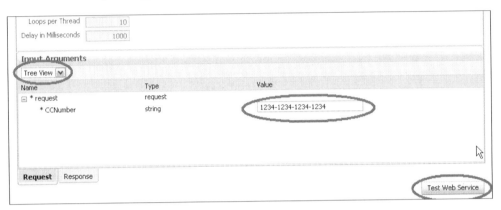

6. In the **CCNumber** field, enter a credit card number. In this case, enter **1234-1234-1234-1234** in the **CCNumber** field, which is a valid credit card and returns the status **VALID**.

7. Click on the **Test Web Service** button.

8. You will get a response from the service, which will indicate if the credit card is valid or not. The following is the output for a valid credit card:

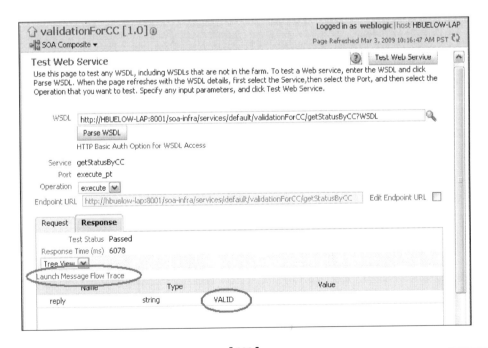

9. Click on **Launch Message Flow Trace** to see the details of the message flow for this instance of your composite. This pops open a new window with the flow trace.

10. Close the **Flow Trace** window.

11. Try another value. Click on the **Request** tab, and this time enter **4321-4321-4321-4321** in the **CCNumber** field, which is an invalid credit card.

12. Click on the **Test Web Service** button to see the output.

13. In an upcoming chapter, you will create a new application that calls this service, so you'll need to know the WSDL location for it. You can see the WSDL location listed at the top of the Test page; in this case:
```
http://localhost:8001/soa-infra/services/CreditCardValidation/
validationForCC/getStatusByCC?WSDL.
```

Web Services Tester: Tree View versus XML View

Note that you can provide input to the Web Services tester using two possible interfaces: the Tree View or the XML View. The Tree View offers a form-based input mechanism. This form is built automatically from the XSD schema in the WSDL describing the service you are testing. It is convenient for small payloads.

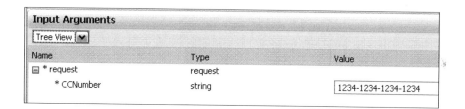

On the other hand, the XML View is a text-based interface. It takes raw XML as input. This is convenient for more complex objects that you might want to save in a text file and just cut and paste in EM for testing. You will be using this mechanism later in the book.

Summary

In this chapter, you were introduced to the SCA assembly and composite applications with some of the basic components: Mediator, File Adapter, and Database Adapter. You also learned to build and test your composite application, as well as review the instance of a running composite using Enterprise Manager. You are now ready to move on to the next level.

Quick-build instructions

This section gives you all of the operations and names for objects created in this chapter. Experienced users can use this to bypass the step-by-step instructions and complete this chapter more quickly. The complete details for any particular operation listed here can be found in the preceding sections. The information is organized in the same manner that it is introduced in the chapter.

- Create a new application:
  - Application Name: **CreditCardValidation**
  - Directory: **C:\po\CreditCardValidation**
  - Project Name: **validationForCC**
  - Directory: **C:\po\CreditCardValidation\validationForCC**
  - Project Technologies: **SOA**
  - Empty Composite

- Add the Database Adapter:
  - DbAdapter Service Name: **getCreditValidation**

- Create database connection details:
  - Connection Name: **soademoDatabase**
  - Connection Type: **Oracle (JDBC)**
  - Username: **soademo**
  - Password: **soademo**
  - Save Password: Checked
  - Enter Custom JDBC URL: Unchecked
  - Driver: **thin**
  - Host Name: **localhost**
  - JDBC Port: **1521** (or the port number of your database)

- ° SID: **XE** (or the SID of your database)
- ° JNDI name: **eis/DB/soademoDatabase**
- ° Operation: **Select**
- ° Import **CREDITCARDINFO** table
- ° Primary key: **CCNUMBER**
- ° Attribute Filtering: **status**
- ° Add a new parameter: **ccnb**
- ° Add Where clause: **ccnumber = #ccnb**

- Add the Mediator Component:
  - ° Create Mediator: **RouteRequest**
  - ° Template: **Define Interface Later**
  - ° Create Web Service: **getStatusByCC**
  - ° Type: **Service**
  - ° WSDL based on: **c:\po\schemas\creditcheck.xsd**
  - ° Request: **creditcardStatusRequest**
  - ° Reply: **creditcardStatus**
  - ° Fault: **error**
  - ° Wire: service to mediator to adapter

- Add a transformation to the Mediator component:
  - ° Mediator transform: Map **CCNumber** from the source side to **ccnb**
  - ° Mediator transform for reply: Map **status** from the source to **creditcardstatus** from the target.

The application is completed. Deploy and test.

6
Accessing Files Using the File Adapter

In the previous chapter, we introduced the Web Service binding, Mediator, and Database Adapter and referred to these as the "basic components" as most SOA applications today involve web services and databases. However, one might have argued that there is another component that would have qualified as "basic": the File Adapter.

Introducing the File Adapter

The File Adapter is used for two main purposes:

1. To *log events* or *persist data*
2. To feed data into a composite application, and act as a *loose integration mechanism*

Indeed, files are at the core of today's computing environments. Everything is stored in files and many things have to be persisted to file—for logging, auditing, bookkeeping, and so on.

Maybe even more importantly: files tend to be the most widely used means of *integrating* disparate technologies. Take the example of a Java application that needs to process information contained in an application running in some mainframe — what are the options to integrate these technologies? You could try to find a Java API to connect to that mainframe application — at best this will come with a certain learning curve, at worst it does not exist. Or you could try to use a database as an intermediary — provided you can find a database that both the Java program and the mainframe application can work with. But the path of least resistance is probably to bridge the two systems via files: one system drops a file at a given time of day and the other one picks it up later on.

Using files for integration is not without challenges though and should be reserved for when:

- There is no transactionality requirement
- Duplicates or missing data can be detected and handled — or are not a major issue
- No tighter integration (via native APIs, messaging, or even database) is available

The File Adapter included in the SOA Suite is bi-directional. It can both write and read files (either on-demand or on a polling basis) and, therefore, can handle a wide variety of usage patterns. In addition, it can leverage the **Native Format Builder**, a shared capability available in other components and products. The role of the Native Format Builder is to translate data to XML (so that it can be processed easily in the SOA Suite) from the variety of formats it could be in when stored in a file, such as text-delimited, fixed-length, Cobol Copybook and so on — and vice-versa.

Select file type:

- ⦿ Delimited (Contains records whose fields are delimited by a special character)
- ○ Fixed Length (Contains records whose fields are fixed in length)
- ○ Complex Type (Contains records whose fields may themselves be records having multiple delimiter types)
- ○ DTD to be converted to XSD
- ○ Cobol Copybook to be converted to native format

This preceding screenshot of the File Adapter wizard shows the various data formats with which the Native Format Builder can operate.

Tutorial: Building the purchase order routing service

Chapters 5-10 must be done sequentially.

In order to follow the tutorial in this chapter you must have either completed the tutorial from the previous chapter, or set up the environment as described in Chapter 4 and deployed the solution for the previous chapter, which can be found in `c:\po\solutions\ch05`.

You have built a credit validation service in the previous tutorial. In this section, you start laying the foundation of the larger PO Processing composite, an application that will eventually be leveraging the credit validation service. You will be adding new features and capabilities to the PO Processing composite in subsequent chapters but in this first iteration it is very simple: it will accept new purchase orders and archive them to disk by using the File Adapter.

The implementation of this service uses a Mediator that receives orders coming over SOAP and writes them to file using the file adapter. At the end of this chapter your composite will look like this:

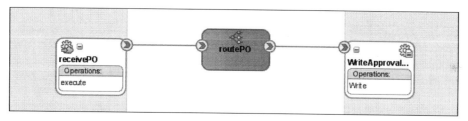

Designing the flow

This service is a one-way service, also called *fire-and-forget* because it does not return any value (or acknowledgement) to the client invoking it. It takes as input a Purchase Order described using an XML schema (`po.xsd`) and writes data to a file using a different schema (`internalorder.xsd`). Having to convert the data from one schema to another gives you an opportunity to work with the data mapper and discover the auto-mapping functionality. You use a pre-defined dictionary named `po2internalorders-dictionary.xml` (available in your schemas directory) to perform the auto-mapping.

Creating a new application

Create a new application for your POProcessing composite. As an alternative, instead of using the **File/New** menu as you did in the last chapter, choose **New Application** from the application list menu.

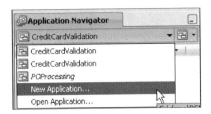

1. Name your application **POProcessing** and make its location in **c:\po**.

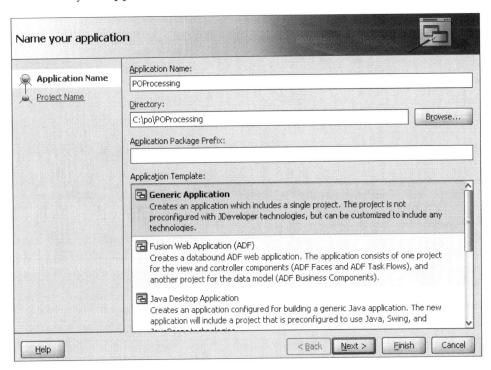

You could elect to make this application an SOA application right from this screen. But let's explore a new path and leave this as **Generic Application** this time around. You would typically use the generic option when you want to combine projects of different technologies in a single application.

2. Click on **Next**.

3. Name the project **POProcessing** and add **SOA** to the list of **Project Technologies**.

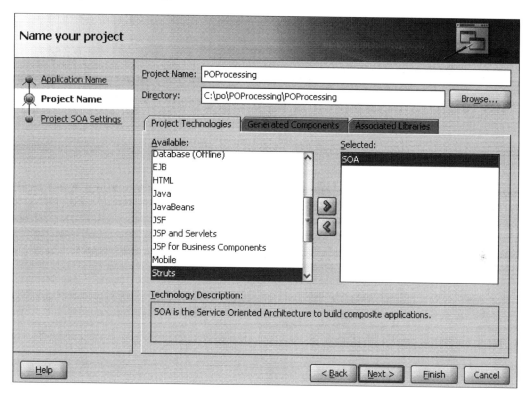

4. Click on **Next** and then click on **Finish** to create the project with an empty composite.

Adding the service interface

1. Start by creating the service end point you will use to expose this composite over SOAP. Drag-and-drop a **Web Service** activity onto the **Exposed Services** swim lane:

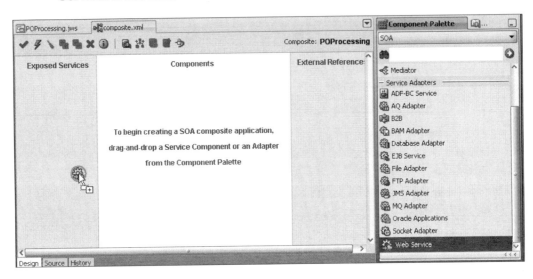

2. Name it **receivePO** and create a WSDL file from a schema by clicking on the cog icon. Creating a WSDL file from a schema allows you to define the input data that your service expects and, at the same time, automatically create the WSDL interface:

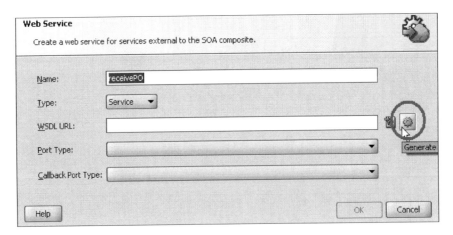

3. In the request tab of the WSDL definition dialog, browse for the schema by clicking on the magnifying lens:

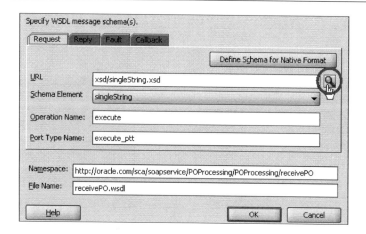

4. Then in the type chooser, import the `po.xsd` schema, which you'll find under `c:\po\schemas`:

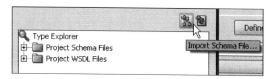

5. Copy it to your project and open it to select the type:

Since you are importing only one file, the **Copy Options** checkbox to maintain the original directory structure can be selected or not selected with the same result.

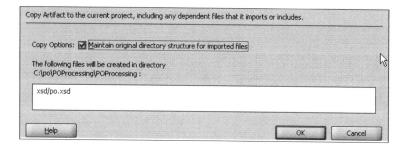

6. Select the **PurchaseOrder** element. This will be the input data for your service.

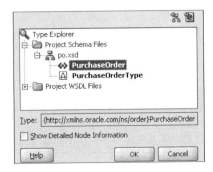

This service is a one-way invocation type, also known as a fire-and-forget service. So there is no need to specify a reply or callback.

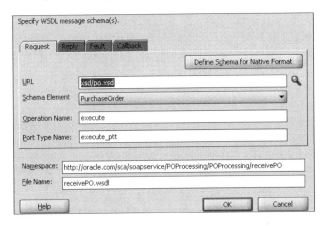

7. Click on **OK** to close the WSDL creation dialog:

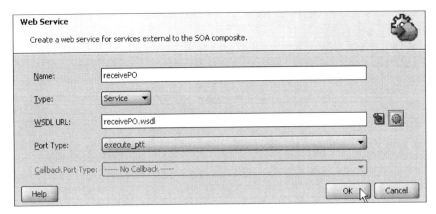

8. Click on **OK** to close the **Web Service** binding dialog.

You have completed the configuration of a web service binding that will be used to expose your composite application over SOAP and accept purchase orders.

Adding the routing component

Now let's add a Mediator routing component that will be used to forward these incoming purchase orders as appropriate.

1. Add a Mediator to the composite by dragging one from the palette to the **Components** swim lane on the canvas:

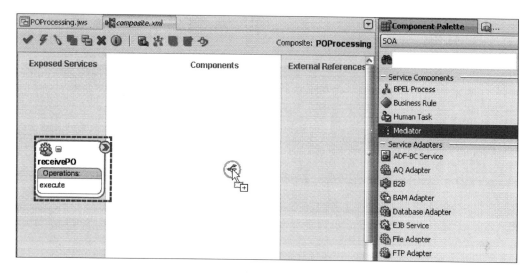

2. Call it **routePO** and select the **Define Interface Later** template:

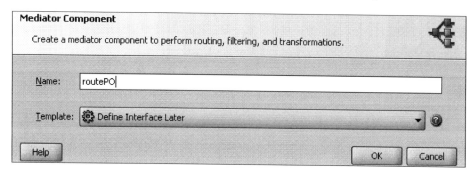

3. Click on **OK.**

Implicit creation of the Mediator's interfaces.

The **Define Interface Later** template is a very convenient feature of the Mediator. When you choose this option, all you have to do is connect the Mediator graphically to the inbound and outbound components, services or references, and interfaces will be automatically derived and created.

Adding the File Adapter

Drag-and-drop a **File Adapter** to the **External References** swim lane. This file adapter will write each new order to a text file.

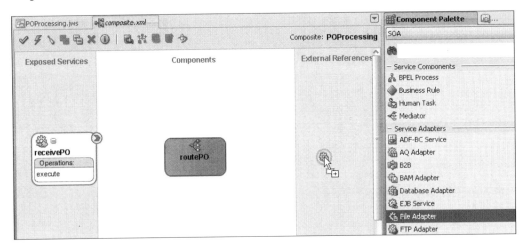

1. Name the service **WriteApprovalResults**.

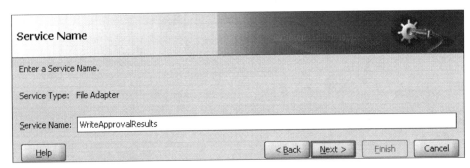

2. Click on **Next**.

3. Select the option to **Define from operation and schema**. This is the most common option for technology adapters and will construct a WSDL file as you step through the wizard.

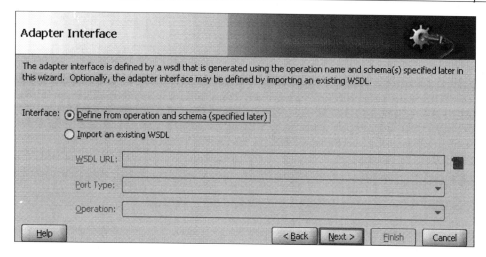

4. Click on **Next**.

5. Select the **Write File** operation.

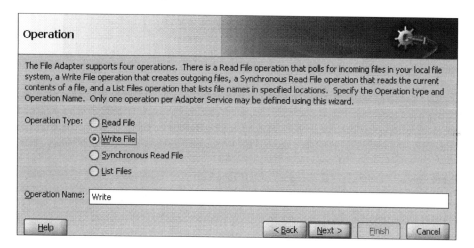

6. Click on **Next**.

7. Specify the following settings, leaving all others with their default values:

    ° **Directory for Outgoing Files**: **c:\temp** (or Linux notation if using Linux).

- File Naming Convention: order_%SEQ%.txt to write the files with increasing sequence numbers. You can see additional options for numbering files in a drop-down menu as soon as you enter % in the field.

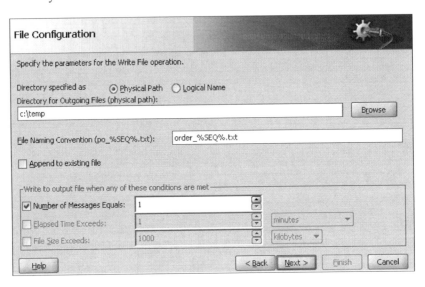

8. Click on **Next**.

9. Browse for the schema that the file adapter will use to format the data to write:

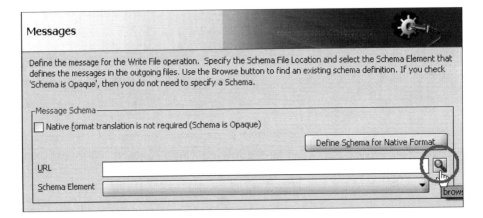

10. Click on the **Import Schema** file button and navigate to `c:\po\schemas\` `internalorder.xsd` to select and copy the schema file, and then select **Order** from the **Type Chooser** dialog.

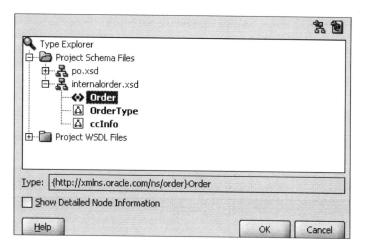

11. Click on **OK**:

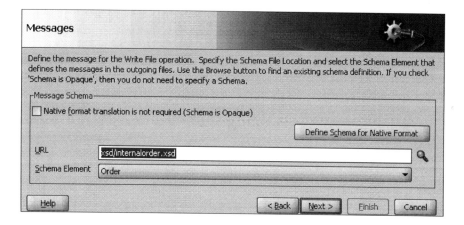

12. Click on **Next**, then **Finish** to complete the File Adapter wizard and return to the composite.

Wiring the components together and adding a transformation

Now that you have created all the components, it's time to graphically assemble all these assets.

1. Connect the Web Service binding to the Mediator:

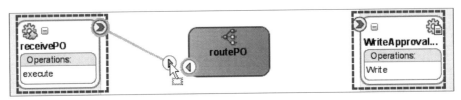

2. Connect the Mediator to the File Adapter:

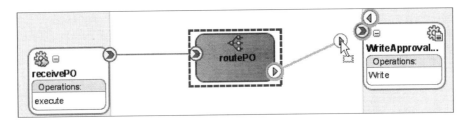

3. The wired components should look like this:

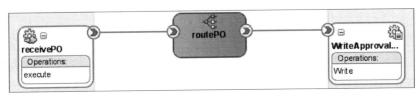

Now that our components are wired together, we need to instruct the Mediator how to map data from the inbound format (expressed using po.xsd) to the format used by the File Adapter (internalorder.xsd):

1. Double-click on the Mediator component to open the Mediator editor and create the mapping between the web service binding and the file adapter. This opens the Mediator configuration screen:

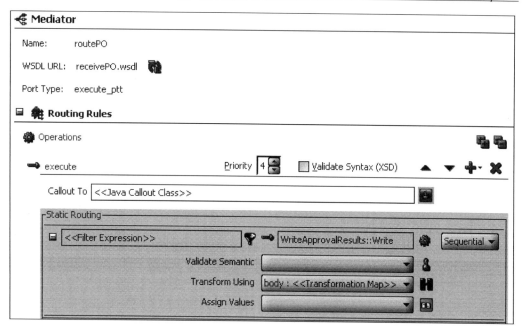

2. Now click on the transformation icon, to the right of the **Transform Using** dialog:

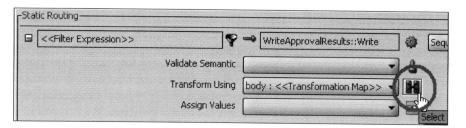

3. Choose to create a **New Mapper File** (you can leave the default filename as-is):

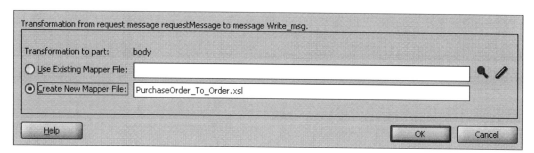

4. Drag a wire from **Purchase Order** on the source side to **Order** on the target side:

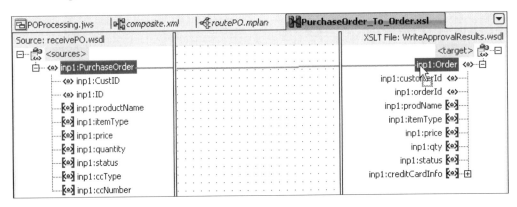

5. You are prompted for auto-mapping preferences:

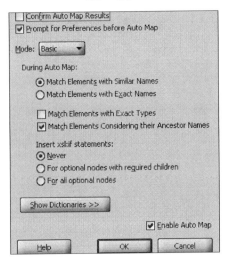

6. To help in the mapping, you are going to leverage a **dictionary** created by the business analysts that lists common synonyms in use across your data objects (for example, "qty" is sometimes used instead of "quantity", some departments use "ID" instead of "orderId", and so on).

7. Deselect the **Match Elements Considering their Ancestor Names** checkbox.

8. Click on **Show Dictionaries**:

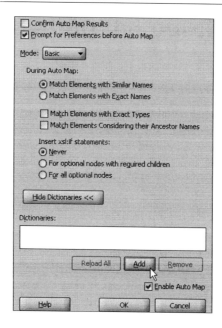

9. Click on **Add**.

10. Browse for `c:\po\schemas\po2internalorders-dictionary.xml`.

11. Click on **Open**.

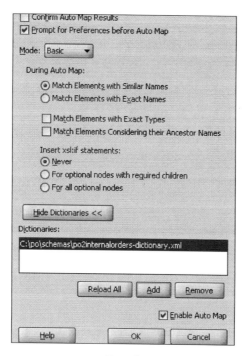

12. Click on **OK** to complete the auto-mapping dialog.

13. You should see that all fields have been auto-mapped, as follows:

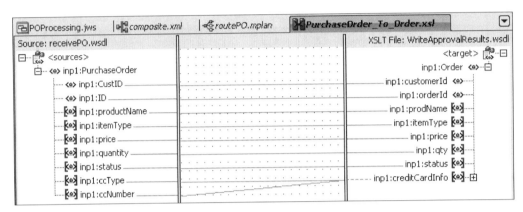

 Notice how the dictionary has helped match fields such as **inp1:CustID** to **inp1:customerId** and **inp1:productName** to **inp1:prodName**.

 Auto-mapping

Even without a dictionary, the **auto-mapping** feature will be able to identify and automatically take care of many of these fields, but a dictionary customized to your company helps improve its accuracy.

14. Save and close both the mapping and the Mediator editor to return to the composite (alternatively, you could use the **Save All** feature of JDev, by depressing the icon at the top left of the toolbar).

At this point in time, you have a fully-functional Mediator flow that can be deployed and tested. In later chapters, you will add more components to it.

Deploying the application

Deploy the application in the same way as in the previous chapter:

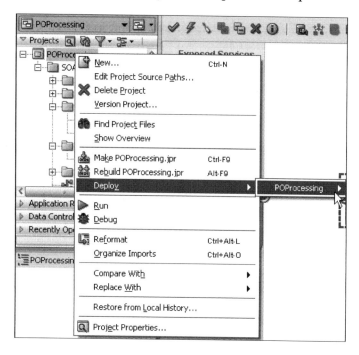

Testing the application

As simple as it is, this new composite is fully functional and can be tested right away to ensure we have the basics right.

1. Once deployment is complete, open Enterprise Manager at the following link: `http://localhost:7001/em`.

2. Locate **POProcessing** in the **SOA** folder in the lefthand side navigation tree. Hit the **Test** button to test your service:

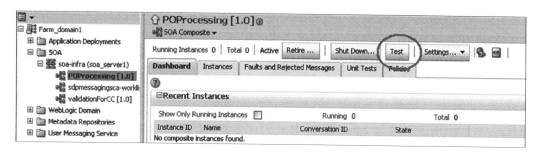

3. Enter a small order by doing one of the following:

   i. Type the values into the HTML form.

   ii. Click on **XML View** so you can paste in the XML payload. This is the recommended way this time around since the object is more complex and typing values in the HTML form could get tedious.

      a. Open the following file in a text editor: `c:\po\input\` `po-small-Headsetx1.txt`.

      b. Copy the entire content and paste it into the large text field in your browser, replacing the blank XML form that is there:

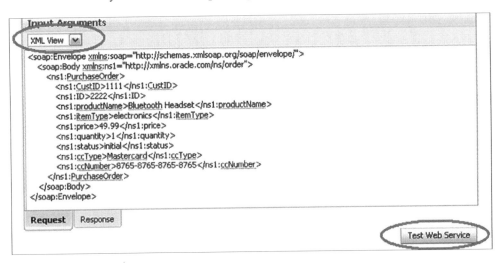

      c. Click on **Test Web Service**.

4. The **Test Result** screen won't have any response — this is normal since this is a one-way invocation with no reply or callback:

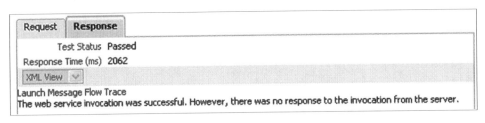

5. You can view the **Flow Trace** by selecting the **Launch Message Flow Trace** hyperlink. You should see the following:

Trace

Click a component instance to see its detailed audit trail.

Show Instance IDs ☐

Instance	Type	State	Time	Composite Instance
⊟ 🔷 receivePO	Service	✓ Completed	Mar 3, 2009 12:41:56 PM	POProcessing of 2
⊟ 🔷 routePO	Mediator Component	✓ Completed	Mar 3, 2009 12:41:58 PM	POProcessing of 2
🔷 WriteA	Reference	✓ Completed	Mar 3, 2009 12:41:58 PM	POProcessing of 2

6. In addition, the call to the File Adapter service should have resulted in a new file in `c:\temp`, called `order_n.txt`, where n is a sequence number like 1, 2, 3, and so on.

You can open that file with a text editor and examine it. Notice how field names have been translated by the mapping and are different from the input XML:

```
?xml version="1.0" encoding="UTF-8" ?>
inp1:Order xmlns:inp1="http://xmlns.oracle.com/ns/order">
  <inp1:customerId>1111</inp1:customerId>
  <inp1:orderId>2222</inp1:orderId>
  <inp1:prodName>Bluetooth Headset</inp1:prodName>
  <inp1:itemType>electronics</inp1:itemType>
  <inp1:price>49.99</inp1:price>
  <inp1:qty>1</inp1:qty>
  <inp1:status>initial</inp1:status>
  <inp1:creditCardInfo>
      <inp1:cardNumber>8765-8765-8765-8765</inp1:cardNumber>
      <inp1:cardType>Mastercard</inp1:cardType>
  </inp1:creditCardInfo>
```

Summary

In this chapter, you have learned how to leverage a very versatile component of the SOA Suite: the File Adapter. As you must have noticed it during the tutorial, the File Adapter has many advanced features that we have not even touched or introduced here but that you are likely to use in your own projects. You have also completed the first iteration of the POProcessing composite that you will be enriching during the subsequent chapters of this book.

Quick-build Instructions

This section gives you all of the operations and names for objects created in this chapter. Experienced users can use this to bypass the step-by-step instructions and complete this chapter more quickly. The complete details for any particular operation listed here can be found in the preceding sections. The information is organized in the same manner that it is introduced in the chapter.

- Create a new application:
    - ○ Application Name: **POProcessing**
    - ○ Directory: **c:\po**
    - ○ Project Name: **POProcessing**
    - ○ Project Technologies: **SOA**
    - ○ Empty Composite

- Add the service interface:
    - ○ Service: **receivePO**
    - ○ Type: **Service**
    - ○ WSDL based on: **po.xsd**
    - ○ Request: **PurchaseOrder**

- Add the routing component:
    - ○ Mediator: **routePO**
    - ○ Define Interface Later

- Add the File Adapter:
    - ○ File Adapter: **WriteApprovalResults**
    - ○ Directory for Outgoing Files: **c:\temp** (or Linux notation if using Linux)
    - ○ File Naming Convention: **order_%SEQ%.txt**
    - ○ Schema file: **c:\po\schemas\internalorder.xsd**
    - ○ Schema: **Order**

- Wire the components and add a transformation:
    - ○ Wire: service to mediator to adapter
    - ○ Mediator transform: Map Purchase Order to Order
    - ○ In Auto-complete: Deselect the **Match Elements Considering their Ancestor** checkbox.
    - ○ In Auto-complete: **Add Dictionary**
    - ○ Dictionary: **c:\po\schemas\po2internalorders-dictionary.xml**

The application is completed. Deploy and test.

7

Creating Processes Using Business Process Execution Language (BPEL)

To derive a new value from existing services and go beyond simple point-to-point integration, you will need to combine and orchestrate these services in a business process. You will want to connect them in a coordinated manner, for example, have the result from one service be the input to another service and have branching logic based on the outcome. Of course you can use Java or another programming environment to call the services and manage the processes and data, but there is an easier, declarative way.

Introducing BPEL

Business Process Execution Language (**BPEL**) is a standard that emerged in 2003 and was developed to enable orchestration of web services using an executable XML-based language. BPEL allows you to separate out the definition of your business process from the implementation of the services that it orchestrates. BPEL provides process flow operators such as conditional branching, parallel flow (split/join), and looping. The resulting BPEL process can itself be exposed as a web service, and therefore, be included in other business processes. You can read the BPEL standard at `http://oasis-open.org/`.

Long-running services

A business process can be short or long, taking minutes, days, or even months. For example, processing a mortgage application can take several weeks and can contain many steps. One of the strengths of BPEL is the way it is designed to handle such long running processes. It has built-in support for asynchronous processing so that when you call another service asynchronously, it waits for the response, even if the server is restarted and no matter how long the wait time is. When the response comes back, the BPEL engine coordinates the response to the BPEL process instance that made the request. You, the business process developer, need not worry about the low-level details of waiting for and correlating the response.

BPEL language

The XML-based language starts with a top-level XML element named **Process**. The elements of a BPEL process are called **BPEL activities**. Web services that the process calls or that call into a process are defined with a **Partnerlink** activity. Within the process, an **Invoke** activity says where to invoke the partnerlink or, if the web service calls the BPEL process, the **Receive** activity shows where the call comes into the process. A BPEL process can have variables and an **Assign** activity is used to assign a value to a variable. Variables are defined as XML elements and are accessed using XPath. Other common BPEL activities are **Switch**: for branching logic, **Flow**: for parallel execution, and **Faulthandlers**: for managing faults.

BPEL Editor

The BPEL Editor gives you a graphical view of the business process flow. In JDeveloper, you create a BPEL component in your composite and when you double-click on the component, the BPEL Editor opens. BPEL is all about XML but you use the graphical editor in JDeveloper to design your process. In fact, although you can edit the BPEL source and enter XML elements directly using text, you usually use the graphical editor for all of your BPEL process editing.

Tutorial: Orchestration of credit card validation service in POProcessing

This chapter adds a BPEL process to your POProcessing composite in order to orchestrate the web service call to `validationForCC`, which is the service implemented by your `CreditCardValidation` composite.

Chapters 5-10 must be done sequentially.

In order to follow the tutorial in this chapter, you must have either completed the tutorial from the previous chapter, or set up the environment as described in Chapter 4 and deployed the solution for the previous chapter, which can be found in `c:\po\solutions\ch06`.

When receiving large orders (greater than $1,000), you want to be more cautious, and:

- Validate the customer's credit card
- Automatically accept or reject the order based on the credit card status

The tool for orchestrating these interactions is the BPEL process manager. The overall flow of the application uses the credit validation service and the purchase order processing service created earlier.

Once completed, your POProcessing composite looks like this:

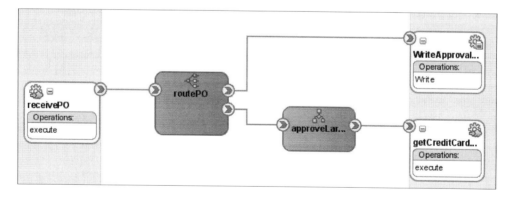

Designing the flow

You will modify POProcessing with the changes outlined earlier. You start by creating a reference using SOAP to the credit card validation service you created in Chapter 5. Then create the BPEL process to orchestrate the call and, based on the returned value, set the return status on the order. Finally, you wire the BPEL process to the Mediator and add a routing rule so that the BPEL process (and the downstream credit card validation service) is called only when the order total is over $1,000.

Invoking the CreditCardStatus service

1. If it is not already open, open your POProcessing application in JDeveloper. Make sure that there are no other files open and then open `composite.xml` for POProcessing. This eliminates any possible confusion as every composite has a `composite.xml` file. Make sure that you are using the one for POProcessing and not the one for `CreditCardValidation`.

2. Start your server and make sure your credit card validation service is running there.

3. Drag-and-drop a **Web Service** activity into the **External References** swim lane:

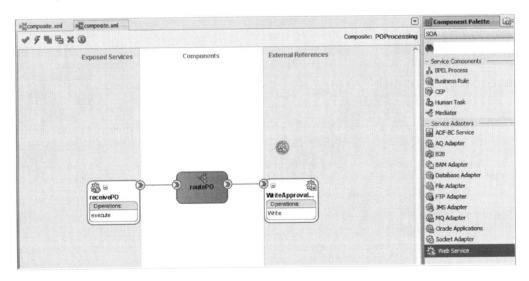

4. Set the following fields:

- **Name**: getCreditCardStatus
- **WSDL URL**: The server must be running and the composite deployed. Navigate to the service using the **Resource Browser** as follows:

    i. Click on the **Find Existing WSDLs** button next to the WSDL field.

    ii. Select **Resource Palette** from the drop-down at the top of the **Resource Browser**.

    iii. Navigate to the **validationForCC** service.

    iv. Select the **getStatusByCC** operation and click on **OK**.

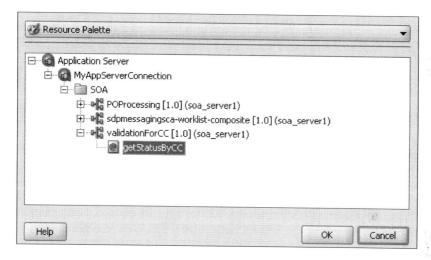

v. Alternatively, you can simply paste the URL to the WSDL into the field. The URL to the WSDL file can be obtained from the **validationForCC** test page in EM.

vi. Be sure to remove any version numbering. The URL will be something like this.

```
http://localhost:8001/soa-infra/services/
CreditCardValidation/ validationForCC/
getStatusByCC?WSDL
```

- ○ **Port Type**: Once you have the WSDL URL, press the *Tab* key to move to the next field. The **Port Type** will be updated automatically based on the WSDL.

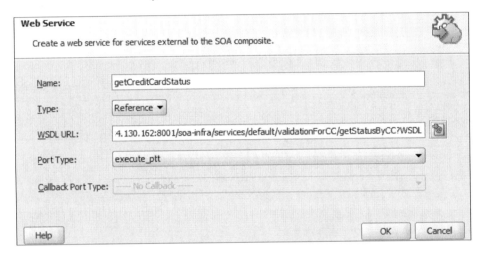

5. Click on **OK**.

   Now create a BPEL process and you can begin the orchestration for large order processing. The input and output to the BPEL process are in the internal order format of the order.

> When you create a BPEL process, you can specify the XSD schema type for the input and output of the process. The process is created with two variables automatically, **inputvariable** and **outputvariable**, with the input and output types you specified. If you do not specify the schema type and use the defaults, `inputvariable` and `outputvariable` are created as a simple string type.

6. Drag-and-drop a **BPEL Process** component on to the **Components** swim lane.

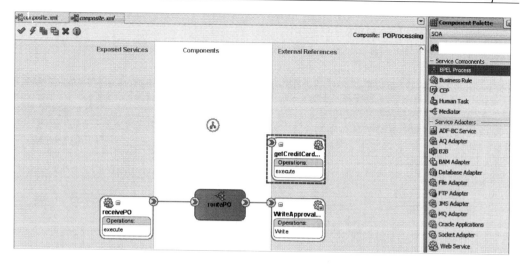

7. In the **Create BPEL Process** dialog, specify the following settings:

  ○ **Name: approveLargeOrder**

  ○ **Template: Asynchronous BPEL Process**

  ○ **Service Name: approveLargeOrder_client**

  ○ **Expose as a SOAP Service**: unchecked

  ○ **Input**: Click on the magnifying glass icon, expand **Project Schema Files | internalorder.xsd**, and select **Order**

  ○ **Output**: Use the **Order** type, as you did for **Input**

The WSDL for this service is created automatically using this information.

 The input and output types specified here go into the WSDL for this service, defining the message types used by the web service.

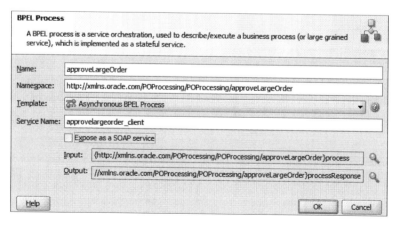

8. Click on **OK**.

9. Wire the BPEL process to the **getCreditCardStatus** service.

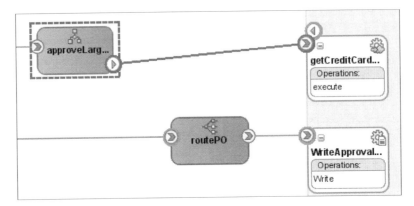

[Wiring a reference to a BPEL component in the composite automatically creates a partner link inside the BPEL process.]

Designing the BPEL approval process

Next, you'll build a simple BPEL process that calls the external **getCreditCardStatus** service.

1. Double-click on the BPEL component to open the BPEL editor.

   Note that the **getCreditCardStatus** partnerlink is already in the References swim lane because you wired it in the composite. The editors keep the references in sync between the BPEL process and `composite.xml`.

2. Drag-and-drop an **Invoke** activity from the **Component Palette** to an insertion point under the **receiveInput** activity:

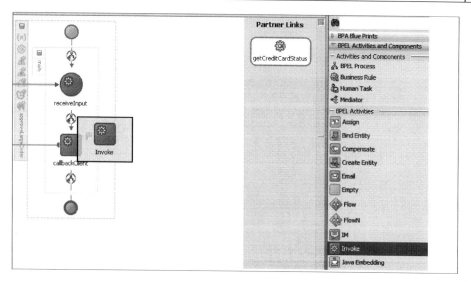

3. Drag the wire from the **Invoke** activity to **getCreditCardStatus**. This tells your BPEL process to invoke that service.

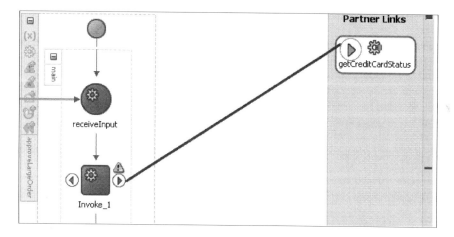

4. In the **Edit Invoke** dialog that opens, specify the following:

   ○ **Name**: **invokeCCStatusService**

   ○ **Input Variable**: Click on the green plus icon and then click on **OK** to create a new global variable, accepting the default name and type.

The variable designated for the input will contain the data that will be sent to the service when it is invoked. It is automatically created with the correct type expected by the service.

○ **Output Variable**: Click on the green plus icon and then click on **OK** to create a new global variable, accepting the default name and type.

This variable contains the data that will be returned by the service, or the output of the service. It is automatically created with the correct type.

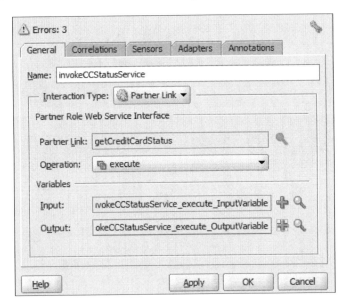

5. Click on **OK**.

Your BPEL process looks like the following screenshot so far:

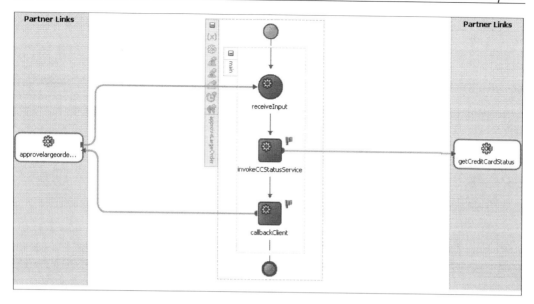

You have created the variables that will be used when interacting with the **getCreditCardStatus** service, but they haven't been populated. The output variable will be populated when the service returns a result, but you need to populate the input variable to pass the credit card number to the service.

In BPEL, you use an **Assign** activity to assign data to a variable. You can assign an element of the schema payload or the entire payload. You can assign data from one variable to another or you can assign an expression that gets resolved at runtime. The **XPath Expression Builder** helps you compose an expression using BPEL language and XPath constructs.

In this case, you want to assign the credit card number that was passed into the **POProcessing** service to the **getCreditCardStatus** service. You will assign the number that is in **inputvariable** to the variable you created using the **Invoke** dialog.

6. Drag-and-drop an **Assign** activity above your **Invoke** activity.

7. Double-click on the **Assign** activity to edit it.

8. Click on the **General** tab and change the name to `assignCCNumber`.

9. Click on the **Copy Operation** tab.

10. Click on the green colored plus icon and select **Copy Operation** to open the **Create Copy Operation** dialog, and specify the following:

   i.   In the **From** side, select **Variables | Process | Variables | inputVariable | payload | Order | creditCardInfo | cardNumber**.

   ii. In the **To** side, select **Variables | Process | Variables | invokeCCStatusService_execute_InputVariable | request | creditcardStatusRequest | CCNumber**.

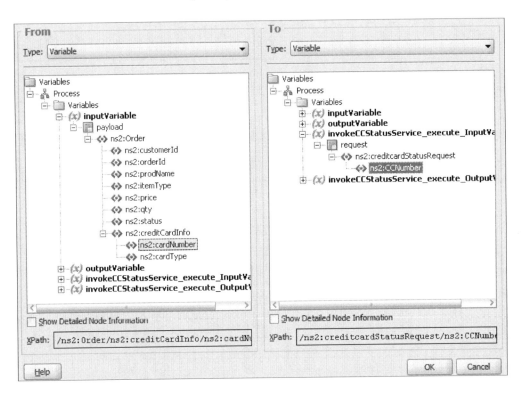

11. Click on **OK**.

12. Back in the **Assign** dialog, add a second copy operation by clicking on the green plus icon and selecting **Copy Operation**, and specify the following.

   i.   In the **From** side, select **Variables | Process | Variables | inputVariable | payload | Order**.

   ii. In the **To** side, select **Variables | Process | Variables | outputVariable | payload | Order**.

You are assigning to **outputVariable** because the BPEL process returns **outputVariable** when it finishes. You will return the input data you've copied here, as well as some updates, which will be made later in the BPEL process.

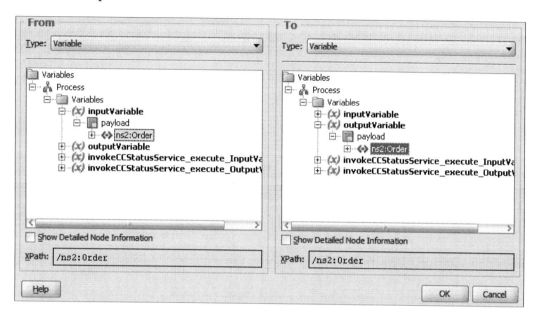

The **Assign** dialog now looks like this:

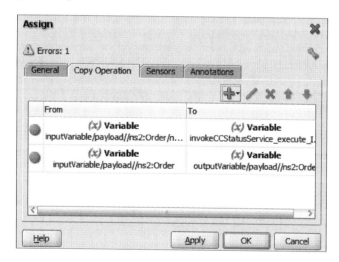

13. Click on **OK** to return to the BPEL process.

14. Click on the green colored check mark in the upper left of the BPEL process to validate the process. All the warnings should go away. It now looks like the following image:

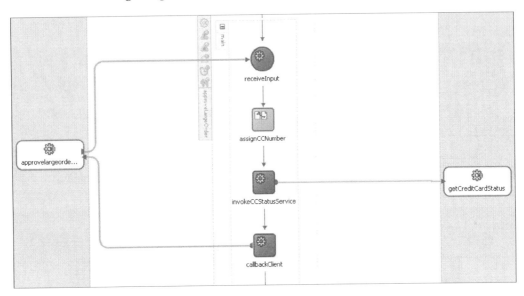

The input variable to **getCreditCardStatus** is now populated. The **Invoke** activity will pass that data to the service. The next step is to process the return data from the service, the output. The return value can be the string 'VALID' or 'INVALID'. You want a **Switch** statement so you can do something different for each case.

15. Drag-and-drop a **Switch** activity underneath **invokeCCStatusService**.

16. Double-click on the name of the switch underneath the icon (which is probably something like **Switch_1**) and rename it to `EvalulateCCStatus`.

> You can also double-click on the Switch icon and change the name in the subsequent dialog, but if you double-click on the text itself, you can change the name in-place.

17. Expand the switch by clicking on the small plus icon next to it.

18. Click on the **View Condition Expression** button.

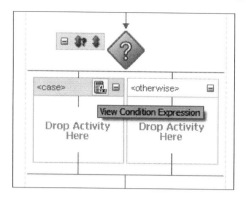

19. Click the **XPath Expression Builder** button.

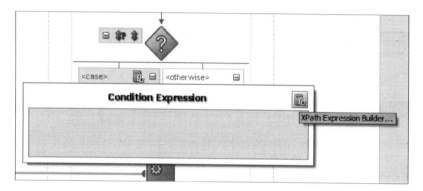

20. In the **BPEL Variables** field, expand **Variables | Process | Variables | invokeCCStatusService_execute_OutputVariable | reply** and select **creditCardStatus**.

21. Click on the **Insert Into Expression** button (it's the wide button under the **Expression** field).

22. Put your cursor in the **Expression** field and at the end and add: = **'VALID'**.

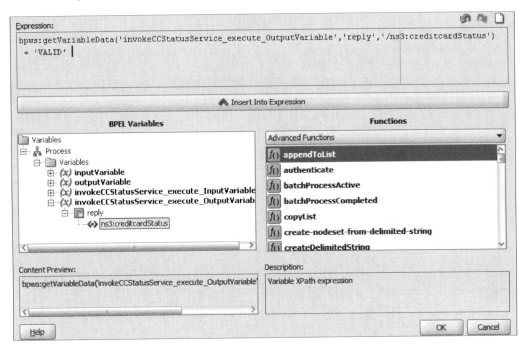

23. Click on **OK**.

24. Click outside the **Condition Expression** pop-up to close it.

   If that condition is true, then BPEL will execute any activities in the **Case** part of the switch. If not, any activities in the **Otherwise** section will be executed.

25. Drag-and-drop an **Assign** activity into the **Case** section of the **Switch**.

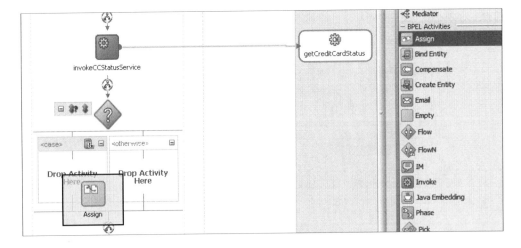

26. Double-click on the name of the **Assign** (which will be something like **Assign_2**) and rename it to **assignApproval**.

27. Double-click on the **Assign** icon to open the **Assign** dialog.

28. Click on the green colored plus icon and add a new copy operation.

29. In the **From** section, change the **Type** poplist to **Expression**.

30. In the **Expression** field, type: **'approved'** (with single quotes).

31. In the **To** section, select **Variables | Process | Variables | outputVariable | payload | Order | status**.

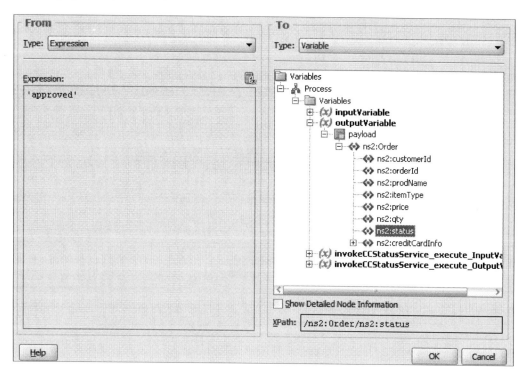

32. Click on **OK.**

33. Drag-and-drop an **Assign** activity into the **Otherwise** section of the switch.

34. Rename it to **assignInvalidCC**.

35. In the same way as you just did, assign the value **'invalidCreditCard'** to the status field of the **outputVariable** variable.

36. At the top of BPEL designer, click on the green colored check mark to validate your process. Any yellow flags you had should disappear and you should not have any warning messages.

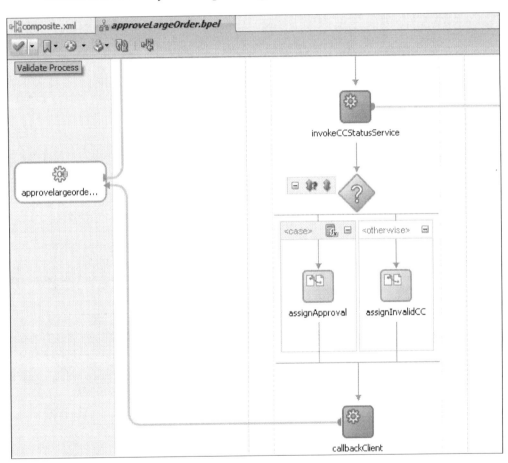

37. Your BPEL process is complete. Save the BPEL process and close the window to return to the composite.

Modifying the Mediator component

1. Wire the Mediator to the BPEL process.

   Your composite now looks like this:

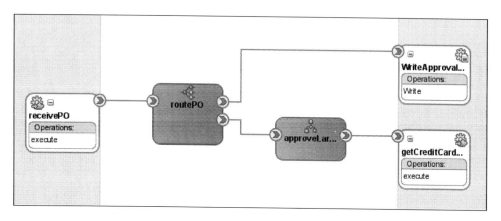

2. Now the Mediator is routing requests to both the **WriteApprovalResults** service and the **approveLargeOrder** BPEL process. Sometimes this is what you want a Mediator service to do, but in this case, a new order should either be automatically approved or have to be approved by going through the **approveLargeOrder** process.

   If you recall, orders under $1,000 should be approved automatically while orders greater than or equal to $1,000 need to go through an approval process. The Mediator is capable of creating a content-based routing service to enable this kind of processing.

3. Double-click on the **routePO** Mediator component to open the Mediator editor.

4. Click on the filter icon, called **Invoke Expression Builder**, which looks like a funnel, for the **WriteApprovalResults::Write request** operation.

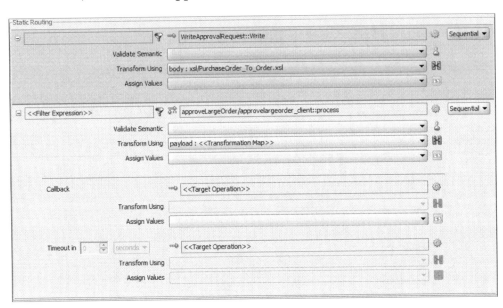

5. In the **Expression Builder** dialog, build up the following expression (don't copy this text into your expression but use the **Variables** frame to select the variables):

```
($in.request/inp1:PurchaseOrder/inp1:price * $in.request/
inp1:PurchaseOrder/inp1:quantity) < 1000
```

 The namespaces (for example, **inp1**) may be different for you.

 Expand the nodes in the **Variables** section to find the field you want and either double-click or press the **Insert Into Expression** button to add them to the expression.

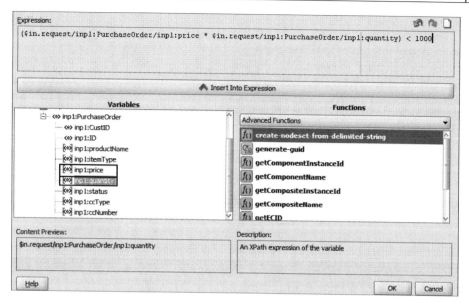

6. Click on **OK**.

7. Similarly, click on the filter icon for the request invocation of **approveLargeOrder/client::process**.

8. Add the following expression:

```
($in.request/inp1:PurchaseOrder/inp1:price * $in.request/
inp1:PurchaseOrder/inp1:quantity) >= 1000
```

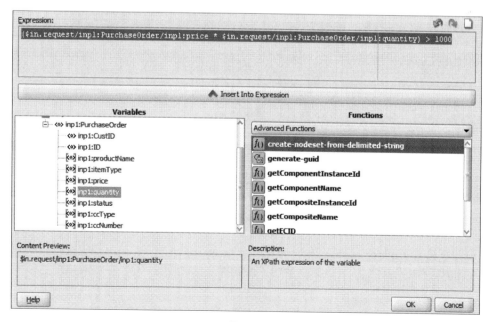

9. Click on **OK**.

    You also need to set the callback of the asynchronous BPEL process to call the file adapter service so that in the case of the large order processing, the order is still written to a file for the fulfillment archive.

10. Click on the cog icon next to the **Target Operation** field in the callback section.

11. In the **Target Type** dialog, click on the **Service** button.

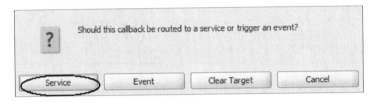

12. In the **Target Services** dialog, select **POProcessing | References | WriteApprovalResults | Write**.

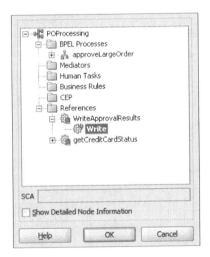

13. Click on **OK**.

    A transformation needs to be added for the operations. It's the same as the transformation done earlier, but the namespaces are different so a new transformation will need to be created.

14. Click on the transformation icon in the request section.

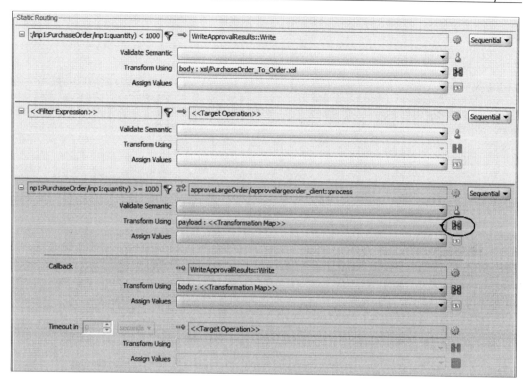

15. Select **Create New Mapper File** and click on **OK**.

16. Drag a wire from **PurchaseOrder** in the source to **Order** in target.

17. In the **Auto Map Preferences** dialog, simply click on **OK** without changing anything since you already added the dictionary in Chapter 6.

    The resulting transformation looks like this:

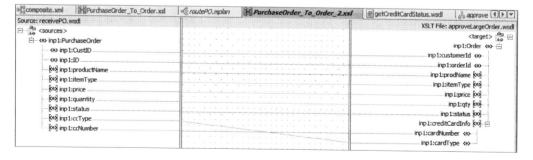

18. Save and close the mapper to return to the Mediator editor.

19. You must also add a transformation for the callback. Click on the transformation icon in the callback section.

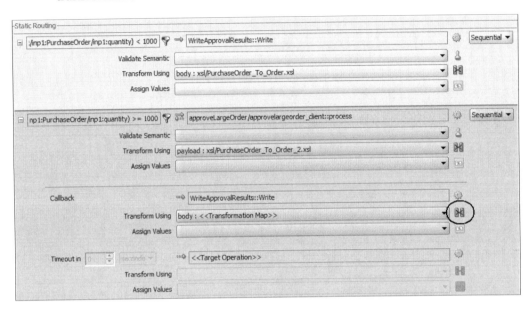

20. Select **Create New Mapper File** and click **OK**.

21. Drag a wire from **Order** in the source to **Order** in the target.

22. In the **Auto Map Preferences** dialog, click on **OK**.

The resulting transformation looks like this:

23. Save and close the mapper.

24. Save and close the Mediator editor to return to the composite.

25. Choose **File | Save All** from the menu or the toolbar just to make sure everything is saved.

Deploying the application

Deploy the application as described in the previous chapter, using the **Deploy** command on the **Project** menu.

Since you have already deployed POProcessing once before, you must either choose a new version number or select **Overwrite any existing composite** when deploying. If you do overwrite the previous composite, the existing instances for the version become stale and can no longer be viewed.

Testing the application

1. After deploying, in the Enterprise Manager console, click on the **POProcessing** application and then open the **Test** page.

2. Click on **XML View**.

3. In the previous chapter, you submitted a small order, which created an order file directly. This time, you'll create a large order, which the Mediator will route to the BPEL approval process.

4. Open the following file in a text editor:

    ```
    c:\po\input\po-large-iPodx30.txt
    ```

5. Copy the entire contents and paste them into the large text field in your browser:

```
Input Arguments
XML View ▾

<soap:Envelope xmlns:soap="http://schemas.xmlsoap.org/soap/envelope/">
  <soap:Body xmlns:ns1="http://xmlns.oracle.com/ns/order">
    <ns1:PurchaseOrder>
      <ns1:CustID>1111</ns1:CustID>
      <ns1:ID>2222</ns1:ID>
      <ns1:productName>iPod shuffle</ns1:productName>
      <ns1:itemType>electronics</ns1:itemType>
      <ns1:price>145</ns1:price>
      <ns1:quantity>30</ns1:quantity>
      <ns1:status>initial</ns1:status>
      <ns1:ccType>Mastercard</ns1:ccType>
      <ns1:ccNumber>1234-1234-1234-1234</ns1:ccNumber>
    </ns1:PurchaseOrder>
  </soap:Body>
</soap:Envelope>

Request   Response

                                    Test Web Service
```

6. Click on **Test Web Service**.

   As before, the **Test Result** screen won't have any response because this is a one-way invocation with no reply or callback. However, a new `order_n.txt` file will have been created in `c:\temp`. You can open it in a text editor and view the results. Note that the value of **<status>** on line 8 has been set to **approved**.

7. Click on the **Request** tab in the browser to return to the request page.

8. Re-run the application using the same input data, but this time change the credit card number to `4321-4321-4321-4321`, which represents an invalid credit card.

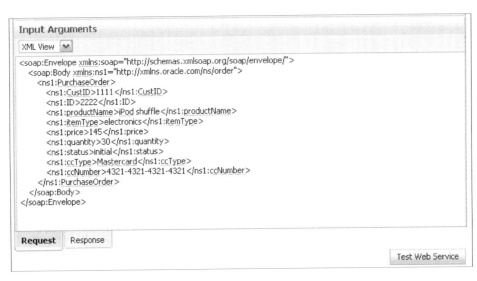

9. Click on **Test Web Service** to run the application.

10. Open the new order file in `c:\temp` and notice what the status is this time. This is the result of the **Switch** statement in your BPEL process.

11. Click on **Launch Message Flow Trace** to see the details of the message flow for this instance of your composite.

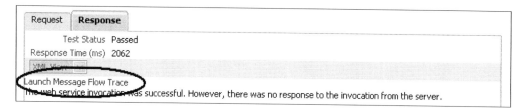

Alternatively, click on the application. In the **Last 5 Instances** section click on the most recent instance to see the message flow in the **Flow Trace** window.

Note that the flow trace shows you the flow through both composites. You can see the composite instance value on the far right.

You can click on the **approveLargeOrder** link to look at the BPEL process instance. You can click on the various activities to see their results.

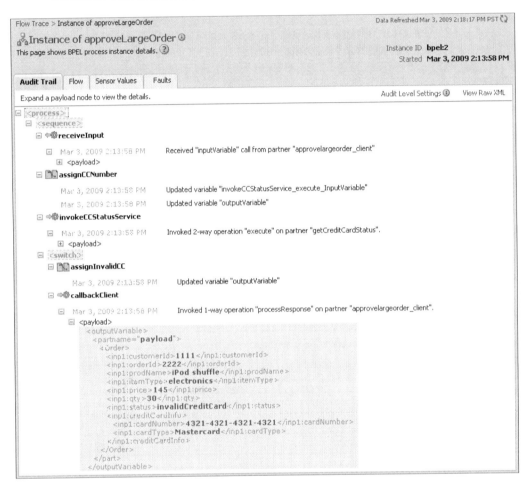

An interesting one to click on is the **getCreditCardStatus** invoke payload.

When you click on the **getCreditCardStatus** invoke payload, it's a synchronous (request-response) call, so you see both the input to the service (that is, what you're passing to the service) and the output (that is, what you're getting back from the service).

In the following screenshots, the input to the service is the credit card number **4321-4321-4321-4321** and the output returned is **INVALID**.

```
⊟ ⇨⚙ invokeCCStatusService
  ⊟  Mar 3, 2009 2:13:58 PM        Invoked 2-way operation "execute" on partner "getCreditCardStatus".
      ⊟ <payload>
           <messages>
            <invokeCCStatusService_execute_InputVariable>
             <partname="request">
              <creditcardStatusRequest>
               <CCNumber>4321-4321-4321-4321</CCNumber>
              </creditcardStatusRequest>
             </part>
            </invokeCCStatusService_execute_InputVariable>
            <invokeCCStatusService_execute_OutputVariable>
             <partname="reply">
              <inp1:creditcardStatus>INVALID</inp1:creditcardStatus>
             </part>
            </invokeCCStatusService_execute_OutputVariable>
           </messages>
```

12. You can also view the BPEL process instance information using the **Flow View**. Click on the **Flow** tab at the top of the BPEL instance **Audit Trail** view:

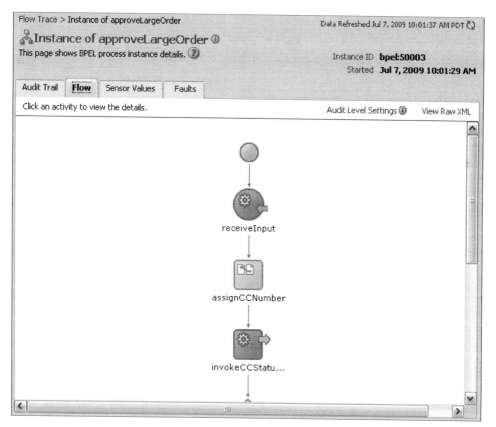

Flow Trace > Instance of approveLargeOrder   Data Refreshed Jul 7, 2009 10:01:37 AM PDT ⟲

🔊 **Instance of approveLargeOrder** ⓘ

This page shows BPEL process instance details. ⓘ

Instance ID **bpel:50003**
Started **Jul 7, 2009 10:01:29 AM**

| Audit Trail | **Flow** | Sensor Values | Faults |

Click an activity to view the details.   Audit Level Settings ⓘ   View Raw XML

receiveInput

assignCCNumber

invokeCCStatu...

13. Then, click on any of the activities in the view to see the payload details. For example, click on the **invokeCCStatus** activity.

14. Back in the main screen of the EM console, run the **Test** page again and this time, use the small order that you used in the previous chapter, which can be found in `c:\po\input\po-small-Headsetx1.txt`

Note that the BPEL process does not get invoked and instead you only get a new order file generated in `c:\temp`. But what is the value of status in this case? This order is automatically approved because it is less than $1,000.

The application is almost complete, but there is an issue. For orders under $1,000, the order is routed directly to the file adapter via the Mediator. For orders over $1,000, the mediator routes to the request to the BPEL process for approval before sending it to the file adapter to be written.

Look at the context of the output file. What is the value for status?

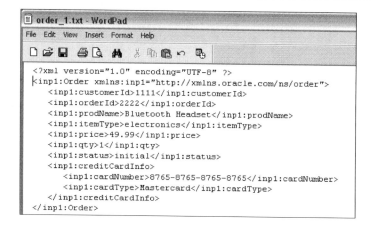

In the case of the large order, the BPEL process sets the status. In this case, the status is **approved**. But in the case of small orders that get routed only through the Mediator, the status is not updated and it still set at **initial**.

This creates inconsistent data. The application should be modified such that small orders are always approved.

Modifying the application for small orders

1. In the composite, double-click on the **routePO** Mediator component to open it.

2. Modify the existing transformation for the **WriteApprovalResults::Write** operation by clicking on the transformation button to the right of the **Transform Using** field:

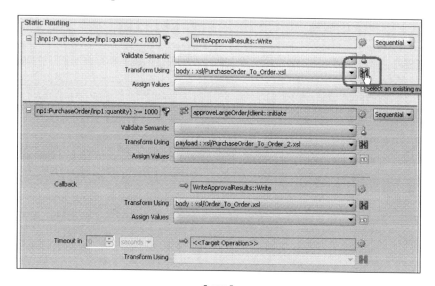

3. Ensure that **Use Existing Mapper File** is selected, and click on the edit button; it looks like a pencil. This will open an existing transformation.

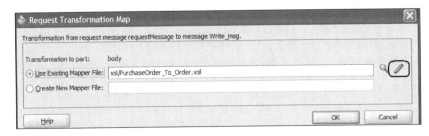

4. Click on the mapping for status to highlight it.

5. Press the *Delete* key on your keyboard to remove it.

6. Right-click on **status** on the target side and select **Set Text** and then click on **Enter Text…**.

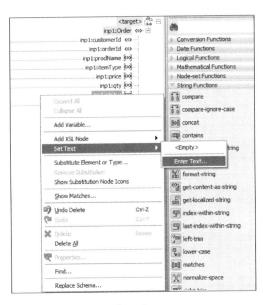

7. Enter **approved** in the **Text** field.

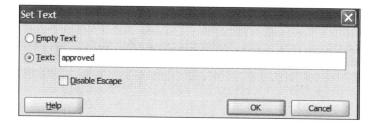

8. Click on **OK**.

   The **status** field has a visual cue to let you know a text value has been assigned.

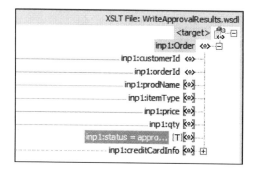

9. Save and close the mapper.
10. Save and close the Mediator editor.

Now, deploy and test your application again for the small order. Review the output file and verify the status is set to approved.

Summary

BPEL orchestration goes a long way in building composite applications by taking your services and putting them together into a business process. Now, you can use your business logic and the declarative SOA tools to connect services in a logical way. With the implementation of the services separate from the business process, you have the flexibility to modify business logic without affecting the detailed implementations. Again, you use Enterprise Manager to monitor and view the details of the composite instance. The same administration console is used no matter which components are in your composite.

Quick-build Instructions

This section gives you all of the operations and names for objects created in this chapter. Experienced users can use this to bypass the step-by-step instructions and complete this chapter more quickly. The complete details for any particular operation listed here can be found in the preceding sections. The information is organized in the same manner that it is introduced in the chapter.

- Invoke the `CreditCardStatus` service:
    - Reference: **getCreditCardStatus**
    - WSDL using Resource Browser—Service: **validationForCC | getStatusByCC**

- Design the BPEL approval process:
    - Name: **approveLargeOrder**
    - Template: **Asynchronous BPEL Process**
    - Service Name: **approveLargeOrder_client**
    - Expose as a SOAP Service: Unchecked
    - Input: **internalorder.xsd - Order**
    - Output: **internalorder.xsd - Order**
    - Wire the BPEL process to the **getCreditCardStatus** service

- In BPEL Editor:
    - Invoke Name: **invokeCCStatusService**
    - Wire: Invoke to **getCreditCardStatus**
    - Input Variable: default
    - Output Variable: default
    - Assign before Invoke: **assignCCNumber**
    - Copy 1 From: **inputVariable | payload | Order | creditCardInfo | cardNumber**
    - To: **invokeCCStatusService_execute_InputVariable | request | creditcardStatusRequest | CCNumber**
    - Copy 2 From: **inputVariable | payload | Order**
    - To: **outputVariable | payload | Order**
    - Switch after Invoke: **EvalulateCCStatus**

- ○ Case Expression: **bpws:getVariableData('invokeC CStatusService_execute_OutputVariable ','reply','/ ns3:creditcardStatus') = 'VALID'**
- ○ Case Assign: `assignApproval`
- ○ Copy From: **'approved'**
- ○ To: **outputVariable | payload | Order | status**
- ○ Otherwise Assign: **assignInvalidCC**
- ○ Copy From: **'invalidCreditCard'**
- ○ To: **outputVariable | payload | Order | status**

- Modify the Mediator component:
  - ○ Wire the Mediator to the BPEL process
  - ○ Filter to **Write:** (`$in.request/inp1:PurchaseOrder/ inp1:price * $in.request/inp1:PurchaseOrder/ inp1:quantity`) `< 1000`
  - ○ Filter to **approveLargeOrder:** (`$in.request/ inp1:PurchaseOrder/inp1:price * $in.request/ inp1:PurchaseOrder/inp1:quantity`) `>= 1000`
  - ○ Callback Target Service: **POProcessing | References | WriteApprovalResults | Write**
  - ○ Request Map from **PurchaseOrder** to **Order**
  - ○ Callback Map from **Order** to **Order**
  - ○ Edit Transform: `PurchaseOrder_To_Order.xsl`
  - ○ Remove wire: **status**
  - ○ **Set Text** on target: **status**
  - ○ Value: **approved**

The application is completed. Deploy and test.

8

Creating Human Tasks

Although some applications may be truly automated without any human intervention, many applications require some level of human interaction, such as escalations, interventions, or simply, manual data entry. Just as a typical service orchestration has a defined flow, so do many human interactions. For example, approving a high-value order may require three levels of approvals, which is a simple three-step flow. There are numerous complex patterns for these types of human interaction flows, which we refer to as **Human Workflow**. Often, the human workflow in your application is integral to the service orchestration and it is a natural fit for within the BPEL process. However, the BPEL standard does not include anything about human interaction and does not apply to people at all. The Oracle SOA Suite Human Task component provides all of these features and more, and your BPEL process can include human workflow and still be 100% BPEL standard based.

Introducing the Human Task component

The Human Task component provides a set of functionality that handles different human interaction patterns within a broader business process. For example, you can assign tasks to users or groups; you can define approval rules such as group voting or management chain approvals; you can set up notification options such as an alert when a task is assigned to you. The Human Task component is available as a service and can be used in your BPEL process component when it needs to initiate a human workflow. It can also be used by other service consumers, as well as by plain old Java objects or in J2EE applications. The Human Task component architecture closely models the BPEL4People specification that is currently being defined. Oracle is a one of the core contributors to the BPEL4People specification.

Functional details

The Human Task component provides two core services:

1. A **Human Workflow Service**, which is responsible for all aspects of executing a workflow consisting of one or more human tasks.

2. A **Worklist Application**, which provides a web-based user interface for working with the tasks created as part of the human workflow.

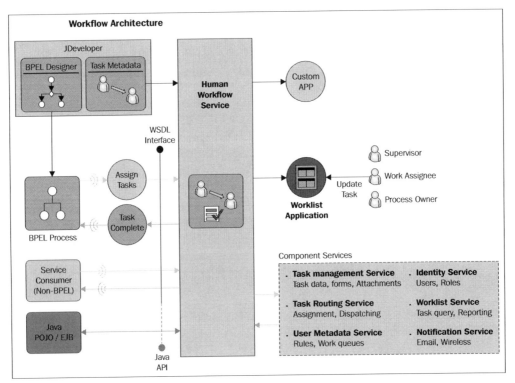

Human Workflow Service

The Human Workflow Service is provided both as a WSDL-based service that can be used by any web service client, as well as a set of Java APIs that can be called from a plain Java or a J2EE application. The workflow service comprises of a number of services. Some of the important ones are listed as follows:

- Task Service provides task state management and persistence of tasks. In addition to these services, the task service exposes operations to update, complete, escalate, and reassign tasks.

- Task Query Service provides operations for querying tasks for a user based on a variety of search criteria such as keyword, category, status, business process, attribute, values, and so on.

- Task Metadata Service provides operations to retrieve metadata information related to a task.

- User Metadata Service provides operations to manage metadata such as user work queues, preferences, vacation, delegation rules, and so on.

- Identity Service provides authentication services and operations for looking up user properties, roles, group memberships, and privileges.

- Notification Service delivers notifications with the specified content to the workflow users using a variety of channels like Instant Messaging (IM), SMS, Email, Voice Mail, and so on. The Notification Service utilizes the User Messaging Service (UMS) in the SOA infrastructure.

Worklist application

The Worklist, an ADF-based web application, is used by users to access and act on tasks assigned to them. For instance, in our POProcessing example, we can introduce a new activity in the flow that requires a manager approval for an order greater than a certain value. When such an order is received and approval workflow is initiated, the manager will use the Worklist application to approve or reject this order.

The approval workflow can be a simple single-step approval or could have a number of steps. For example, you may want to escalate the approval to a vice president if the manager doesn't attend to the assigned task within a given time period. The Worklist application provides different functionality based on the user's profile, which means that the manager would have different functions available to him or her as compared to the vice president. Standard user profiles include task assignee, supervisor, process owner, and administrator. Some examples of the functions attached to different roles are:

- Update of payloads
- Attaching documents or comments

- Routing tasks to other users
- Completing tasks by providing conclusions such as approvals or rejections

Supervisors or group administrators can also use this application to analyze the tasks assigned to a group and route them appropriately.

Users that have tasks assigned to them can use the application to:

- Perform authorized actions on tasks in the worklist, acquire and check out shared tasks, define personal to-do tasks, and define subtasks
- Filter tasks in a worklist view based on various criteria
- Define custom work queues
- Gain proxy access to part of another user's worklist
- Define custom vacation rules and delegation rules
- Enable group owners to define task dispatching rules for shared tasks
- Collect a complete workflow history and audit trail

Tutorial: Adding Manual Approval in PO Processing

 Chapters 5-10 must be done sequentially.

In order to follow the tutorial in this chapter you must have either completed the tutorial from the previous chapter, or set up the environment as described in Chapter 4 and deployed the solution for the previous chapter, which can be found in `c:\po\solutions\ch07`.

In this next iteration of the application, you will add a Human Task to the composite in order to review large orders manually.

Once completed, your POProcessing composite will look like this:

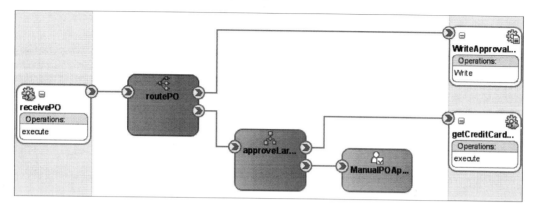

Designing the flow

To review large orders manually, you add the Human Task to the BPEL process after the credit card has been validated and only for VALID cards. You also create an ADF task form as a separate project in the application to be used at runtime with the worklist application.

Adding a Human Task to the composite

1. In JDeveloper, drag-and-drop a **Human Task** component onto the composite.

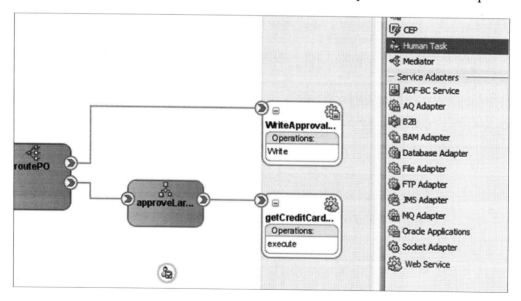

2. Specify the following:
    ◦   **Name**: **ManualPOApproval**
    ◦   **Namespace**: Leave as default
    ◦   **Create Composite Service with SOAP Bindings**: Unchecked

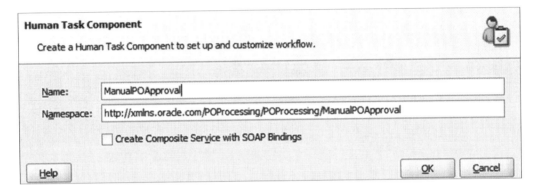

3. Click on **OK**.
4. Wire the BPEL process to the **Human Task**.

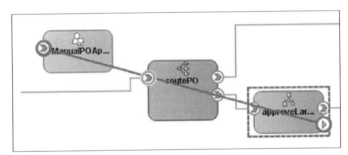

5. Double-click on the Human Task to open the **Task Definition** editor.

6. Specify the following settings:

- Using the expression builder button on the right, enter '**Approve Order**' for **Title** and click on **OK**. You will see <%'**Approve Order'**%> entered as the value.

- Enter **Manual approval task for large orders** in the **Description** field.

- Enter **Order** in the **Parameters** field.

  i. Use the green plus sign to open the **Add Task Parameter** dialog. Select **Element** and then browse for the **Order** element in `internalorder.xsd`.

  ii. Select the **Editable via worklist** option. (This is optional and only so that you can see the functionality. Our application does not need to edit the payload.)

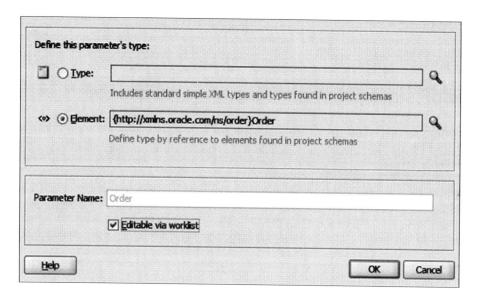

7. Click on **OK**.

8. In the **Assignment and Routing Policy** section, double-click on the **<no participant>** box in the diagram.

9. In the **Edit Participant Type** dialog, specify the following:
    ◦ **Type**: **Single**
    ◦ **Label**: **Large Order Approver**

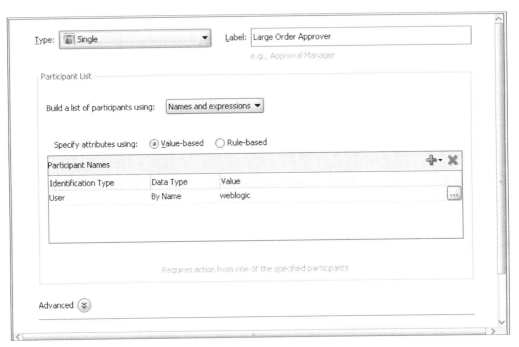

10. Use the green plus sign next to **Participant Names** to add a user:
    i. Set the **Identification Type** to **User** (already set)
    ii. Set **Data Type** to **By Name** (already set)
    iii. In the **Value** field, enter **weblogic** (no quotes)

 Normally you would browse for users set in the server. However, in your current installation, you haven't yet created any users other than the default weblogic user. To browse for users, you must create a server connection to the SOA-Managed server (usually at port 8001) and when you test that connection, some protocols will fail. But you will be able to use it to browse for users. For now, only the weblogic user is returned. Later, if you have added more users to the system, they will be returned as well.

11. Click on **OK**.

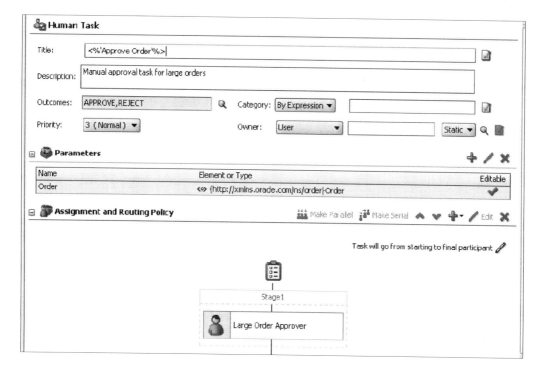

12. Save and close the **Task Definition** editor and return to the composite.

Calling the Human Task from BPEL

Now that the Human Task is defined, you can add an activity in your BPEL process that references the task and invokes the Human Task service at that point in the process. In JDeveloper, this looks like a single BPEL activity but is really a set of activities within a BPEL Scope activity to assign the input, invoke the service, and assign the output data.

1. Double-click on the BPEL component to open the BPEL designer.

2. Drag a **Human Task** into the **<case>** branch of the Switch, underneath the **assignApproval** Assign activity (you will be moving this Assign activity shortly).

3. The **Create a Human Task** dialog opens. Select **ManualPOApproval** from the **Task Definition** drop-down. This action automatically creates a service interface to the Human Task service that you created. In BPEL, a partnerLink appears for the service reference.

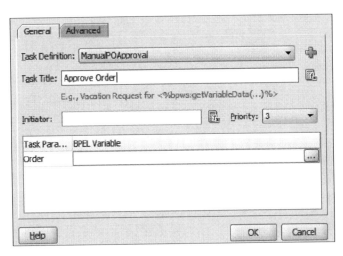

4. Select the BPEL variable to pass the input parameter by clicking on the [...] button on the right of **Order**.

5. Select **Variables | Process | Variables | outputVariable | payload | Order**. **outputVariable** has all of our information collected so far.

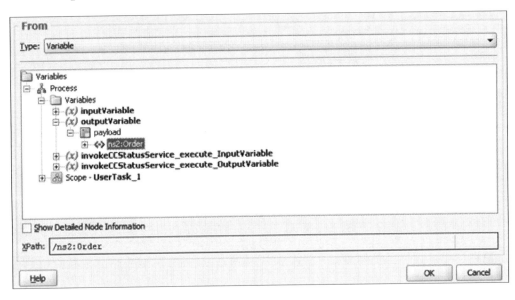

6. Click on **OK**.

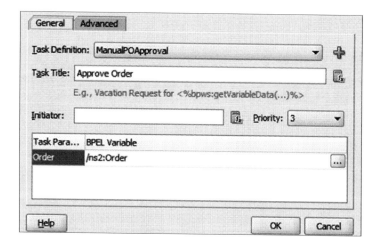

7. Click on **OK**.

   You will have two new activities in your BPEL process: a **Human Task** and a **Switch** activity. The **Human Task** activity handles getting the approval (or rejection) from users using a work list application. The **Switch** activity can then be used to evaluate the results from the **Human Task**, for example, what to do if it's approved and or what to do if it's rejected.

8. You just configured the **Human Task**, so the next step is to take appropriate actions in the **Switch** activity.

9. Click on the plus icon next to the **Switch** to expand it.

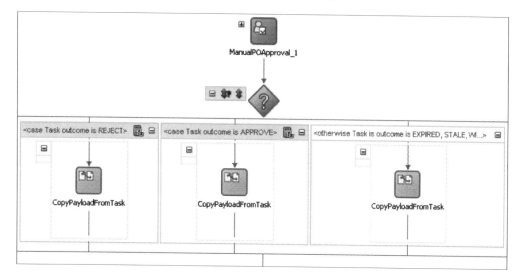

Notice the three outcomes this Human Task was configured for: APPROVE; REJECT; or EXPIRED, STALE, WITHDRAWN, or ERRORED. You will set the status for each of those cases.

 The Task outcome status values can be set to any value you prefer when you complete the task definition. In this chapter, the default values of APPROVE and REJECT were used. Once you have completed the task definition and added the task to the BPEL project, the Switch statement is created automatically with the correct case expressions. The outcome values cannot be changed without editing the Switch statement manually.

10. The approved case was already done earlier, so you can reuse that. Drag the **assignApproval** Assign activity underneath the **CopyPayloadFromTask** Assign activity in the **APPROVE** branch of the **Switch**.

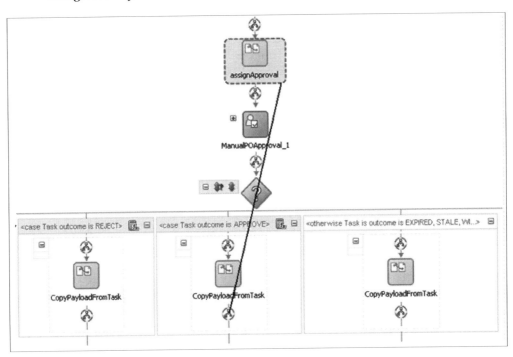

11. Double-click on the **CopyPayloadFromTask Assign** activity in the **REJECT** branch.

12. Click on the green plus icon and add a new copy operation.

13. Set the **status** field of the **outputVariable** variable to **'rejected'**.

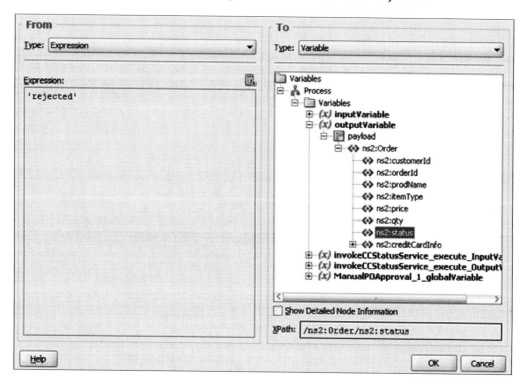

14. Click on **OK**.

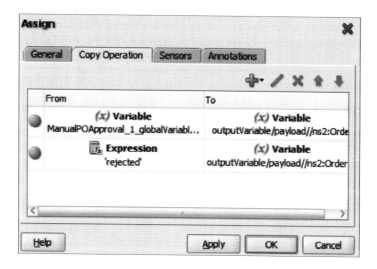

15. Click on **OK**.

16. Now for the third branch. Double-click on the **CopyPayloadFromTask Assign** activity in the **EXPIRED, STALE, WITHDRAWN**, or **ERRORED** branch.

17. Click on the green plus icon and add a new copy operation.

18. Set the **status** field of the **outputVariable** variable to **'expired'**.

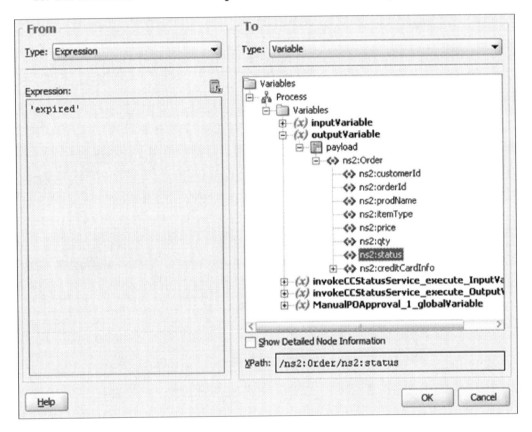

19. Click on **OK**.

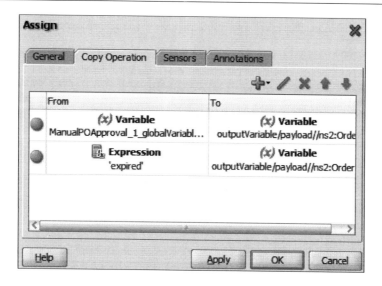

20. Click on **OK**. The **Switch** activity now looks like the following figure:

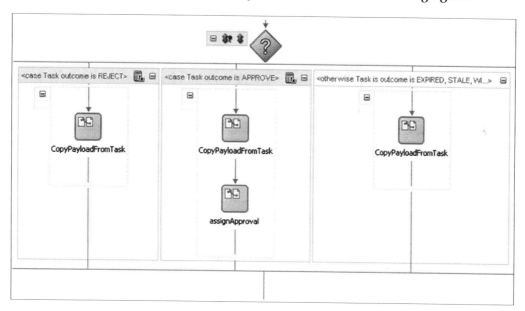

 The **APPROVE** branch could have been done the same way
as the other two, but in this case there are two separate **Assign** activities.
The end result is the same.

21. Save the BPEL process.

Creating the task form for task details

The Task is an ADF form that is created in a separate project. You create a JSF project to manage the task form and point it to the task file you create in your composite.

When you want a default form that includes the task payload and actions you just defined in the task definition, this is a simple one-click operation. For this lab, you want the default form. Complete the following:

1. In the BPEL process (not the composite), right-click on the human task **ManualPOApproval** and select **Auto-generate task form**.

2. Enter a project name **ApproveTaskDetails** for your task form and select **OK**.

   Stand back and watch the magic (it may look like nothing is happening at first but be patient and don't touch anything). You can watch your disk activity light.

3. The project is created and all of the artifacts needed for the form start to show up there. The **Task Flow** diagram will open and then the task form itself. When you see the task form **TaskDetails1.jspx** page open with the payload form elements, the form is created. Click on the **Save all** button and close the task form and task flow windows.

4. In the **Application** navigation pane, you see lots of files listed in the new task form project and the pane may be scrolled to the right. Scroll the pane to the top and left and close the folders for the **ApproveTaskDetails** project to clean up the navigation view and allow you to see your composite project files again.

5. Now that you have created the form, you have the option to customize the form but for this lab, you can jump ahead to the next section to deploy and test.

If you would like to learn how to create the form in a step-by-step manner, for non-default choices, read on. The step-by-step method for creating the task form is included here for your information. Otherwise, just skip ahead to the next section.

Creating a form from a **Human Task** definition is easy; simply accept the defaults for the different steps or customize as desired. A default form layout is created automatically. You have the option to edit this as desired.

1. From the **Application Menu,** select **New Project**.

2. Select **General** in the **Categories** column and **Generic Project** under **Items**.

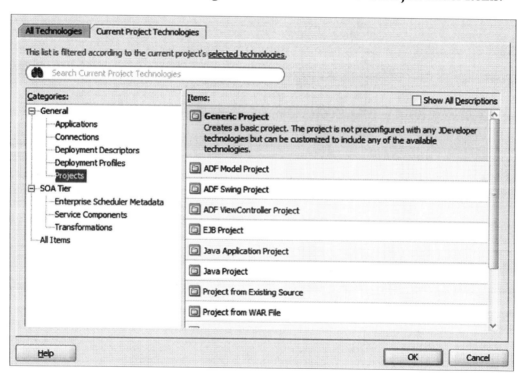

3. Click on **OK**.

4. Enter the project name as **ApproveTaskDetails**.

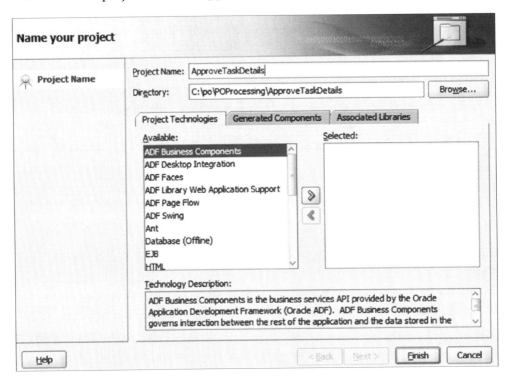

5. Click on **Finish**.

6. Right-click on the new project and select **New**.

7. In the **New Gallery**, scroll to the **Web Tier** category and select **JSF**. Under **Items**, select **ADF Task Flow Based on Human Task** (and click on **OK**).

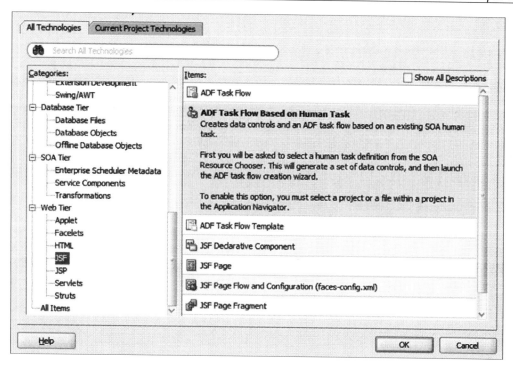

8. In the **SOA Resource Lookup** dialog, browse to the **ManualPOApproval. task** file that you created in the **POProcessing** project. This file is in the **POProcessing** folder.

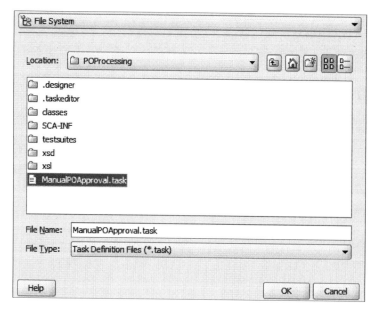

9. Click on **OK**.

10. In the **Create Task Flow** dialog, accept all defaults and click on **OK**.

11. The task details page is initialized and all of the artifacts needed for the form are added to your new project. Close the folders of the task details project in the navigation bar.

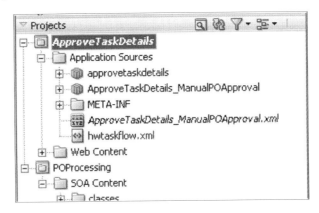

12. Double-click on the **taskDetails1.jpsx** icon in the **Task Flow** view to finish creating the task flow.

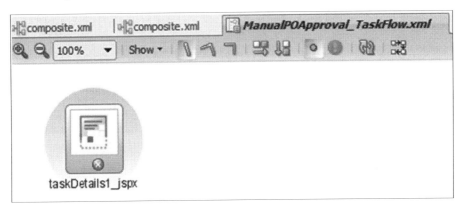

13. In the **Create JSF Page** dialog, accept all defaults and click on **OK**.

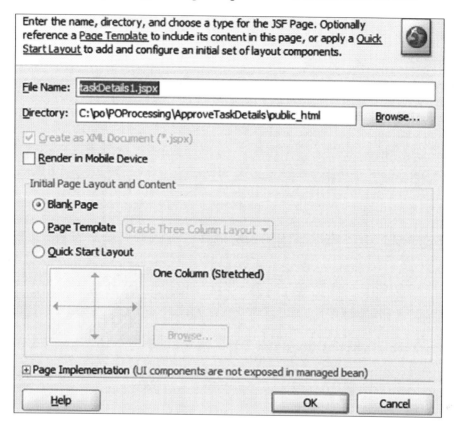

Now the empty task flow page is open. You will drag the task definition to this page to create all of the elements of the order payload that you specified as the task payload when you created the task in the composite project.

14. Locate the **Task** definition in the **Data Controls** section of the **Application Navigator** as shown in the following figure:

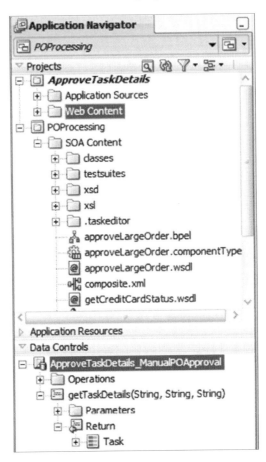

15. Drag the **Task** object to the empty task flow page and drop it anywhere.

16. In the menu that opens, select **Human Task | Complete Task with Payload**.

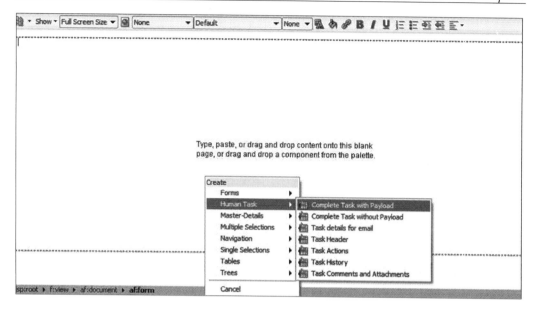

17. In the dialog, **Edit Action Binding**, accept all defaults and click on **OK**. Click on **OK** again to finish creating the task form.

18. Edit the form as desired. Click on the **Save All** button and close any task windows that are still open.

19. In the **Application Navigation** pane, you see lots of files listed in the new task form project. Scroll the pane to the top and left and close the folders for the project to clean up the navigation view and allow you to see your composite project files again.

Deploying and testing the application

1. Deploy the **POProcessing** composite from its project menu. Enter a new version number or select the checkbox to overwrite the existing version.

2. Next, deploy the **ApproveTaskDetails** task form project by selecting **Deploy** from the **Application** menu in the toolbar.

3. STOP—did you select deploy from the project menu or the application menu? Task forms are deployed using the **Application** menu, not the **Project** menu. You can find the **Application** menu in the toolbar or you can right-click on the application name to bring up the menu, or you can click the drop-down menu icon to the right of the application name to open the application menu.

4. In the **Deployment Configuration** dialog, set the managed server **soa_server1**.

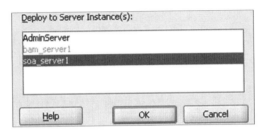

5. Click on **OK**.

   If you chose to deploy the task form project from its project menu, you will see an error message and deployment will not complete. You must deploy task forms from the **Application** menu in the toolbar. Go back to step 2.

6. Once deployed, open the **EM** console to test the application using the input for a large order as you did in the previous chapter. This will create a new order that's over $1,000. Copy the input data into the **XML View** in the **Test** page from: `C:\po\input\po-large-iPodx30.txt`.

7. As usual, the **Response** tab won't show any results as this is a one-way invocation with no reply or callback. Also notice, however, that a new order file was not created in `c:\temp`. That's because the application hasn't completed running yet. To see what's going on, you need to look at the instance audit trail.

8. Click on **Launch Message Flow Trace** to see the details of the message flow for this instance of your composite. Alternatively, click on the latest instance from the composite page. You'll notice the status for **approveLargeOrder** and **ManualPOApproval** are both still **Running**. They are waiting for the human task to be processed.

9. Now it is time to "change hats" and log on to the Worklist application as a customer service representative to approve the task. Using a browser, open `http://localhost:8001/integration/worklistapp` (use the correct port for your installation).

10. Log on using the following credentials:

    ○ **Username**: **weblogic**

    ○ **Password**: **welcome1** (or as appropriate for your machine)

> The Worklist application is an out of the box application where users can view and manage their tasks.

11. Click on the most recent task to highlight it.

> Selecting the task opens it in the lower frame of the Worklist application. The first time that the task is opened, there will be a delay of a minute or so while the pieces of the form are compiled and loaded.

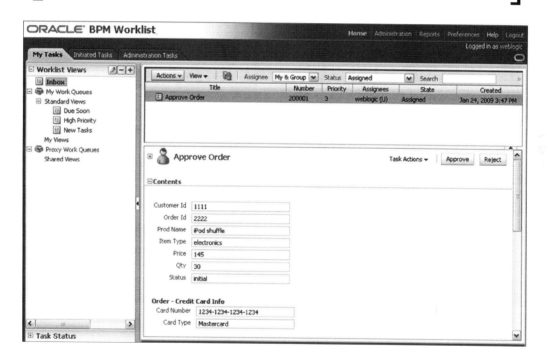

12. When the form opens, you can see the task details and the different options. Select **Reject** or **Approve** as desired. This will submit the task and notify the BPEL process it can continue. If you have edited the task data, using the buttons will also save the data before submitting. If you use the **Actions** menu to submit the task, you must save manually first.

13. Return to the task flow in the **EM** console. If you still have it open, you can just refresh the page. Notice that it is now complete.

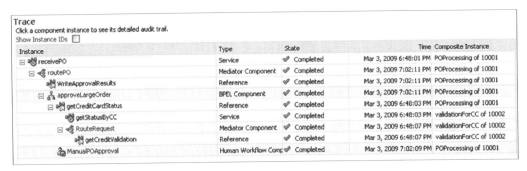

You will also have a new order file in `c:\temp`.

Summary

No business process solution is complete without some human involvement in the completion of the processes. Standards such as BPEL have evolved for addressing modeling and execution of automated processes. Although there are specifications like BPEL4People in the works, currently there is no standard way for handling workflows involving human participants. Oracle has addressed this by providing a service-based approach via the Human Task component that allows you to add human workflow easily to an automated flow in BPEL without deviating from the BPEL standard. Additionally, the ADF-based Worklist application provides an easy way to work with and manage task assignments. SOA Suite 11*g* also provides wizard-based tooling for easily defining a workflow, including any ADF-based UI components that need to be embedded in the Worklist application for specific task assignments. All these features make it fairly easy to model automated processes with complex human interactions.

Quick-build Instructions

This section gives you all of the operations and names for objects created in this chapter. Experienced users can use this to bypass the step-by-step instructions and complete this chapter more quickly. The complete details for any particular operation listed here can be found in the preceding sections. The information is organized in the same manner that it is introduced in the chapter.

- Add a Human Task to the composite:
  - Name: **ManualPOApproval**
  - Namespace: Leave as default
  - Expose as Composite Service: Unchecked
  - Wire: BPEL to task
  - Title: **<%'Approve Order'%>**
    (enter **'Approve Order'** using the expression builder)
  - Description: **Manual approval task for large orders**
  - Parameters: **internalorder.xsd | Order**
  - Editable via worklist: Checked
  - Participant Type dialog, specify the following:

    Type: **Single**

    Label: **Large Order Approver**

    User: **weblogic**

- Call the Human Task from BPEL:
  - In case statement, after **assignApproval**, Human Task: **ManualPOApproval**
  - Task Parameter: **Variables | Process | Variables | outputVariable | payload | Order**
  - Move **assignApproved** to APPROVE branch after **CopyPayloadFromTask**
  - **CopyPayloadFromTask** Assign REJECT branch
  - Copy from: **'rejected'**
  - To: **outputVariable | payload | Order | status**
  - **CopyPayloadFromTask** Assign Otherwise branch
  - Copy from: **'expired'**
  - To: **outputVariable | payload | Order | status**

- Creating the Task form for task details:

    ○ Right-click on **Human Task**, select **Auto-generate task form**

    ○ Project Name: **ApproveTaskDetails**

OR

    ○ **Application** menu | **New Project** | **Generic project**

    ○ Project Name: **ApproveTaskDetails**

    ○ **Project menu** | **New**

    ○ **JSF** | **ADF Task Flow Based on Human Task**

    ○ **POProcessing** | **POProcessing** | **ManualPOApproval.task**

    ○ Double-click on **taskDetails1.jspx** icon in **Task Flow** view; click on **OK**

    ○ Open **Data Controls** | **getTaskDetails** | **Return** | **Task**

    ○ Drag **Task** to the **Open Task Details** page

    ○ Select **Human Task** | **Complete Task** with **Payload**

    ○ Click on **OK** for remaining dialogs, accepting defaults

The application is completed. Deploy and test.

9

Business Rules

Suppose suddenly there is a positive review of one of your products that causes a very high number of requests to your POProcessing application. If this product happens to cost more than $1,000, then your manual task processing will suddenly be more than your agents can handle. You want to change the application logic temporarily to include auto-approval for this particular product until demand goes back to normal. Or, suppose your company is growing faster than you can hire agents to handle the manual tasks and besides, your risk level has changed such that you can afford to increase the limit for manual approval. You want to change this limit and may want to change it again for other reasons, such as during holidays when you get high volumes of requests.

If you could handle this type of business logic outside of the application logic in a declarative manner, then you would have greater control over your business by not having to change the application logic at all when business conditions change.

Introducing Business Rules decision service

Your composite application does logical branching while processing the application flow and this branching falls into two distinct categories—implementation logic and business logic. Implementation logic is what the developer adds to implement the flow of the application. Business logic is what the business user adds and changes based on business data outside of the application.

The Oracle Business Rules component is most often used from BPEL processes but it can also be used outside of BPEL. It can be used by other service consumers as well as by plain old Java objects or in J2EE applications. With Oracle Business Rules, when business rules need to change, you change only the rule component, not any of the other services or components that call it. Your implementation logic stays the same.

 Business Rules de-couples decision services from SOA applications.

Rules design

You can use JDeveloper to design your rules or you can create a web-based custom user interface to create or edit rules. A web-based rule composer will be provided in a post-R1 release. Using JDeveloper, open your composite and add a Rules component and then double-click on the component to open the Rules editor.

Based on what you specified for the input and output schemas, the rule facts and other data elements are created for use within the rules. The rules run on a Jess-based inference engine and can be simple or complex.

Jess is a rule engine and scripting environment written in Java. Using Jess, you can build Java software that has the capacity to "reason" by using knowledge you supply in the form of declarative rules. Jess uses an enhanced version of the **Rete** algorithm to process rules. Rete is a very efficient mechanism for solving the difficult many-to-many matching problem. Read more about Jess here: http://www.jessrules.com/

When you design your rule, you take your input fact and compare it against other values until you have your result. The result is assigned to the output fact and returned by the decision service. It is simple to create the rules using JDeveloper, which offers you variables and facts that are in context with your expression as you enter the expression. You can use a date or effective date range, aggregation and other formulas, and decision tables.

Decision tables are an efficient way to describe a rule when there are more than a few cases to your evaluation. You set up the table with each case in a column and for each, you specify the action. The decision table calculates where there are conflicting cases, where your ranges overlap, and also calculates where you have a hole, where your cases miss a value or range in the input data. Decision tables help you design your evaluation with the confidence that you have done it correctly.

Tutorial: Adding an approval rule using the decision service in POProcessing

Chapters 5-10 must be done sequentially.

In order to follow the tutorial in this chapter you must have either completed the tutorial from the previous chapter, or set up the environment as described in Chapter 4 and deployed the solution for the previous chapter, which can be found in c:\po\solutions\ch8.

This chapter has two labs—one for an if-then-else rule and one for a decision table. In the first lab you add a Business Rule to the composite to make the decision of whether the human task is required for manual approval or not. When you added the human task, it would be called for orders greater than $1,000. Now, the Business Rule will determine whether or not the human task is required.

When this lab is completed, the composite looks like this:

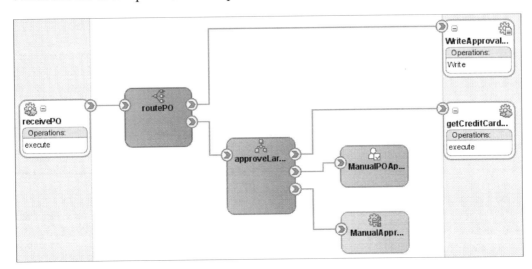

Designing the flow

The Business Rule uses the order total to determine whether or not manual approval is required. Orders over $5,000 require manual approval; otherwise, the order is approved automatically. The BPEL process only sends orders to the Business Rule that have already had the credit card validated.

Adding a Business Rule to POProcessing

You first add the Business Rule component to the composite and then you invoke the rule from the BPEL process.

1. Add the **Business Rule** component to the composite by dragging it to the Components section.

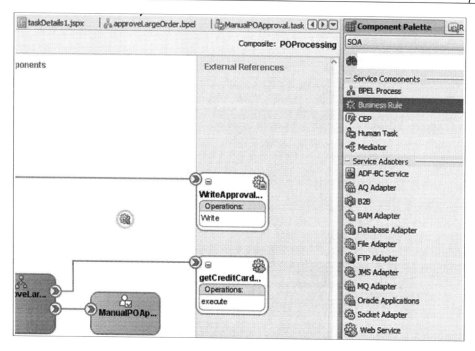

2. In the Create dialog, enter **ManualApproval** for the Dictionary name.

3. Now set the input and output schema. Selecting **Input** from the green plus sign drop-down opens the **Type chooser** for choosing the schema. Select the top right button to import a schema and then browse to the schema location: `c:\po\schemas\OrderBookingDiscount.xsd`.

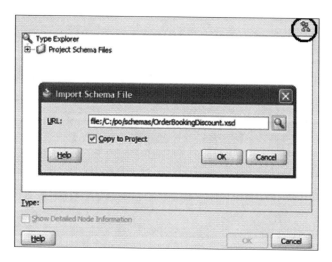

4. Select **price** for the input schema type.

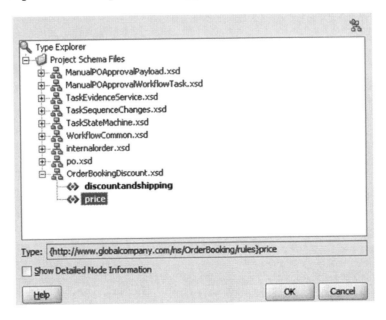

5. Repeat the steps for the output schema. This time, you do not need to import the schema type. Just select the type **discountandshipping**. If you do not see the schema in the list of **Project Schema Files**, go through the import steps again but deselect the checkbox to rename duplicate files. Sometimes JDeveloper will not refresh the schema file list for you at this step.

6. Once the dialog is complete, click on **OK** to close it.

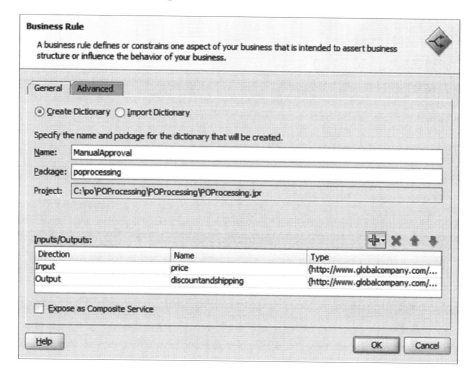

7. Double-click on the **Rules** component to open the rule editor. Select **RuleSet_1**.

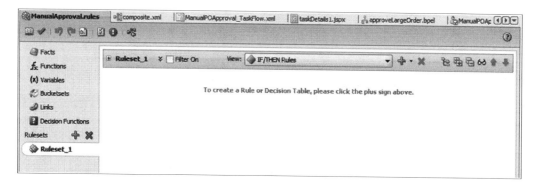

8. Click on the green plus sign to add a rule template.

9. Select **insert test** and then select **operand** in the IF statement, and select the **price.price** object.

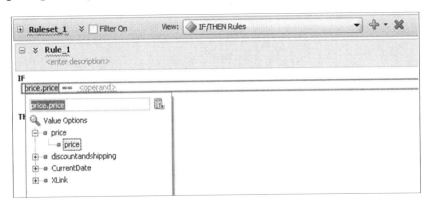

10. Complete the test for **>= 5000** by pressing *Enter* key to enter the value and adding the THEN clause to create the return result.

11. Select **<insert action>** and select **assert new**. Select **<target>** and select **discountandshipping**.

12. Select the **<add property>** box. A dialog box will come up to set the property values. Set the values as shown. We are not using discount or shipping in this composite application, so set those values to **0** (use the *Enter* key to enter the value). For orders of $5,000 or more, set the approval required to true. You can also set the price value to the input price:

- **approvalRequired** = **true**
- **discount** = **0**
- **price** = **price.price**
- **shipping** = **0**

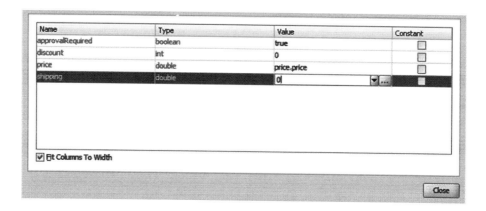

13. Repeat the process to add a second rule for orders under $5,000. In this case, approval is not required.

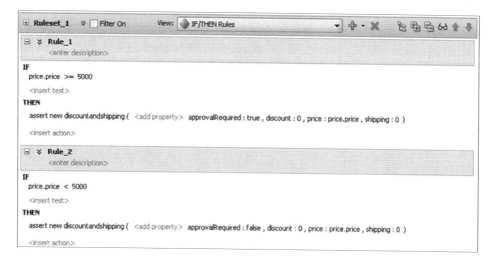

14. Save and close the **Rules** editor.

15. Next, double-click on the BPEL icon to open the BPEL process. You will be adding a Rule activity just before the existing Human Task. First create a variable to store the output from the RuleSet.

16. In the **Structure** palette, open **Variables/Process** and select the **Variables** node. If the Structure palette is not open, select it from the **View** menu.

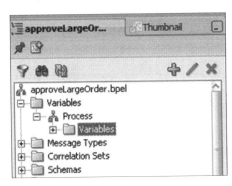

17. Select the green plus sign to add a variable named **approvalRequired** of type **discountandshipping**.

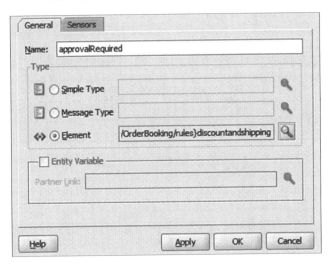

18. Now drag the **Business Rule** to the location just before the **Human Task**, within the case block of the **Switch** activity.

19. The **Rule** dialog will open. Set the **Name** and select the **Business Rule Dictionary** you just created in the composite. Next, complete the **Input Facts** and **Output Facts**.

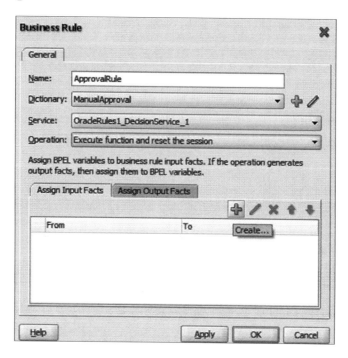

20. The input fact will be the price value. You create an expression using the expression builder to multiply the item price by the quantity.

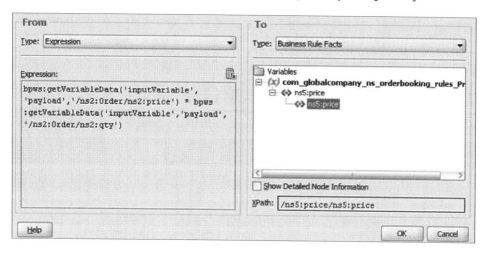

21. After the **RuleSet** is evaluated, the output fact is returned. Set the value of the output fact to the variable you just created. Make sure that you select the whole payload to copy all the values over (although we are only interested in the **approvalRequired** value).

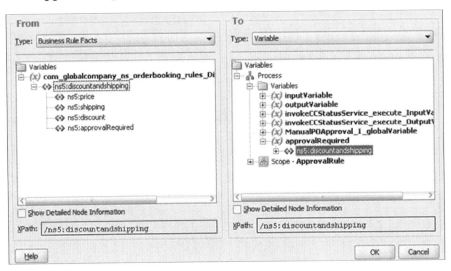

22. Click on **OK** to close the dialog.
23. Now, drag a **Switch** activity to the location just after the **Rule** activity.

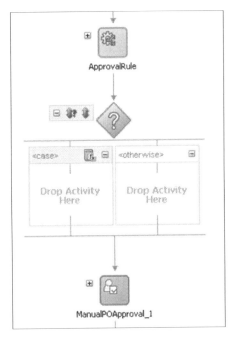

24. Select **Save All** before continuing.

25. You will be moving the human task and switch statement into the case block of this new **Switch** activity. Before you do that, drag a **Sequence** activity to keep the moved activities in the proper order.

26. Drag a **Sequence** activity from the palette into the case block.

27. Move the **Human Task** into the **Sequence** block for this switch so that it only executes when the test case is true.

28. There is a **Switch** activity that follows **Human Task** for processing the **Human Task** results, which sets the status to approved or rejected accordingly. Move this into your new Sequence block in the **Switch** activity case statement as well.

29. Select **Save All** before continuing.

30. Use the **Expression Builder** to set the test case expression in the case block. You want to invoke the human task only when manual approval is required. This is the result from the previous Rule evaluation:

    ```
    bpws:getVariableData('approvalRequired','/ns5:discountandshipping/
    ns5:approvalRequired') = 'true'
    ```

31. Next, create an **Assign** activity in the **Otherwise** block of your new **Switch**. Call this Assign **AutoApproved**. This assigns the status value approved for the case where the manual task is not required. Set the status to **'approved'**.

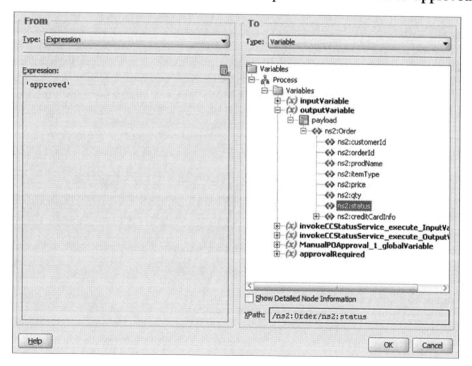

32. Your completed BPEL changes look like the following screenshot:

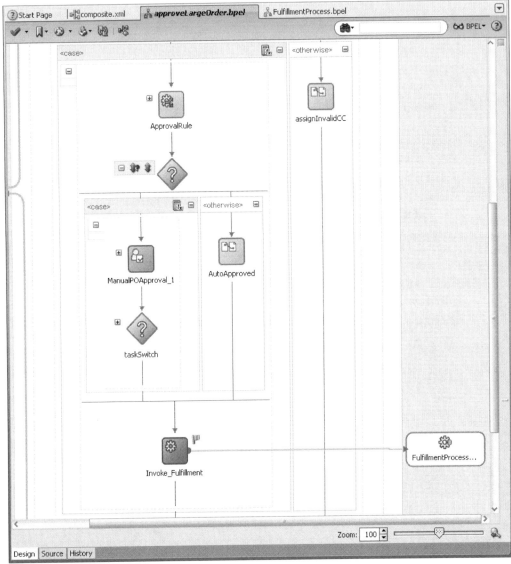

Review the logic of the changes you made: when the credit card is valid, you ask the Rule to tell you if manual approval is required. If manual approval is required, call the Human Task service to take care of that and set the status based on the returned value. If it isn't required, auto-approve the order in the otherwise block.

You have completed all changes and are ready to deploy. Continue with the next section.

Deploying POProcessing composite

1. In the same way as you did in previous chapters, deploy your newly updated POProcessing. Using the project menu, select **Deploy**.

2. When you see the **Deployment Plan** dialog, enter a new version or select the **Overwrite Version** checkbox and click on **OK**.

Running the application

1. Once the application is deployed, you are ready to try running it. Open the EM console at `http://localhost:8001/em`.

2. Click on **POProcessing** and then on the **Test** button to test your service.

3. Enter an extra large order (greater than or equal to $5,000) by doing one of the following:

   i. Type the values into the HTML form.

   ii. Click on **XML View** so you can paste in the XML payload. This is the recommended way.

4. Open the following file in a text editor:

   `c:\po\input\po-xtralarge-HDTVx10.txt`

5. Copy the entire contents and paste them into the large text field in your browser, replacing the defaulted XML:

Input Arguments

XML View ▼

```
<soap:Envelope xmlns:soap="http://schemas.xmlsoap.org/soap/envelope/">
  <soap:Body xmlns:ns1="http://xmlns.oracle.com/ns/order">
    <ns1:PurchaseOrder>
      <ns1:CustID>1111</ns1:CustID>
      <ns1:ID>2222</ns1:ID>
      <ns1:productName>HD TV</ns1:productName>
      <ns1:itemType>electronics</ns1:itemType>
      <ns1:price>2250</ns1:price>
      <ns1:quantity>10</ns1:quantity>
      <ns1:status>initial</ns1:status>
      <ns1:ccType>Mastercard</ns1:ccType>
      <ns1:ccNumber>1234-1234-1234-1234</ns1:ccNumber>
    </ns1:PurchaseOrder>
  </soap:Body>
</soap:Envelope>
```

Request   Response

Test Web Service

6. Click on **Test Web Service**.

   ○ The **Response** screen won't have any response because this is a one-way invocation with no reply or callback.

   ○ There is also no file written to the output directory. That's because the application hasn't completed running yet. To see what's going on, you need to look at the instance audit trail.

7. Click on **Launch Message Flow Trace** to see the details of the message flow for this instance of your composite. Alternatively, click on the latest instance from the composite page. You'll notice the status for **approveLargeOrder** and **ManualPOApproval** are both still running. They are waiting for the human task to be processed.

8. Log in to the worklist app at `http://localhost:8001/integration/worklistapp` (use the correct port for your SOA server; the default value is 8001) with user **weblogic/welcome1** and approve the task.

9. Return to the task flow in the **EM** console. If you still have it open, you can just refresh the page. Notice that it is now complete.

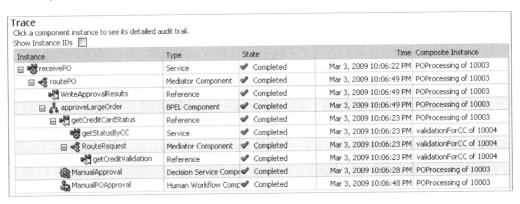

Additional Test Cases.

10. There are now four test cases for your application depending on the input data value of the total price:

    i. Under $1,000 (price x quantity) — auto-approval without BPEL component

    ii. Invalid credit card (and over $1,000) — auto-reject using BPEL but no Rules or Task components

    iii. $1,000 to under $5,000 — auto-approval using BPEL and Rules but no Task

    iv. $5,000 and over — manual approval using BPEL, Rules, and Task components

An invalid credit card number is: **4321-4321-4321-4321**. A valid one is: **1234-1234-1234-1234**. Continue with different input data values and try all the test cases. What happens when the credit card is invalid and the order under $1,000? What happens when the card is invalid and the order is over $1,000, over $5,000?

Quick-build instructions

This section gives you all of the operations and names of the objects created in this lab. Experienced users can use this to bypass the step-by-step instructions and complete this chapter more quickly. The complete details for any particular operation listed here can be found in the preceding sections. The information is organized in the same manner that it is introduced in the chapter.

Add a Business Rule to **POProcessing**:

- **Composite Business Rule: ManualApproval**
- **Input: OrderBookingDiscount.xsd | price**
- **Output: OrderBookingDiscount.xsd | discountandshipping**
- **RuleSet_1: Rule 1**:
  - **If price >= 5000 then assert new discountandshipping**
  - **with approvalRequired = true**
- **RuleSet_1: Rule 2**:
  - **If price < 5000 then assert new discountandshipping**
  - **with approvalRequired = false**
- BPEL variable: **approvalRequired** of type **discountandshipping**
- Business Rule **ApprovalRule** before Human Task **ManualApproval**
- **Input fact: price*quantity to price**
- **Output fact: discountandshipping to approvalRequired > discountandshipping**
- **Switch** below **Rule**
- Case expression: **bpws:getVariableData('approvalRequired', '/ ns5:discountandshipping/ns5:approvalRequired') = 'true'**
- **Case**: add **Sequence**, move Human Task and human task switch
- **Otherwise: Assign: AutoApproved, Copy From: 'approved'**

The application is completed. Deploy and test.

Introducing Business Rules decision table

In this second lab, you will add a BPEL process to the composite that includes a Business Rule using a decision table to make the decision of which fulfillment carrier to use for fulfilling the order. Orders under $1,000 use USPS, orders from $1,000 and under $5,000 use UPS, and orders equal to or over $5,000 use FedEx.

When finished, the composite will look like this:

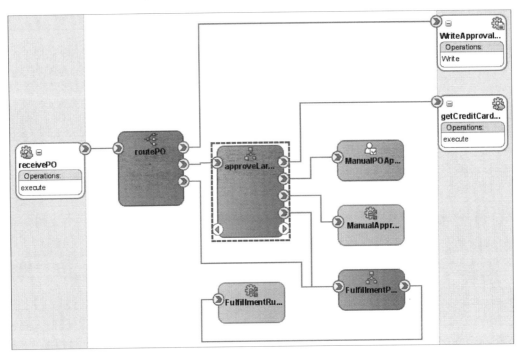

Designing the flow

The Business Rule uses the order total to determine which fulfillment vendor to choose. Three order total ranges are used, which means there would be multiple IF-THEN clauses to create to cover all of the cases. Instead, you use a decision table to create the three values in the Bucketset and then create only three rules.

The fulfillment process must be called whenever the order is approved. This is in the BPEL approveLargeOrder process but is also in the first case, in the routePO mediator when the order is under $1,000 and automatically approved.

Adding a BPEL Process and a Business Rule

You first add the BPEL Process component to the composite and then you add the Business Rule.

1. Add the BPEL Process component to the composite by dragging it to the **Components** section. Complete the dialog as follows:

    ○ **Name**: **FulfillmentProcess**

    ○ **Template**: **Asynchronous BPEL Process**

    ○ **Service Name**: **fulfillmentprocess_client**

    ○ **Expose as a SOAP Service**: Unchecked

    ○ **Input**: Click on the magnifying glass icon, in the **Type Chooser** dialog, click on the **Import Schema File** button and import `c:\po\schemas\fulfillment.xsd` in the same way as you have previously imported an XSD. Select **Fulfillment** as the input type.

    ○ **Output**: Use the **CarrierSelection** as the output type.

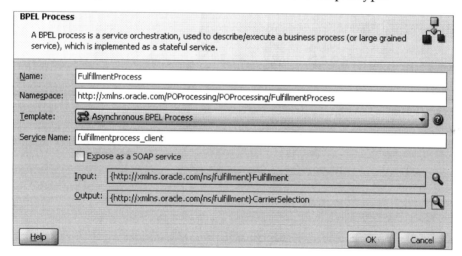

2. Click on **OK**.

3. Now drag a **Business Rule** component to the **Components** section. Complete the dialog as follows:

   ○ **Name: FulfillmentRules**

   ○ **Package: fulfillmentrules**

   ○ **Input: Fulfillment**

   ○ **Output: CarrierSelection**

   ○ **Advanced tab | Service Name: OracleRulesFulfillment**

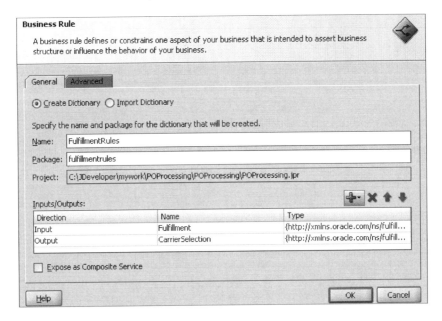

This is the second Rule in the composite and you cannot reuse the defaulted value for Service Name. You must set it to a unique value.

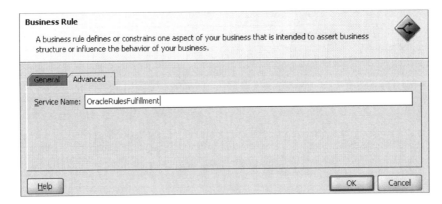

4. Click on **OK**.

5. Drag a wire from the new BPEL process to the new rule.

6. Drag another wire from **ApproveLargeOrder** to the new BPEL process.

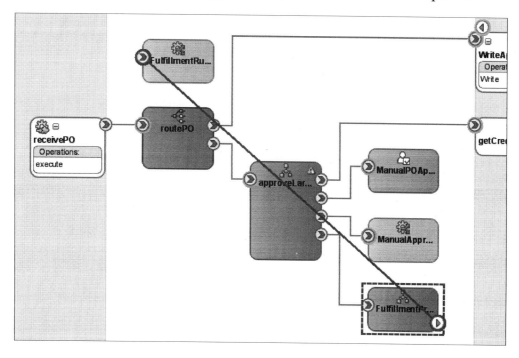

Defining the Business Rule

Now, you define the Business Rule. You need a rule that will distinguish between three carriers based on the order total. Rather than write out multiple exclusive IF-THEN statements in the Ruleset, you can do this easily with a decision table.

First define the three ranges of the order total that you want to use for evaluation. Use those ranges in the decision table to determine the carrier.

1. In the composite, double-click on **FulfillmentRules** to open the rule editor.

2. Click on **Bucketsets**.

3. Notice that one Bucketset has already been created. In the fulfillment. xsd schema, **CarrierValue** is a restricted **String** type and is, therefore, represented as a Java **enum**. All imported Java enums are used to create a Bucketset of their values. You use this Bucketset to assign the return value, **CarrierSelection**.

4. Add a **List of Ranges** and then click on edit to define the values in the new Bucketset.

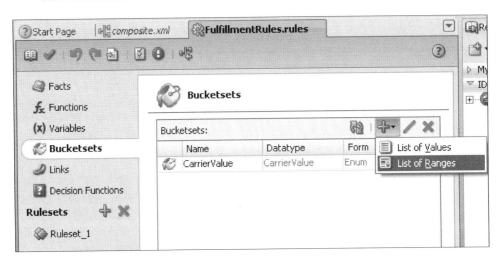

5. Enter the **Name** as **OrderTotal** and **Data Type** as **double**.

6. Click the green plus icon twice to add two buckets and edit the values as follows:

   ○ **Endpoint: 5000, Alias: xtralarge**

   ○ **Endpoint: 1000, Alias: large**

   ○ **Endpoint: -Infinity, Alias: small**

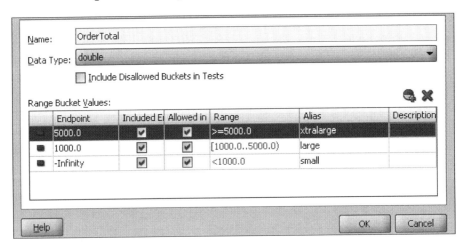

7. Click on **OK**

8. Now you have to associate this Bucketset with the input fact. Click on **Facts** and select and edit **FulfillmentType**.

9. Set the **Bucketset** for **total** to **OrderTotal**.

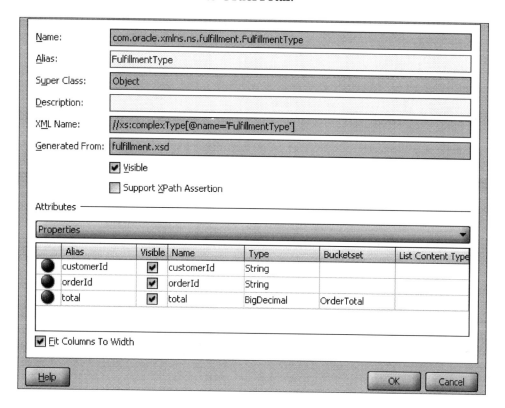

10. Click on **OK**.

11. Select **CarrierSelection** and click on edit. You see the value **carrier** has already been associated with the Bucketset **CarrierValue**. All imported Java enums are automatically associated with properties of their type.

12. Click on **OK**.

13. Now you are ready to create the table. Click on **Ruleset_1** and select the drop-down menu on the green plus icon. Select **Create Decision Table**.

14. Insert a condition and choose **FulfillmentType.total**.

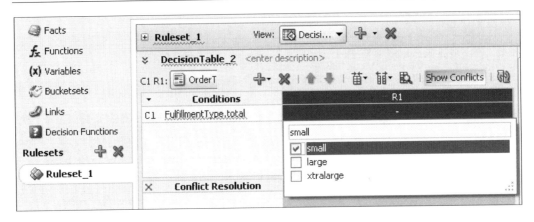

15. Select the cell under **R1** and choose **small**—the range you created previously.

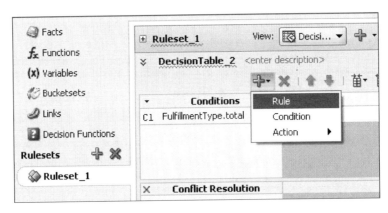

16. Select the menu for the green plus icon just above the rule and select **Rule** to add a second rule. Set this one to **large**.

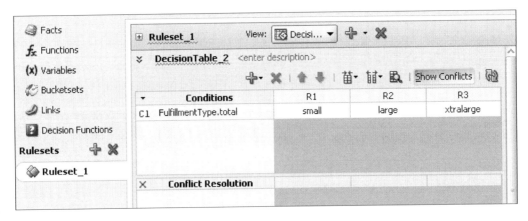

17. Add a third rule and set it to **xtralarge**. These three rules, which are the ranges defined earlier, are evaluated against the condition **FulfillmentType.total**.

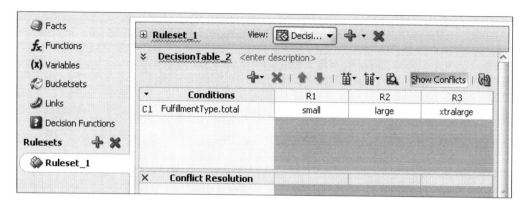

18. Now set the **Actions** for these three rules. **Insert Action** and select **Assert New**. Select **CarrierSelection**.

19. Select the checkbox for **Parameterized**.

20. Select the checkbox for **Always Selected**.

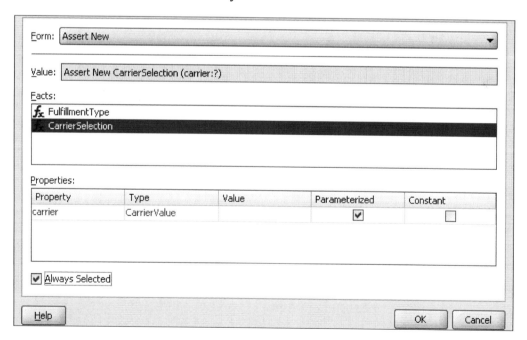

21. Click on **OK**.

22. Now set the values. Select the cell for each of the three rules and set the carrier value for each one: **small=USPS, large=UPS, xtralarge=FED_EX**.

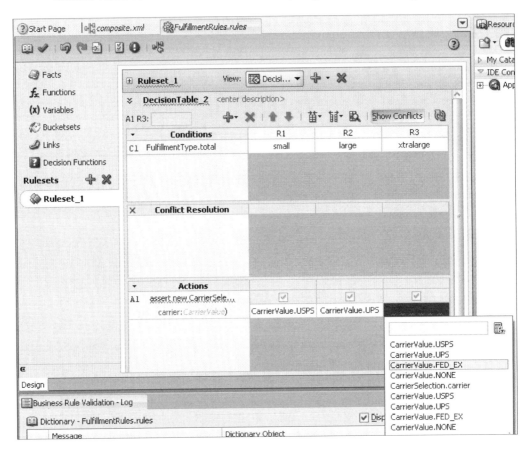

23. That's it! The Decision Rule is complete. Click on **Save All** button and close the rule editor.

Defining the BPEL process

Now define the fulfillment BPEL process that will use this Business Rule. At first, this simply calls the business rule you just created. In the next chapter, you add additional functionality to send the fulfillment message.

1. Double-click on **FulfillmentProcess** to open the BPEL editor.

2. Drag a **Business Rule** activity to the process flow.

3. In the Business Rule dialog, leave the default name and select the **FulfillmentRules** rule.

4. In the **Assign Input Facts** tab, click on the green plus icon to add an assignment to assign the BPEL **inputVariable** to the rule input fact.

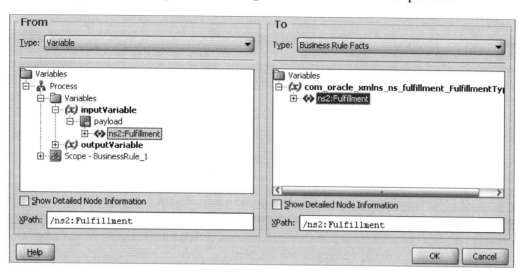

5. In the **Assign Output Facts** tab, assign the output fact to **outputVariable**.

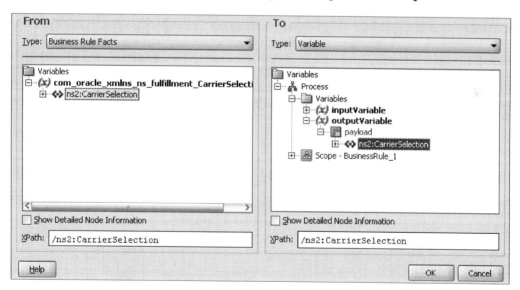

6. In the Business Rule dialog, click on **OK**.

Invoking FulfillmentProcess

Now invoke your new fulfillment process. It should be called whenever you have an approved order. There are two places, one in the **approveLargeOrder** BPEL process and one in the **routePO** mediator for small orders that are automatically approved.

1. You've already wired it to **ApproveLargeOrder**, so let's start there. In the composite, double-click on **approveLargeOrder** to open the BPEL editor.

2. Locate the switch branch for valid credit cards. Drag an **Invoke** activity to the end of this branch, at the end of the branch scope.

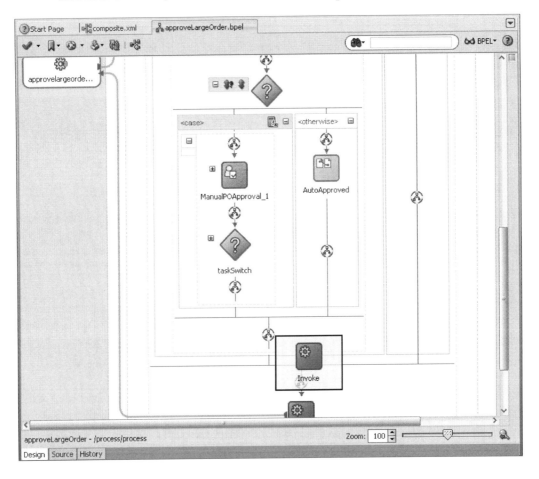

3. Wire the **Invoke** to the **partnerLink** for **FulfillmentProcess**, which was added for you when you wired the processes earlier.

4. In the **Invoke** dialog, set the **Name** to **Invoke_Fulfillment** and create the input variable using the default values.

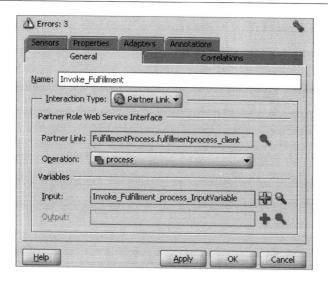

5. Click on **OK**.

6. Do you remember what input the **FulfillmentProcess** service is expecting? It is the **FulfillmentType**, which contains customer ID, order ID, and order total. The easiest way to set this input value is using a **Transform**. Drag a **Transform** activity just before the **Invoke**.

7. Set the source for the transformation to **inputVariable** and the target to the fulfillment input variable you just created in the **Invoke** dialog.

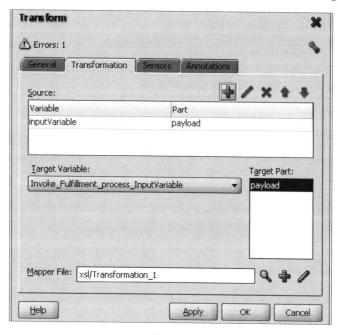

8. Click on the green plus icon to create the mapper file.

9. Drag wires to copy the customer ID and order ID values.

10. For total, you have to multiply price and quantity so use a mathematical function. First, drag the **multiply** function into the middle area. Then drag the wires for **price** and **qty** values into the function, and drag a wire from the function to **total**. The multiplication is complete.

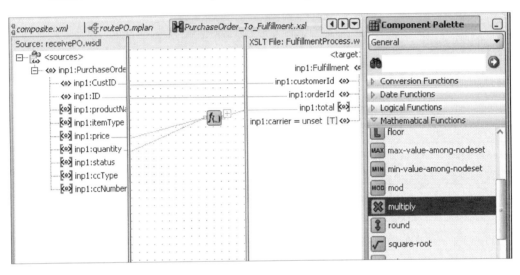

11. Save and close the transformation mapper.

12. Take a look at the completed process. This isn't quite complete because there should be fulfillment only when the human task is approved. You need to add a switch statement to check for the approved status for both the auto-approved and the human task-approved cases.

13. Drag a **Switch** activity directly below the **Invoke_Fulfillment**, call it **Switch_Fulfillment**, and expand the case.

14. Since you are going to move both the **Transform** and the **Invoke** activities into the **Switch**, drag a **Sequence** activity block into the case to hold them.

15. Drag the **Transform** and **Invoke** activities into the **Sequence** block within the case block.

16. Add the condition statement to the case block to check the status. It should look like this:

```
bpws:getVariableData('outputVariable','payload','/ns2:Order/
ns2:status') = 'approved'
```

17. Remove the otherwise case because there is no action to take here. Just right-click on the otherwise block and select **Delete**.

18. The changes to the BPEL process are complete. Return to the composite.

19. Now you invoke fulfillment from the mediator. Double-click on **routePO** to open the mediator editor.

20. Select the green plus icon and choose **static routing rule**.

21. Select **Service** as the type and in the dialog, navigate to **POProcessing | BPEL Processes | FulfillmentProcess | Services | fulfillmentprocess_client | process**.

22. Click on **OK**. A new routing rule is added to the table. You want to call fulfillment from here only in the auto-approval case, so you set the filter to the same thing as in the first case, that is, for orders under 1000. Click on the filter icon to open the expression builder and enter:

    ```
    ($in.request/inp1:PurchaseOrder/inp1:quantity * $in.request/
    inp1:PurchaseOrder/inp1:price) < 1000
    ```

23. Click on **OK**.

24. Click on the transform icon on the right and create a transformation mapping in the same way as earlier, using the multiply function to set the value for **total**.

25. Save and close the transformation mapper.

26. The new routing rule is complete. You don't need to set the callback because you are not interested in the return value here.

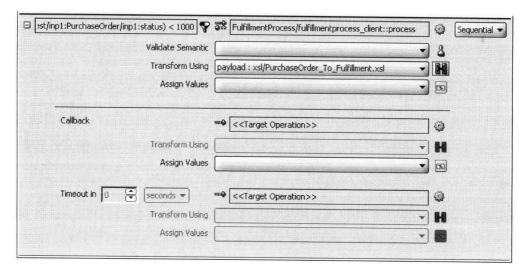

27. Save and close the mediator routing rule editor.

28. All done! Now you are ready to test.

Deploying the application

Deploy the **POProcessing** in the same way as in previous chapters using the **Deploy** command on the **Project** menu.

Testing the application

So far, the fulfillment process determines the delivery carrier but doesn't really do anything with the information. So you have to use the flow view in the EM console to see that everything is working correctly (in the next chapter, you finish the fulfillment process).

1. Open **EM** console and click on **POProcessing**.

2. Click on **Test**.

3. Using the input files in `c:\po\input`, run three tests, with small, large, and extra large orders.

4. Click on **Launch Message Flow Trace** to view the instance data.

5. For the extra large order, submit the approval task to complete the process.

6. Verify that **FulfillmentRules** returns **USPS**, **UPS**, and **FedEx** as the delivery carrier, appropriately.

7. Submit a second extra large order, and this time, reject the order approval. Verify that **Fulfillment** is not called.

8. Submit an order with an invalid credit card and verify that **Fulfillment** is not called.

Quick-build Instructions

This section gives you all of the operations and names for objects created in this lab. Experienced users can use this to bypass the step-by-step instructions and complete this chapter more quickly. The complete details for any particular operation listed here can be found in the preceding sections. The information is organized in the same manner that it is introduced in the chapter:

- Add a BPEL Process and a Business Rule:
    - BPEL Name: **FulfillmentProcess**
    - Template: Asynchronous BPEL Process
    - Service Name: **fulfillmentprocess_client**
    - Expose as a SOAP Service: Unchecked
    - Input: **c:\po\schemas\fulfillment.xsd | Fulfillment**

- ° Output: **CarrierSelection**
- ° Rule Name: **FulfillmentRules**
- ° Package: **fulfillmentrules**
- ° Input: **Fulfillment**
- ° Output: **CarrierSelection**
- ° **Advanced** tab | **Service Name**: **OracleRulesFulfillment**
- ° Wire: **FulfillmentProcess** to **FulfillmentRules**
- ° Wire: **ApproveLargeOrder** to **FulfillmentProcess**

- • Define the Business Rule:
  - ° Bucketset: List of Ranges
  - ° Name: **OrderTotal**
  - ° Data Type: **double**
  - ° Endpoint: **5000**, Alias: **xtralarge**
  - ° Endpoint: **1000**, Alias: **large**
  - ° Endpoint: **-Infinity**, Alias: **small**
  - ° Facts: **FulfillmentType** | **Bucketset**: total to **OrderTotal**
  - ° Ruleset_1: **DecisionTable_1**: Condition: **FulfillmentType.total**
  - ° R1: **small**, R2: **large**, R3: **xtralarge**
  - ° Actions > Assert New: CarrierSelection
  - ° Checkboxes: **Parameterized, Always Selected**
  - ° Values: small=USPS, large=UPS, xtralarge=FED_EX

- • Define the BPEL Process:
  - ° **FulfillmentProcess**: **Business Rule**: **FulfillmentRule**, **FulfillmentRules**
  - ° Input fact: **inputVariable** | **Fulfillment** to **Fulfillment**
  - ° Output fact: **CarrierSelection** to **outputVariable** | **CarrierSelection**

- • Invoke **FulfillmentProcess**:
  - ° BPEL: **ApproveLargeOrder**
  - ° Drag Invoke: into switch branch for valid credit cards
  - ° Wire Invoke: to **FulfillmentProcess**
  - ° Name **Invoke_Fulfillment**
  - ° Input variable: defaulted

- ○ Transform before Invoke: **inputvariable** to **Invoke_ Fulfillment_process_InputVariable**
- ○ Wire: customer ID and order ID values
- ○ Multiply: **price*quantity** wired to total
- ○ Switch: **Switch_Fulfillment** below **Invoke_Fulfillment**
- ○ Case expression: **outputVariable | status** = **'approved'**
- ○ Case: add Sequence, move Transform, and Invoke
- ○ Otherwise: delete branch
- ○ Mediator: **routePO**
- ○ static routing rule < Service: **FulfillmentProcess | fulfillmentprocess_client | process**
- ○ Filter: orders < 1000
- ○ Transform: **PurchaseOrder_To_Fulfillment.xsl**

The application is completed. Deploy and test.

Summary

In this chapter, you saw how to create flexible composite applications that allow changing the process flow using decision services provided by Business Rules. You used a simple `if-then-else` construct to determine the outcome, as well as used a decision table for a more complex decision. Both ways use a declarative method of defining the rules that allows you to separate cleanly rule-based decision making from your control-flow logic. The business rule can be defined outside of the application logic and can be changed as your business situation changes without affecting the application code. This allows for non-intrusive changes and greater reliability and flexibility when making changes.

10
Using the JMS Adapter

SOAP over HTTP, also commonly called Web Service, and messaging technologies are complementary technologies that tend to be present in most service-oriented architectures.

A Web Service is typically used for **synchronous interactions** and has the clear advantage of not requiring any intermediary—the communication is directly established between the two parties. However, this advantage also has its limitations: what happens when one of the parties is not reachable? Also, what if the data needs to be fanned out to multiple recipients? It would be highly inefficient for the sender to contact each recipient one after the other. Furthermore, this also implies that the sender knows about all the possible recipients. Messaging technologies address these limitations and are the perfect fit for:

- **Asynchronous interactions**—when the response might not come back instantly—or not at all when dealing with one-way flows
- **Fan-out** and distribution of a given piece of data to many recipients
- True decoupling of producers and consumers—a sender might be sending some data without having to be aware of who will be consuming it or even if anyone will be consuming it

- Push-based models (as opposed to a polling-based model) and publish-subscribe interactions
- Dealing with environments where consumers and producers might not all be online at the same moment, therefore, requiring some intermediary to act as buffer

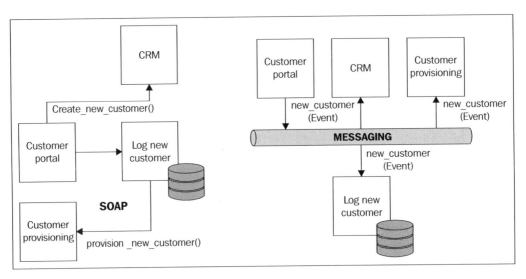

The preceding figure shows the contrast between a tightly coupled architecture based on Web Services and RPC compared to the same system implemented using messaging.

Examples of popular messaging technologies include older technologies such as IBM MQ Series and TIBCO Rendezvous or newer JMS-based messaging solutions such as WebLogic JMS.

Introducing the JMS Adapter

JMS, or **Java Message Service**, is often described as a messaging technology. While a convenient shortcut, this is actually not quite correct: JMS is in fact a standard (JSR 914), vendor-agnostic messaging API to messaging technologies—not a messaging protocol or infrastructure. Its main benefit is to allow developers to work with a simple and consistent API to messaging, regardless of the vendor product used underneath as the messaging provider.

Without going too far into the capabilities of JMS, it is important for the reader to understand the two main messaging models or "**domains**" (in JMS terminology): **queues** and **topics**. Queues are typically used for transactions, when a given piece of data needs to be consumed once and only once. Topics on the other hand are the perfect vehicle for notifications, when a signal needs to be broadcasted to multiple consumers at once. By default, queues persist data until it is consumed, while data on a topic is transient and offline subscribers will not see the data that they might have missed while they were offline. The model is refined with the concept of durable subscribers. The JMS provider will persist all messages that a durable subscriber might have missed while offline and redeliver them the next time the subscriber connects.

The following figure shows JMS Queues and JMS Topics:

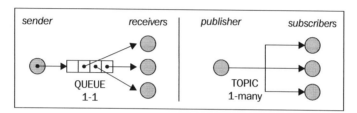

WebLogic JMS

Oracle WebLogic Server includes a full-fledged messaging provider with a JMS interface. In addition, it allows the JEE application it hosts to interact with most other JMS providers, such as AQ JMS or TIBCO EMS, through the concept of a foreign JMS provider.

Oracle WebLogic JMS has many compelling features. Some of the most important are the following:

- Complete transactional support, including support for distributed transactions between JMS applications and other transaction-capable resources

- Choice of file or database to use as a persistent message storage (both fully transaction capable)

- Message **Store-and-Forward (SAF)** to locally store messages sent to unavailable remote destinations

- Uniform Distributed destinations that provide high availability, load balancing, and failover support in a cluster

- Unit-Of-Work and Unit-Of-Order to allow the re-sequencing of messages across multiple applications

JMS Adapter

The Oracle SOA Suite includes a JMS Adapter that can be used within a composite application to send or receive messages. This adapter can be either a service (to receive) or a reference (to send) in an SCA composite.

The adapter supports both one-way and request-response interactions, byte, text, and map messages, and is XA-capable.

The JMS Adapter is certified with most JMS providers available today: Oracle WebLogic JMS, Oracle AQ JMS, TIBCO EMS, IBM WebSphere MQSeries, Apache JMS, and Active MQ (check the documentation for an up-to-date list), and is a key element of interoperability.

Tutorial: Orchestration of JMS services in the fulfillment process

In this chapter, you will send the fulfillment information to a JMS queue at the end of the fulfillment process. The delivery carrier was determined in the previous chapter. You will use this selected carrier to send the message to an appropriate queue depending on the carrier. The message sent to the shipping carrier is sent over JMS for reliable delivery. Shipping carriers can be UPS, USPS, and FedEx. To make this easier to test, however, we just use the same queue configuration for all three carriers.

Chapters 5-10 must be done sequentially.

In order to follow the tutorial in this chapter, you must have either completed the tutorial from the previous chapter, or set up the environment as described in Chapter 4, and deployed the solution for the previous chapter, which can be found in `c:\po\solutions\ch09`.

When finished, the composite will look like the following figure:

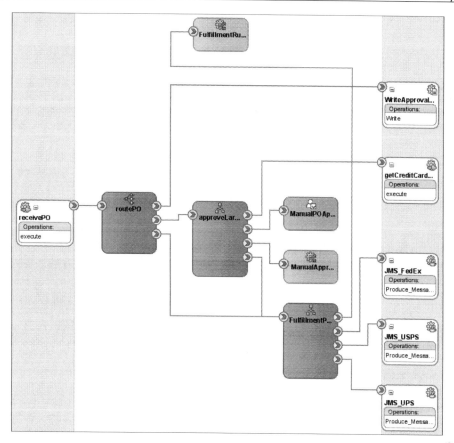

Adding the JMS adapters to the composite

The fulfillment process was left in the last chapter just after having determined the carrier. To add the JMS messaging, add the three JMS services for USPS, UPS, and FedEx and then invoke the appropriate service from the BPEL process.

You add a JMS adapter for each carrier. If you have your server running, the adapter wizard will be able to look up the JMS destination queue.

1. In JDeveloper, open the **POProcessing** composite.
2. Drag a **JMS Adapter** to the right swim lane of the composite.

3. Name the service: JMS_USPS.

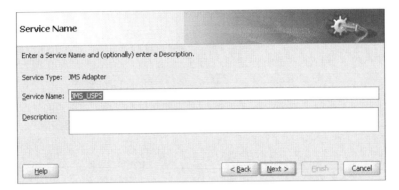

4. Click on **Next**.

5. Select the **OEMS** service **Oracle Weblogic JMS**.

6. Click on **Next**.

7. Select the **Connection**.

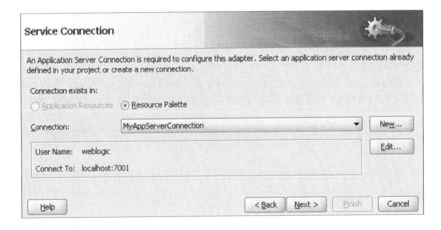

8. Click on **Next**.

9. For the **Interface**, select the radio button for defining this later.

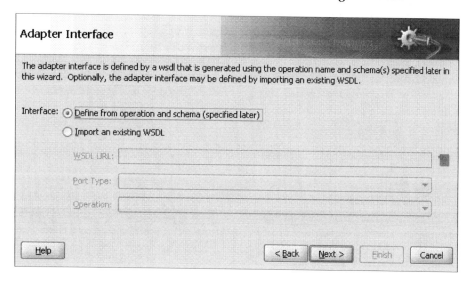

10. Click on **Next**.

11. For the **Operation Name**, select **Produce Message**. The name is filled in automatically.

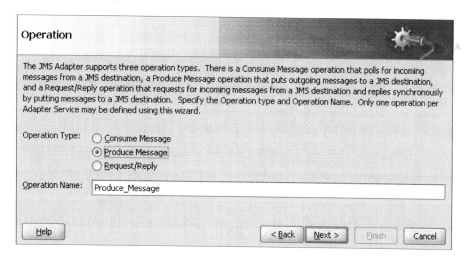

12. Click on **Next**.

13. For the **Produce Operation Parameters**, click on **Browse** to look up the JMS destination queue and select **demoFulfillmentQueue**.

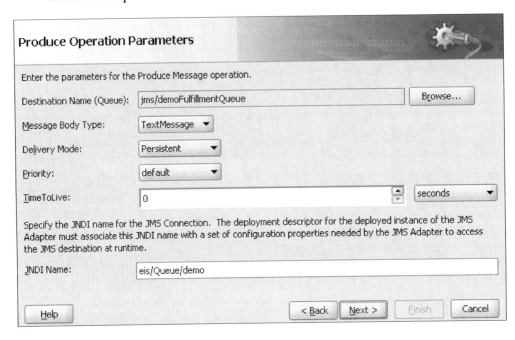

14. Click on **OK**.

15. Enter the **JNDI name** associated with the JMS Adapter: `eis/Queue/demo`.

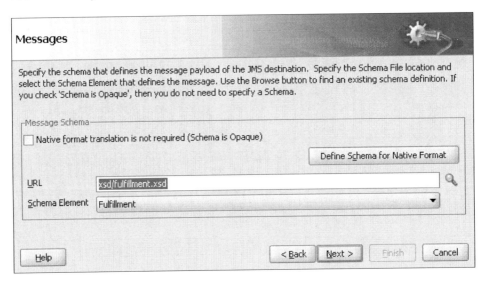

16. Click on **Next**.

17. For the message schema, use the magnifying glass to browse to `fulfillment.xsd` and select the **Fulfillment** element.

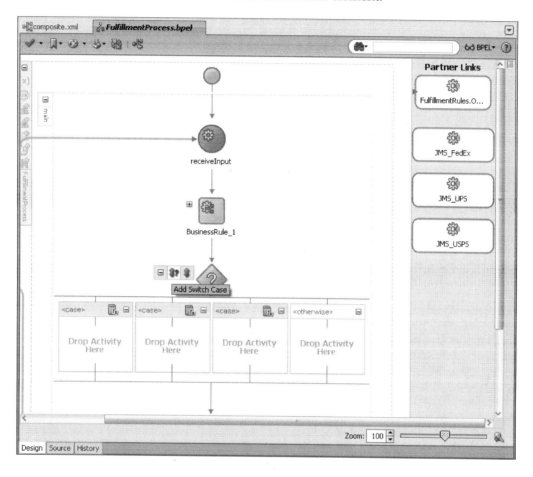

18. Click on **Next** and then click on **Finish**. This completes definition of the first adapter service.

19. Repeat the process to create two more services, JMS_UPS and JMS_FedEx.

20. From **FulfillmentProcess**, drag a wire to each of the three JMS services.

These services represent the three carriers and the message that is sent is the order information for fulfillment. As mentioned earlier, normally the three carriers would all have individual destination queues, but for easier testing, just use one queue for all of them.

Your composite now looks like the following figure:

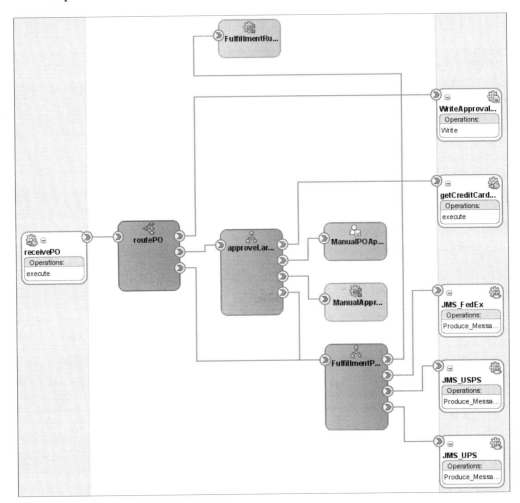

Invoking the services from BPEL

Next, go into the BPEL process and invoke the three services according to the value of carrier returned from the decision service.

1. Open the **FulfillmentProcess** BPEL process and drag a **Switch** activity below the **Business Rule** activity.

2. Expand the **Switch** and add two more switch cases.

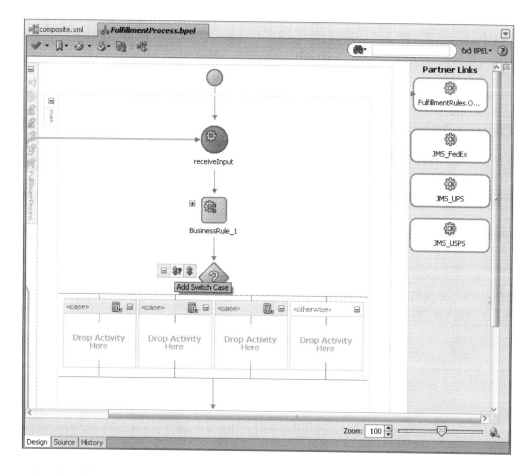

3. Double-click on the first **Case** bar and set the **Name** to USPS.

4. Select the Expression Builder icon to set the condition expression for the first case. Enter the expression as follows:

```
bpws:getVariableData('outputVariable','payload','/
ns2:CarrierSelection/ns2:carrier') = 'USPS'
```

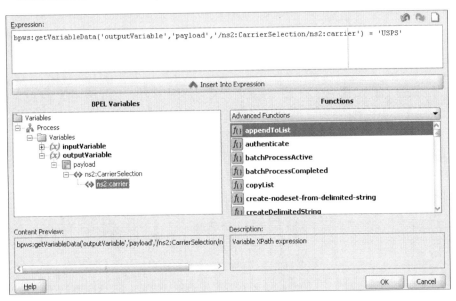

5. Click on **OK**. Repeat for the next two cases, setting the condition for UPS and FedEx, respectively.

6. Drag an **Invoke** activity into the first case for **USPS**. Drag a wire from the **Invoke** to the **JMS_USPS** partner link. The **Invoke** dialog opens.

7. Set the name to Invoke_USPS and create the input variable using the default values. Click on **OK**.

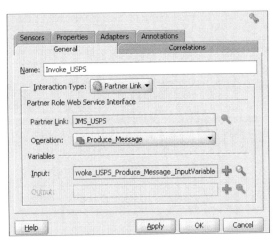

8. Repeat for **UPS** and **FedEx**.

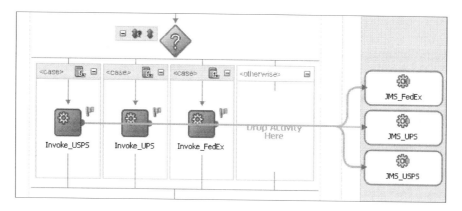

Now you need to assign data to the input variables for the three service invokes.

1. Drag an **Assign** activity into the first case just before the **Invoke**.

2. Open the **Assign** and create a copy operation to copy the fulfillment data to the input variable for the USPS service.

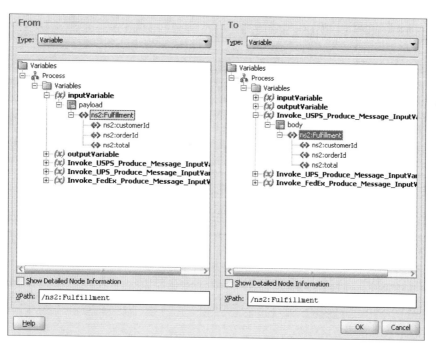

3. Repeat for the remaining two services.

The final case, the **Otherwise** case, can be handled in one of the two ways. You could choose to do something at this point such as raise a fault. That would be appropriate if in the future there is a fourth carrier setting returned from the rule and you wanted to be sure to flag it so that code could be added to handle it. Alternatively, when you do not anticipate future changes, you can remove the otherwise block or put an **Empty** activity there.

4. Remove the **Otherwise** case block to do nothing in the otherwise case.

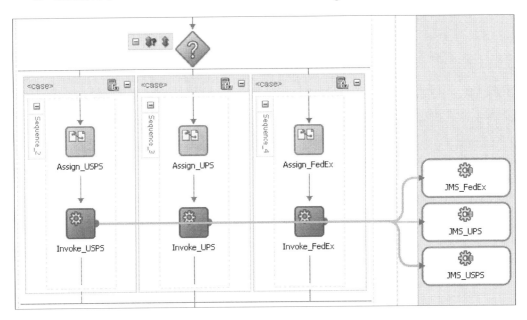

Deploying the application

Deploy the **POProcessing** application as in the previous chapter using the **Deploy** command in the **Project** Menu.

Testing the application

Again, use the flow view in the EM console to see that everything is working correctly.

1. Open the EM console and click on **POProcessing**; click on **Test**.

2. Using the input files, which you will find in `c:\po\input`, run three tests with small, large, and extra large orders.

3. View the instance data using EM console. For the extra large order, you have to submit the approval task to complete the process.

4. Verify that the `FulfillmentRules` returns USPS, UPS, and FedEx as the delivery carrier appropriately.

5. Verify the JMS message is sent appropriately by viewing the instance flow details and the message using one of the following three methods.

You have multiple options to ensure that messages are being sent over JMS:

You can use the WLS console:

1. Open **Services | Messaging | JMS Modules | SOAJMSModule**.

2. Click on **demoFulfillmentQueue/Monitoring**.

3. Select the checkbox for **SOAJMSModule!demoFulfillmentQueue**.

4. Click on **Show Messages** to view the messages waiting in the queue.

You can consume the messages using the SOA composite `ConsumeJMSFulfillmentApp`:

1. Go to the `c:\po\solutions\ch10` directory and locate the `ConsumeJMSFullfillmentApp` composite. Deploy this composite using JDeveloper. This application has been set up to listen on the JMS queue used in this tutorial. Whenever a message shows up, this composite fires off an instance that you can view in the EM console using **Flow Trace** and **Flow Details**. It also writes a file.

2. When you no longer want this application to consume messages (it polls as long as it is running), use EM to shut the composite down. The **Shut Down** button is next to the **Test** button. You can **Start Up** again later as desired.

You can use the command-line send/receive utility included in the tutorial material:

1. Go to the `c:\po\solutions\ch10` directory and locate and unzip `jms-send-receive.zip`.

2. Using a text editor, edit the `oems.properties` file to reflect your environment. You might have to update `java.naming.provider.url` to reflect your server location and the username and password.

3. Using a text editor, edit `setenv.bat` and set the path to your JDK and your WebLogic server.

4. From a command prompt, go to the unzipped location of `jms-send-receive` and run the `setenv.bat` file. Then, start the receive program using the following command:

```
java Receive "jms/demoFulfillmentQueue"
```

Summary

In this chapter, you have learned the key capabilities of WebLogic JMS. You have learned how to use the WebLogic console to configure the JMS adapter and define queues and connection factories. You have also learned how to view (or otherwise manipulate) JMS messages using the WebLogic console. You have used the adapter to send fulfillment messages to one of the three carriers from the composite.

Quick-build Instructions

This section gives you all of the operations and names for objects created in this chapter. Experienced users can use this to bypass the step-by-step instructions and complete this chapter more quickly. The complete details for any particular operation listed here can be found in the preceding sections. The information is organized in the same manner that it is introduced in the chapter.

- Add the JMS adapters to the composite.
- Create adapter for USPS:
  - **Name**: `JMS_USPS`
  - **OEMS service**: `Oracle Weblogic JMS`
  - **Service Connection**: `MyApplicationServer`
  - Define this Adapter Interface later
  - **Operation**: `Produce_Message`
  - **Queue name**: `demoFulfillmentQueue`
  - **JNDI name**: `eis/Queue/demo`
  - **Message schema**: `Fulfillment`
- Repeat for: `JMS_UPS` and `JMS_FedEx`; wire all from `FulfillmentProcess`.
- Invoke the services from BPEL.

- Add the switch in `FulfillmentProcess` below the business rule:
  - ○ Expand the **Switch** and add two more switch cases
  - ○ Double-click on the **Case** bar and set **Name**: USPS
  - ○ **Expression**: `bpws:getVariableData('outputVariable',` `'payload',` `'/ns2:CarrierSelection/ns2:carrier') = 'USPS'`
  - ○ Repeat for the next two cases, setting the condition for UPS and FedEx, respectively

- Add the invoke inside the case:
  - ○ **Invoke**: `Invoke_USPS` inside case block; wire to `JMS_USPS`.
  - ○ **Input variable**: defaulted
  - ○ Repeat for UPS and FedEx
  - ○ **Assign**: `Assign_USPS` just before **Invoke_USPS**
  - ○ **Copy From**: **inputvariable > fulfillment**
  - ○ **Copy to**: `Invoke_USPS_Produce_Message_InputVariable`
  - ○ Repeat for UPS and FedEx

The application is completed. Deploy and test.

11

Reusing and Virtualizing Services with Oracle Service Bus

ValidateCredit

One of the fundamental concepts of SOA is *service re-use*, which can lead to very significant *cost benefits*. For a service to be re-usable, it has to be well designed and exposed through a generic-enough interface. However, a large number of services available within your enterprise might have been designed with little thought to re-use. It would not be realistic to reengineer all your existing applications to ensure they expose better and more standard interfaces. But a similar goal can be attained by fronting these legacy services with a service virtualization layer that can map arcane interfaces to more re-usable ones, as well as expose them over more standard protocols (SOAP or REST, for instance) than what they natively exposed (MQSeries for instance).

Another problem is that application interfaces change over time as business requirements evolve. However, in a successful SOA practice, these applications are heavily re-used by many clients and a simple change to an interface can have dramatic ripple effect across all the clients. What is required is an intermediate layer, a buffer that can absorb the change. Such a layer is the key to delivering the *agility* required for IT systems to meet new business requirements rapidly.

Finally, for re-use even to take place, existing services need to be discoverable in the first place.

The key element to build this virtualization layer is a **service bus**, coupled to a service registry and repository to ensure governance and discoverability.

Introducing Oracle Service Bus

Oracle Service Bus (OSB) is a high-performance stateless enterprise service bus that provides service virtualization and ensures IT agility. OSB can work with all types of data formats, from XML to binary and structured text (SWIFT FIN or CSV for instance) or protocols, from SOAP to JMS, and from MQSeries to t3.

What are the types of changes that OSB can absorb?

OSB can largely absorb all of the following conditions:

1. Changes to the document format, say due to XML schema changes or even changes to the version of structured binary data. Transformation can be done by Java code, XSLT, XQuery, or MFL to convert between structured binary and XML. OSB supports any to any bridging between formats.

2. Changes to packaging say from SOAP 1.1 to SOAP 1.2 or even from REST to SOAP.

3. Changes to the routing or load-balancing logic.

4. Changes to the location of a service (change in address).

5. Changes to the security scheme, say from HTTP basic authorization to web services security username token.

6. Changes to the transport, say from HTTP to JMS. OSB supports a large number of transports and you can also seamlessly plug in new custom transports. OSB supports any to any bridging between transports.

7. Changes to the invocation style say from one-way to request/response. OSB supports any to any bridging between supported invocation styles.

8. Changes to the data the message is enriched with. OSB has a variety of ways to look up data. You can look up data in a databases or invoke web services or Java code to do lookups.

9. Changes to the parallelization or sequence of requests. A service can be split into multiple services or operations to be invoked in sequence or in parallel—or a mix of the two. Such parallelization can be used to greatly reduce response time.

10. Spikes in traffic. As service re-use increases, services might get overloaded during peak hours. The service bus can shape the traffic through throttling strategies.

Who are the users?

OSB is targeted towards system integrators and administrators who can make changes to the service virtualization quickly through a zero-install web-based console. In addition, Oracle Service Bus also offers an IDE targeted towards developers with versioning and visual debugging. OSB offers a powerful customization scheme to support advanced life cycle management, and changing of environmental properties when migrating projects across environments.

OSB also has a monitoring console supported both locally in the OSB console and centrally through **Oracle Enterprise Manager** (**EM**) to report performance, traffic statistics, and errors.

OSB terminology: Business services and proxies

Two important concepts in Oracle Service Bus are **Business Services** and **Proxies**.

A **business service** describes the endpoint being virtualized, its policies, and interfaces. A **proxy service** is what the service bus exposes to service consumers and implements the virtualization logic:

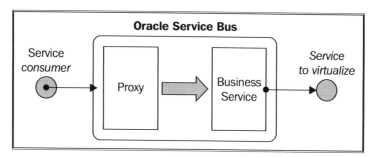

What about governance and discovery?

Re-usable services need to be governed and discovered. OSB services are harvested by **Oracle Enterprise Repository (OER)** for visibility, impact analysis, and approval of the interfaces by architects. OSB proxy services are auto-uploaded to **Oracle Service Registry (OSR)**. Business services are auto-imported into OSB when the registry entry for the endpoint service changes.

OSB for Financial Services

Oracle Service Bus for Financial Services is a vertical solution that enables the parsing, validation, and transformation of financial messages (SWIFT, FIX, FpML) within a service-orientated architecture. The product bundle includes Oracle Service Bus as the core product (which includes a native MQ and file transport for SWIFT connectivity), the Financial Message Designer (a design environment that provides pre-defined financial services message formats plus the capabilities to set up custom messages and transformations) and the Message Format Adapters (SWIFT adapter, FIX adapter, Payments adapter, and Derivatives adapter) to be used at runtime within Oracle Service Bus.

Tutorial: Virtualization of services

Now that you have completed the design of the POProcessing composite application, you should switch gears and think about how this application will behave once it is deployed in production.

- Does it have dependencies that will change frequently?
- Could these dependencies require modifications and re-deployment, creating a disruption of service to the consumers of the POProcessing application?

If so, we should leverage the Oracle Service Bus to make our composite more resilient to change.

Upon inspection, the credit validation service is a good candidate to decouple from the POProcessing composite. While the interface for the credit validation service is fairly stable, the service provider may be replaced frequently. In fact, we already have been alerted that the credit validation service may be moved to another division and Visa cards would be processed differently. We should not have to re-deploy our application every time the credit validation provider is moved or the interface and routing is changed in a way that is not relevant to our own application. Being able to insulate from these types of changes will make our application more agile, more robust, and adaptable.

In addition, credit validation is a service that could be re-used by many business processes and making it available for enterprise-wide re-use could lead to cost reductions.

In this tutorial, you register the credit card validation service as a Business Service with Oracle Service Bus. You then create a Proxy Service and re-wire the POProcessing composite to access this service indirectly through Oracle Service Bus. This is called service virtualization.

Service virtualization provides loose coupling and allows the POProcessing composite to be more agile and resilient to change once put into production.

 Chapters 11-19 can be done in any order after completing Chapter 10. In order to follow the tutorial in this chapter you must have either completed the tutorial from Chapter 10 or higher, or set up the environment as described in Chapter 4 and deployed the solution for Chapter 10, which can be found in `c:\po\solutions\ch10`.

Designing the flow

The following figure illustrates the high-level flow we are implementing:

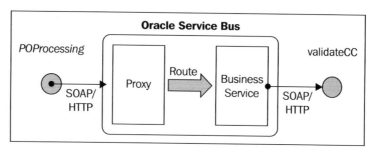

During this tutorial, you will accomplish the following tasks:

1. Import Resources.
2. Configure and test a business service for `validationForCC`.
3. Create proxy and message flow to process incoming messages with data validation, reporting of the incoming message, and error handling by sending an alert in the event of a validation failure.
4. Re-wire the POProcessing composite to invoke the credit card validation service through Oracle Service Bus.
5. Test the end-to-end application.

Once completed, the overall message flow of the Oracle Service Bus Proxy should look like the following picture:

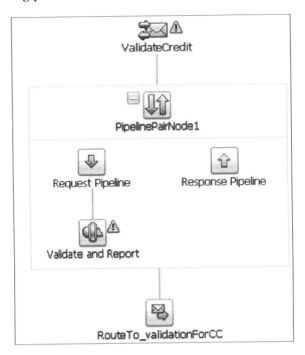

Creating the project and importing resources

If not already running, start the OSB Examples Server from the start menu. If not already running, start your SOA server.

1. Log into OSB Web Console (`http://localhost:7021/sbconsole`) with username as `weblogic` and password as `weblogic`.

2. Click on the **Create** button in the lefthand corner of the screen to start a new session. In OSB, all changes are done in a sandbox called a session. You first create the sandbox by creating a session in the **Change Center**. After a set of related changes is done, you deploy all the changes in the session as a unit by clicking on **Activate** in **Change Center**.

You first need to create a project with sub-folders. You could create it using the console, but instead you will import this to illustrate how configuration can be imported into OSB. If you decide to go directly to the solution, you can import the solution in the same way.

3. Scroll down the lefthand pane and click on **System Administration**.

4. Click on **Import Resources**:

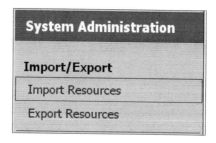

5. Click on **Browse** and navigate in your local file system to where you unzipped the materials. Select c:\po\solutions\ch11-OSB\Lab 11 OSB starting sbconfig.jar.

6. Click on **Next** then click on **Import**.

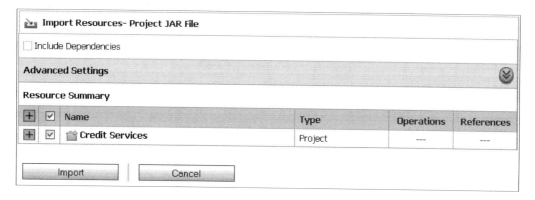

7. Click on the **Activate** button to deploy the OSB configuration change. Then click on the **Submit** button.

8. Click on **Project Explorer** then **Project Folders**. You should see a top-level project called **Credit Services** with a sub-folder called **BusinessServices**.

9. Start a new session in **Change Center**. Click on **Credit Services**. Add **ProxyServices** and **Resources** folders under the **Credit Services** folder by typing each folder name in the **Enter New Folder Name** field and clicking on **Add Folder**. When finished, the project looks as depicted in the following screenshot:

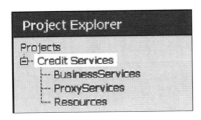

10. Navigate to the **Resources** folder. Click on the **Create Resources** drop-down box and select **Resources from URL**.

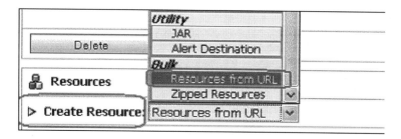

11. You will import resources from the WSDL URL of SOA Suite Server. You can simply paste the URL to the WSDL into the **URL/Path** field as depicted in the following screenshot. The precise URL to the WSDL file can be obtained from the `validationForCC` test page in the Enterprise Manager console. Be sure to remove any version numbering. It will be something like this:
    `http://localhost:8001/soa-infra/services/default/`
    `validationForCC/getStatusByCC?WSDL`

12. Enter the Resource Name, **ValidateCredit_WSDL** and the Resource Type, WSDL.

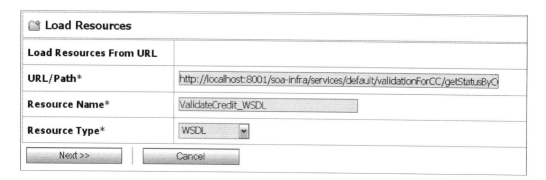

13. Click on **Next**. Click on **Import**. You have now imported the WSDL and schema needed to create the Business Service for the credit card validation service on Oracle Service Bus.

Configuring Business Service

A business service defines the interface and connection information for an endpoint that OSB invokes. It is similar to a composite reference.

1. Navigate to the **Business Services** folder. From the **Create Resources** drop-down, select **Business Service**.

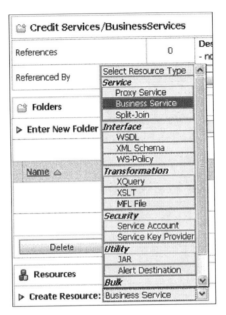

2. On the **General Configuration** tab, fill in the **Service Name** and **Description**. Set **Service Type** to WSDL web service. Click on the **Browse** button. This will bring up a window to select the WSDL for the Business Service:

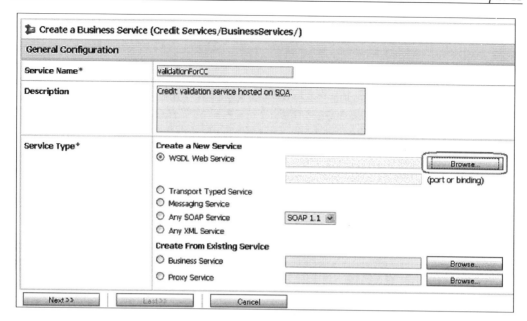

3. Click on the link to the WSDL imported in the previous step, **ValidateCredit_WSDL**:

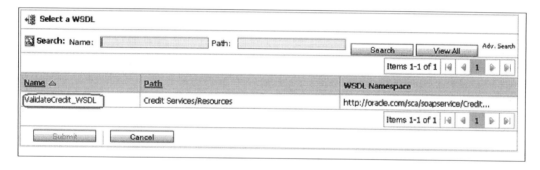

4. Select **execute_pt** under the **Ports** and then click on **Submit**:

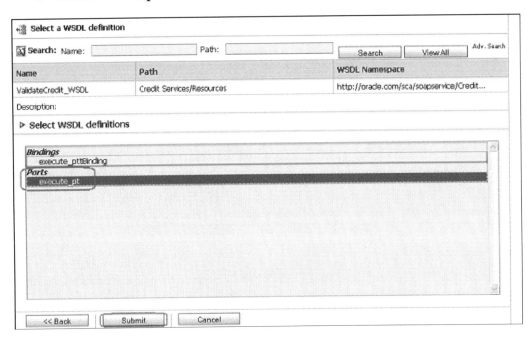

5. Click on **Next** through each of the remaining configuration screens. Review options available to business services. Accept all of the defaults.

6. Finally, on the last screen showing all the options together in a table format, scroll down and click on **Save** (don't forget this step and navigate away from this page before hitting **Save** or you'll lose your changes):

7. From the **Project Explorer** view, click on your new Business Service:

8. Click on **Operational Settings** tab at top of page:

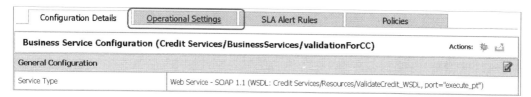

9. Select the **Enabled** checkbox next to **Monitoring**. Change the **Aggregation Interval** to greater than ten minutes.

 The aggregation interval is the moving window of time over which metrics are computed. Enabling monitoring will collect metrics for your service such as average response time, number of messages, and number of errors. You can define SLA alerts on these metrics.

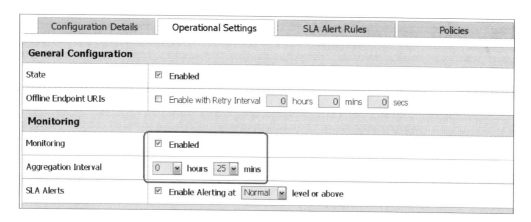

10. Click on the **Update** button to save your changes.

11. Activate your changes by clicking on the **Activate** button in the lefthand corner of the screen. Add a **Description** before clicking on **Submit** to document what was done. This will help you identify it later in the **Change Center** in case you would like to undo or redo your changes.

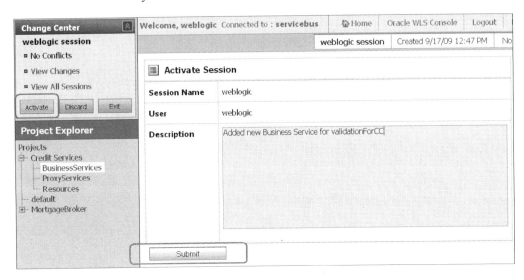

12. Select the **Launch Test Console** button next to your new Business Service to bring up the test console. Make sure the SOA server is running.

13. Set the credit card number to `1234-234-1234-1234`. The payload XML should look like this:

```
<cca:creditcardStatusRequest xmlns:cca="http://www.globalcompany.
com/ns/CCAuthorizationService"><cca:CCNumber>1234-1234-1234-1234</
cca:CCNumber></cca:creditcardStatusRequest>
```

14. Click on the **Execute** button:

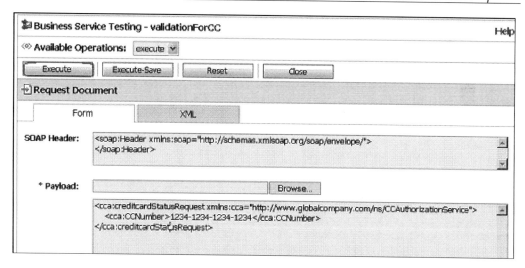

15. Review the **Response Document** for **VALID**.

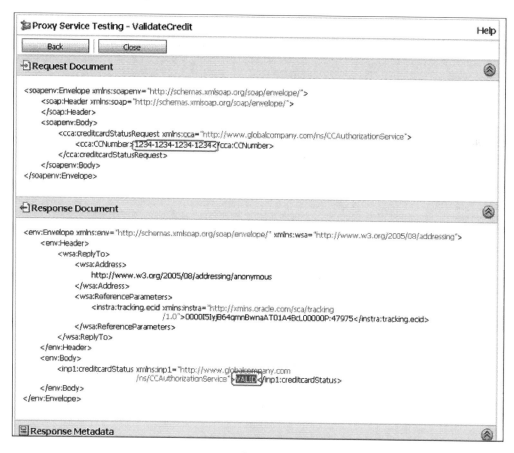

Configuring the Proxy

A proxy service is the OSB mediation and virtualization logic that virtualizes the endpoints that OSB routes to and decouples them from the client. You first create a proxy service exposed to the client that just routes to the business service. Later you add more logic in the proxy service.

1. Click on the **Create** button in the **Change Center** to start a new session.

2. Navigate to the **ProxyServices** folder. Click on the **Create Resources** drop-down box and select **Proxy Service**.

3. On the **General Configuration** page, enter the **Service Name**: ValidateCredit. Set **Service Type** to WSDL Web service. Click on the **Browse** button, select the WSDL you just imported, select **execute_pt** under **ports**, and click on **Submit**.

4. Click on **Next** through the remaining configuration screens, making note of some of the settings for Proxy. Notice that you can configure security for your services, as well as enable content and attachment streaming.

5. On the **Summary** page, click on the **Save** button at the bottom of page:

6. Navigate to the newly created Proxy Service through **Project Explorer**.

7. Click on the Message Flow icon next to **ValidateCredit.** This will take you to the Message Flow editor:

8. Click on the **ValidateCredit** icon and select **Add Route**.

9. Click on the **RouteNode1** icon and select **Edit Name and Comments**. Change the name to **RouteTo_validationForCC** and click on **Save**.

10. Click on **RouteTo_validationForCC** and select **Edit Route**.

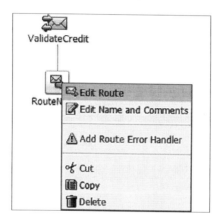

11. Click on **Add an Action**, select **Communication,** and then select **Routing**.

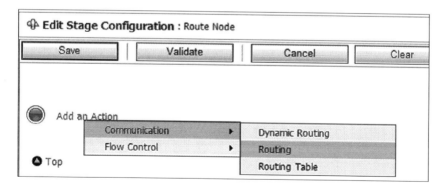

12. Click on **service** link and select **validationForCC** and click on **Submit**.

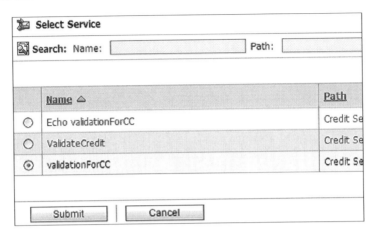

13. Select the **Use Inbound operation for outbound** checkbox. Click on **Save All**.

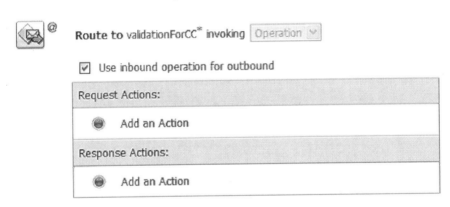

14. Click on **Activate** in the Change Center and Confirm to deploy your changes to the session. You are now ready to test your new Proxy!

15. Navigate to the new Proxy Service and click on the icon to bring up the Test Console.

16. Cut and paste the same XML as in previous step into the **Payload** text box.

17. Click on the **Execute** button. You should see output similar to when you tested your Business Service.

18. Instead of the previous steps, an alternative way to create the same proxy service is to auto-generate it from the business service. When creating the proxy service, on the **General Configuration** page, select **Create From Existing Service** and click on **Browse** to select the business service you created.

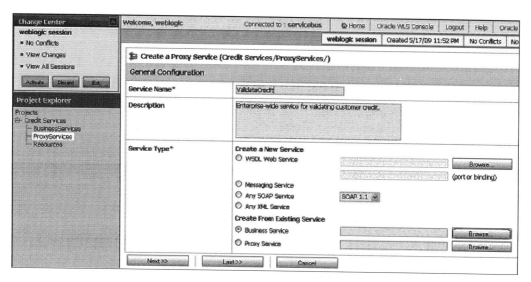

Configuring Message Flow

Now that the Proxy Service is creater and working, change the message flow to add reporting and input validation.

1. Navigate to the newly created Proxy Service through **Project Explorer**.

2. Click on **Create** to start a new session in **Change Center**.

3. Click on the Message Flow icon next to **ValidateCredit**. This will take you to the Message Flow editor.

   Next you will add some processing steps to the Message Flow.

4. Click on the envelope above **ValidateCredit**. Select **Add Pipeline Pair**.

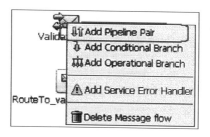

5. Click on **Request_Pipeline** to the left and select **Add Stage**. The request pipeline does the processing of the request and the response pipeline does the processing of the response. A pipeline contains a sequence of stages:

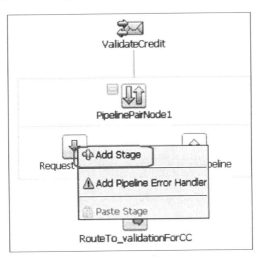

6. Click on the new Stage and select **Edit Stage**.

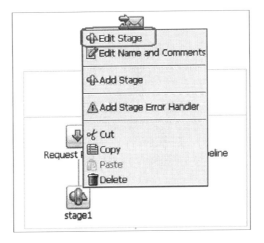

Now we will add two actions: **Report** and **Validate**. The **Report** action allows you to record any payload elements along with key-value pairs to a database. **Validate** allows you to check for valid input (by a schema) to credit card validation service and throws an error if an invalid input message is detected.

7. Click on **Add Action | Reporting | Report**.

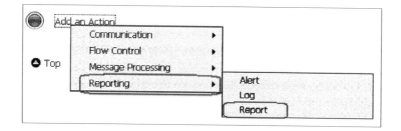

8. Fill in fields as follows:

   ○ **Expression**: **$body**

   ○ **Key Name**: **CCNumber**

   ○ **Key Value**: **./cca:creditcardStatusRequest** in variable **body**

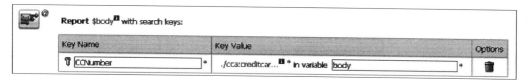

9. Add a **Validate** action.

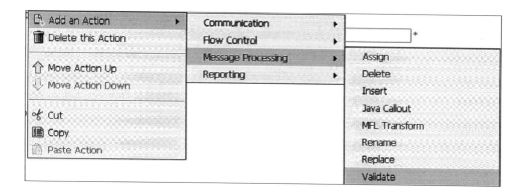

10. Fill in fields as follows:
    ○ **XPath**: **./*** (dot slash star)
    ○ **variable**: **body**
    ○ **Resource**: **XMLSchema –248516241* (Element = "creditcardStatusRequest")**

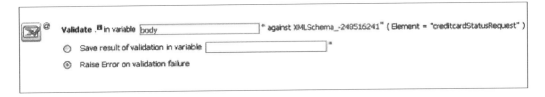

11. Click on the **Save** button.
12. Navigate to the top of the message flow and click on the envelope. Select **Add Service Error Handler**. Click on **Error Handler**. Select **Add Stage**.

 An error handler can be attached to a stage, pipeline, or the whole service. The error handler consists of a sequence of stages with actions. If control passes past the last stage, a SOAP fault is returned to the client (if the operation is a request/response WSDL operation).

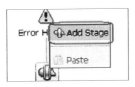

13. Click on the stage and select **Edit Stage**.

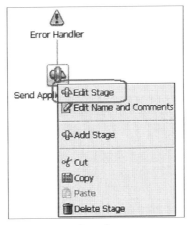

14. Click on **Add an Action | Reporting | Alert**.

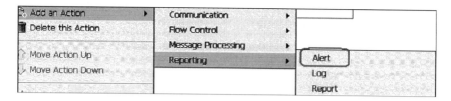

15. Fill in **Alert** as depicted below and click on **Save All**.

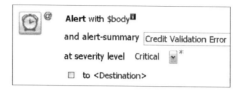

16. **Activate** the session in **Change Center**.

Re-wiring POProcessing composite

Next, open your POProcessing composite and change the **getCreditCardStatus** reference to invoke the virtualized service from Oracle Service Bus.

1. Open JDeveloper if not already open. Navigate to the POProcessing application. Double-click on composite.xml in the lefthand pane to open the composite editor.

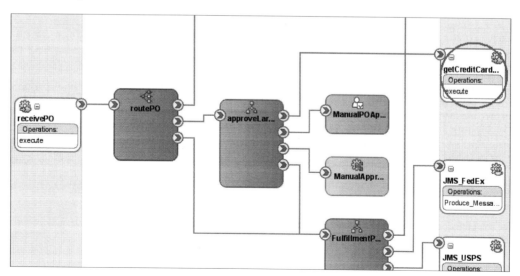

2. Double-click on the **getCreditCardStatus** reference link. Edit the **WSDL URL** field to point to your new Proxy in Oracle Service Bus.

To find your WSDL URL, navigate to the Proxy Service and locate the End-point URI to use for the WSDL URL. For example, if you named your Proxy as recommended in the tutorial, the URL would be: `http://localhost:7021/Credit_Services/ProxyServices/ValidateCredit?WSDL`.

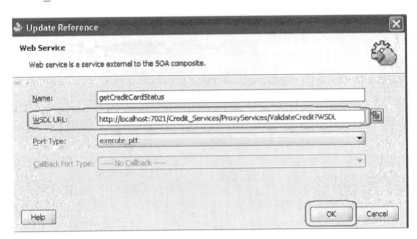

3. Click on **OK**.

4. Re-deploy the `POProcessing` composite. You are now ready to test your end-to-end scenario with Oracle Service Bus.

Testing the end-to-end application

To test, execute an instance of POProcessing and see that it calls the Proxy Service on the Oracle Service Bus by reviewing the report you added to the message flow.

1. After deploying, in the EM console, click on the **POProcessing** application and then open the test page. Test with the sample input `c:\po\input\po-large-iPodx30.txt`.

2. Navigate back to the Oracle Service Bus console. Log in. Navigate to **Operations**.

3. Review the **Message Reports**.

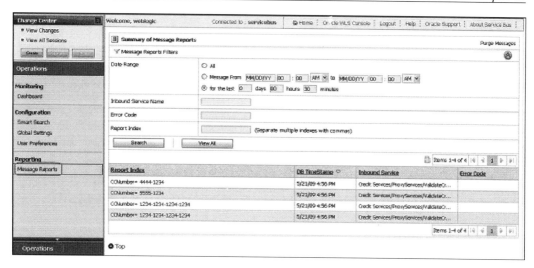

4. Navigate to the **Dashboard**. No Alerts have been generated yet. Try sending your proxy bad data (XML that does not conform to the schema) using the OSB Test page and see the alert you coded into the proxy.

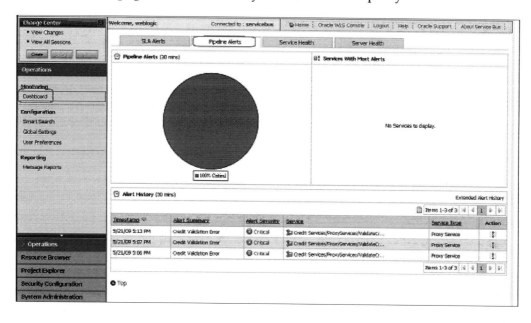

Summary

In this chapter, you have learned the role of the Oracle Service Bus (OSB) in an end-to-end SOA architecture, and seen how it can increase re-usability and agility through service virtualization.

Quick-build Instructions

This section gives you all of the operations and names for objects created in this chapter. Experienced users can use this to bypass the step-by-step instructions and complete this chapter more quickly. The complete details for any particular operation listed here can be found in the preceding sections. The information is organized in the same manner that it is introduced in the chapter:

- Create project and import resources:
    - Import JAR to create project:
        - **Name:** `po\solutions\ch11-OSB\Lab 11 OSB starting sbconfig.jar`
    - Create folders in project **Credit Services**:
        - Name: **ProxyServices**
        - Name: **Resources**
    - Import WSDL of credit service from URL:
        - WSDL Resource Name: **ValidateCredit_WSDL**
- Configure Business Service:
    - Name: **validationForCC**
    - WSDL: **ValidateCredit_WSDL**
    - Port: **execute_pt**
    - Default the rest
- Configure the Proxy Service:
    - Create proxy service:
        - Name: **ValidateCredit**
        - WSDL: **ValidateCredit_WSDL**
        - Port: **execute_pt**
        - Default the rest

- º Create route node:
  - º Name: **RouteTo_validationForCC**
- º Create route action
  - º ˊService Name: **validationForCC**
  - º Set inbound operation for outbound.
- Configure Message Flow:
  - º Add the pipeline pair and request stage. Use default names
  - º Add the report action in the request stage:
    - º Expression: **$body**
    - º KeyName: **CCNumber**
    - º Key Value: `./cca:creditcardStatusRequest` in variable `body`
  - º Add Validate action after Report action:
    - º XPath: `./*` (dot slash star)
    - º variable: `body`
    - º Resource: `XMLSchema –248516241*` (Element = `"creditcardStatusRequest"`)
  - º Add service-level fault handler with one stage with default name.
  - º Add Alert action in fault handler:
    - º Expression: **$body**
    - º Alert Summary: `Credit Validation Error`
    - º Severity Level: `Critical`
- Re-wire POProcessing Composite:
  - º Change WSDL URL in reference to proxy service WSL URL.

The application is completed. Deploy and test.

12
Exploring Application Life Cycle Management

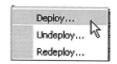

Every piece of software progresses through phases, such as requirement analysis, design, development, testing, and production. This is called the software development life cycle. In traditional development approaches like J2EE, management of this software development life cycle has become quite mature. In the case of service-oriented application development, tools and techniques for managing software life cycle are still evolving. Although tools and techniques used for traditional development are perfectly valid and usable for SOA, SOA does put additional requirements on the overall management. For starters, there tend to be more artifacts to worry about. For instance, in the world of Java, you manage Java classes and resource bundles, whereas in SOA composites, you manage composite definitions, component definitions, XML schemas, WSDLs, and so on. And this is just the source code management aspect of the life cycle management.

When it comes to deployment and runtime management, things become more complex. For example, if a composite is using an existing service, it may be referring to the WSDL and end point on a development server. When the composite goes into the testing phase and then into production, the same service references will have to be changed to point to the corresponding test and production servers.

These are just some examples of challenges in managing the software development life cycle of a SOA composite application that Oracle SOA Suite 11*g* addresses.

Introducing life cycle management features

Software development life cycle management is a broad subject. This chapter focuses on the deployment aspect of it.

Deploying the composite to the development, test, and production environments requires modifying the composite to change environment-specific properties, policies, and URLs. Also, an IDE is the tool of choice for developers, but deployment to test, stage, and production environments is typically done by administrators who prefer command-line tools and scripts or the administration console.

Oracle SOA Suite provides multiple facilities to help in this area:

- It offers a variety of deployment methods:
    - From JDeveloper, the development environment
    - From Enterprise Manager, the management and monitoring environment
    - From the command line, in an interactive fashion
    - From ANT or Python scripts

- It offers the ability to deploy multiple versions of a given composite simultaneously, and specify a default version.

- It offers **configuration plans** that are composite-wide to customize environment-specific values (for example, a web service URL that is different in the test environment than in the production environment). You can modify all of the following with a configuration plan:
    - Binding and other properties associated with references, components, and services
    - URLs in WSDL, imports and schema imports, includes and redefines
    - URLs in `composite.xml`
    - JCA adapter properties
    - OWSM WS-Policies can be enabled, disabled, or new ones attached

- It offers built-in support in JDeveloper for version control systems to version the composite artifacts.

Tutorial: Solution deployment

In this tutorial, you create a configuration plan, which can be used for deploying the composite to your Development, Test, and Production systems with environment-specific changes applied. The following figure illustrates a typical code promotion scenario:

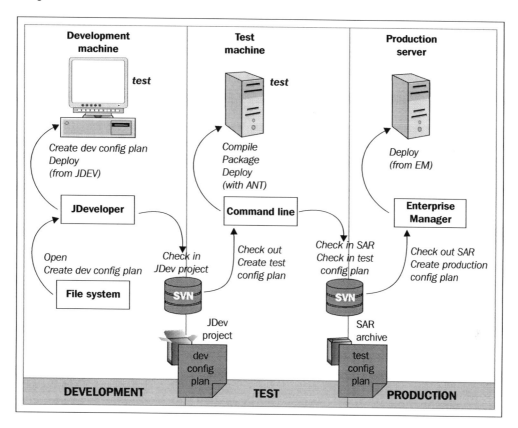

The configuration plan that you create in this lab performs the following tasks:

1. Modifying properties that can take on different values in different environments.

2. Modifying the file naming convention and the destination directory for the file adapter.

You apply the configuration plan by using three deployment methods:

- JDeveloper
- ANT scripts
- Enterprise Manager Console

> Chapters 11-19 can be done in any order after completing Chapter 10.
> In order to follow the tutorial in this chapter, you must have either completed the tutorial from Chapter 10 or higher, or set up the environment as described in Chapter 4, and deployed the solution for Chapter 10, which can be found in `c:\po\solutions\ch10`.

Development environment approach

You first explore the development environment tasks.

Surfacing binding properties at the composite level

If the developer knows which properties need to be customized, then the properties can be surfaced at the composite level for easy customization.

1. In JDeveloper, open the **POProcessing** composite.
2. Select the **WriteApprovalResults** reference (a file adapter).
3. View the properties using the **Property Inspector** in the lower right pane. You may need to enlarge or scroll the pane to see all of the sections. If you do not see the **Property Inspector**, select it from the **View** menu in the toolbar.
4. You are going to add a binding property using the **Property Inspector**.
5. Scroll to the **Binding Properties** section and select the add icon.

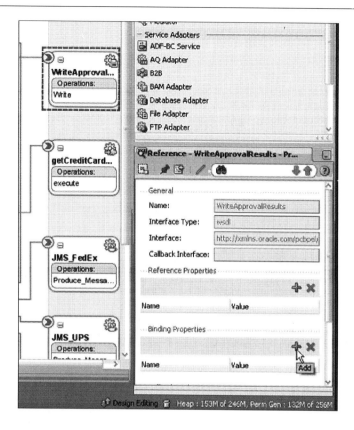

6. Select **FileNamingConvention** for the property name and `test_%SEQ%.xml` for the value.

7. Click on **OK**.

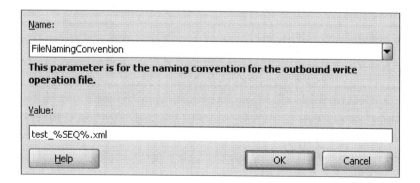

8. Check the source of `composite.xml` to see the result of this operation. With this change, you have surfaced a binding property in `composite.xml`.

The term "surfacing a property" means exposing a component-level property and making at available in the composite as a composite property.

```
<reference name="WriteApprovalResults"
           ui:wsdlLocation="WriteApprovalResults.wsdl">
   <interface.wsdl interface="http://xmlns.oracle.com/pcbpel/adapter/file/POProcessing/POProces
   <binding.jca config="WriteApprovalResults_file.jca">
    <property name="FileNamingConvention" type="xs:string" many="false"
              override="may">test_%SEQ%.xml</property>
   </binding.jca>
```

9. Click on **Save all**.

Generating and modifying a configuration plan

We will now generate a configuration plan in JDeveloper.

1. From **Projects Explorer**, select **composite.xml**.

2. Right-click on **composite.xml** and choose **Generate Config Plan**.

3. Name your plan POProcessing_dev_cfgplan.xml.

4. It should automatically open in text mode in JDeveloper.

5. Locate the reference for **WriteApprovalResults** and edit the **FileNamingConvention** property to **orderoutput_%SEQ%.xml**.

```
<reference name="WriteApprovalResults">
    <!--Add search and replace rules for the binding properties-->
   <binding type="jca">
      <property name="FileNamingConvention">
         <replace>orderoutput_%SEQ%.xml</replace>
      </property>
   </binding>
</reference>
```

6. In addition, in the **wsdlAndSchema** section, add the **PhysicalDirectory** JCA property (this is the directory that you configured for the file adapter to write to) and replace it with another directory, for instance, **C:\tmp\out**:

```
104 <wsdlAndSchema name="approveLargeOrder.wsdl|FulfillmentProcess.wsdl|getStatusByC
105    <jca:property name="PhysicalDirectory">
106       <replace>c:\tmp\out</replace>
107    </jca:property>
108    <searchReplace>
109          <search></search>
110          <replace></replace>
111    </searchReplace>
112 </wsdlAndSchema>
```

You can also restrict the scope of this global replace to a single file by only leaving **WriteApprovalResults_file.jca** in the list of files to consider for this search and replace.

Now it is time to validate your new config plan to ensure it works as expected.

1. Right-click on **composite.xml**.

2. Select **Validate Config Plan**.

3. Select **OK** in the **Composite Configuration Plan Validator** dialog.

4. The `report.log` file opens automatically. You should see the following screen:

```
                Reference  [ WriteApprovalResults ]
                    Reference Bindings
                        Binding  [ jca ]
                    Property [ FileNamingConvention ]
                        Old [ test_%SEQ%.xml ]
                        New [ orderoutput_%SEQ%.xml ]
                Reference  [ getCreditCardStatus ]
                    Reference Bindings
                        Binding  [ ws ]
            Attribute name=port
                    No change in old and new value http://oracle.
            Attribute name=location
                    No change in old and new value http://localho
                Reference  [ JMS_USPS ]
                    Reference Bindings
                        Binding  [ jca ]
                Reference  [ JMS_UPS ]
                    Reference Bindings
                        Binding  [ jca ]
                Reference  [ JMS_FedEx ]
                    Reference Bindings
                        Binding  [ jca ]
---End Match for composite [ POProcessing ] in config plan---
Checking for replacement in wsdl and schema files
            WSDL WriteApprovalResults_file.jca JCA properties
            Property [ PhysicalDirectory ]
                    Old Value [ c:\temp ]
                    New Value [ c:\tmp\out ]
```

5. Finally, deploy from JDeveloper and attach this configuration plan. Give this new deployment a different revision ID and ensure the behavior is as expected (that is, the file adapter now writes all messages to `c:\tmp\out` with a name `orderoutput_<number>.xml`).

Test environment approach

Test system administrators typically do not want to work with an IDE and prefer to operate from the command line or with scripts. Let's take the role of a test administrator in this section and exclusively work from the command line.

Compiling and packaging from the command line with ANT

1. First, open a DOS prompt and set your environment for command line deployment via ANT.

   ```
   Set PATH=
   C:\Oracle\Middleware\jdev_11gR1\modules\org.apache.ant_1.7.0\
   bin;%PATH%
   ```

2. Navigate to the following directory:

   ```
   cd C:\Oracle\Middleware\jdev_11gR1\jdeveloper\bin
   ```

3. Look at the available ANT commands. Use `ant -f <command> help` to get usage information for a given command:

   ```
   dir ant-sca*
   ant-sca-compile.xml    ant-sca-deploy.xml    ant-sca-mgmt.xml
   ant-sca-package.xml    ant-sca-test.xml      ant-sca-upgrade.xml
   ```

4. Compile and package `POProcessing` using the `ant-sca-package` command. This command also sets the version number. You will need to have `JAVA_HOME` set to run ant. For instance (but adjust this to your own environment and application paths):

   ```
   ant -f ant-sca-package.xml
   -DcompositeDir=C:\po\POProcessing\POProcessing
   -DcompositeName=POProcessing
   -Drevision=1.0
   -Dscac.application.home=C:\po\POProcessing
   ```

5. If successful, you should see a **BUILD SUCCESSFUL** message.

6. Check for the `[jar]` message that will tell you where the script is writing the resulting SAR file:

   ```
   [jar] Building jar: C:\po\POProcessing\POProcessing\deploy
   \sca_POProcessing_rev1.0.jar
   ```

Deploying from the command line with ANT

Now deploy this SAR file from the command line using `ant-sca-deploy.xml`.

1. Use `ant-sca-deploy.xml` to deploy the previously packaged SAR file. Adjust the following command to your own environment:

```
ant -f ant-sca-deploy.xml
-DserverURL=http://localhost:8001
-DsarLocation=C:\po\POProcessing\POProcessing\deploy\sca_
POProcessing_rev1.0.jar
-Doverwrite=true
-Duser=weblogic
-Dpassword=welcome1
-DforceDefault=true
-Dconfigplan=C:\po\POProcessing\POProcessing\POProcessing_dev_
cfgplan.xml
```

Production environment approach

Production administrators typically want to use EM to do tasks. Let's take the role of a production administrator in this section and exclusively work from EM.

Deploying from Enterprise Manager

In this section, we will explore the deploy options from Enterprise Manager.

1. Right-click on **soa-infra** and select the **Deploy** option.

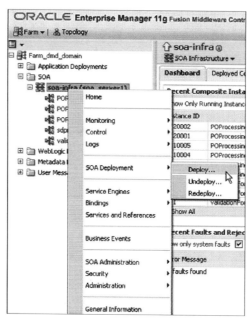

2. Point EM to your local SAR file and configuration plan and deploy.

 If you are redeploying an existing version of the composite, use the **Redeploy** option instead of the **Deploy** option.

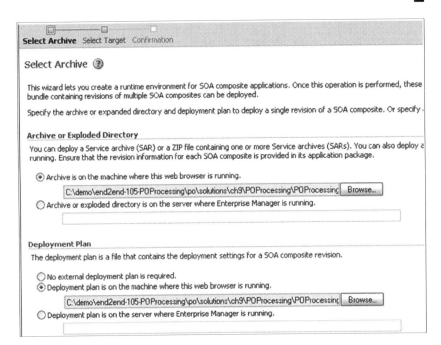

Summary

In this chapter, you learned how to customize your deployment when going from development to test to production. This is just one aspect of the overall software development life cycle management. For managing your complete end-to-end life cycle, you should consider an enterprise repository solution like the Oracle Enterprise Repository, which integrates with JDeveloper and related tools. You can get more information on Oracle Enterprise Repository at this web address: `http://www.oracle.com/technology/products/soa/repository/index.html`.

Quick-build Instructions

Unlike other chapters in this book, this chapter does not have you implement a set of changes to your POProcessing composite, but rather shows you how to implement deployment using the IDE and command line. As such, instructions summarizing the edits made in this chapter are not applicable.

13

Unit-testing the Composite Application

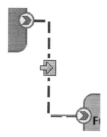

A comprehensive framework for creating test scenarios and carrying out testing by using these test suites to test your applications is an essential part of any integrated development environment. A number of tools like JUnit are available to perform unit testing of your Java code. You need something similar that provides a framework for your composite application.

Introducing the built-in testing framework

Oracle SOA Suite 11g provides a testing framework that allows you to:

- Define tests, assertions, and emulations using JDeveloper
- Run these tests either from the EM console or on the command line using ANT
- Review the test results from the EM console or as a JUnit report

There are three parts to a test case:

1. An *Initiation* of a composite defines the service and operation invoked along with the test data.

2. *Emulation* defines the message or fault returned from a reference or component invoked through a synchronous response or a callback without executing the component or referenced service.

3. An *Assertion* compares the message or part of the message over an SCA wire against the expected data.

A single test includes definitions of the initiation, emulations, and assertions. The test suite is defined in the composite project and is deployed along with the composite to the server, so it can be initiated from the EM console.

Tutorial: Automated unit testing

The best way to learn how to build and execute a unit test is to try an example.

Modify POProcessing to add a unit test, which sets the inbound message, the simulation message, and two assertions. The inbound message is a valid order with a valid credit card and order total between 1000 and 5000. This triggers the approveLargeOrder process but not the human task.

The simulated message is the message returned from the credit validation service as a VALID response.

The first assertion is on the data being passed to the WriteFile service, checking that the value of status = 'approved', which is the expected value for this input data.

The second assertion is on the data being passed to FulfillmentProcess, checking that the customer ID is 9999 — since the customer ID is actually 1111, this test will always fail. This last assertion shows what happens when the data being checked is not the expected value.

> Chapters 11-19 can be done in any order after completing Chapter 10.
>
> In order to follow the tutorial in this chapter you must have either completed the tutorial from Chapter 10 or higher, or set up the environment as described in Chapter 4 and deployed the solution for Chapter 10, which can be found in `c:\po\solutions\ch10`.

Creating the unit test

Use JDeveloper to create a unit test for POProcessing.

1. Open the **POProcessing** project in JDeveloper. In the Application navigator expand the **SOA Content** folder and right-click on the **test suites** folder.

2. Select **Create Test Suite**.

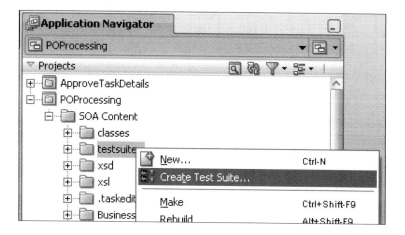

3. Name the test suite **logicTest**.

4. Click on **OK**.

5. Name the test **TestDelivery**.

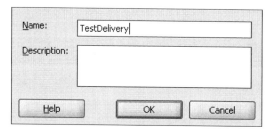

6. Click on **OK**.

Notice that the composite view changes slightly to show you are in Unit Test creation mode now. The swim lanes on the left and right are yellow. You can return to the normal composite editor by selecting the **Return to SOA composite diagram** button at the top of the window.

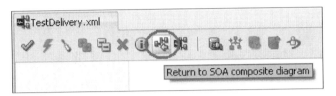

Setting the inbound message

First create an inbound message for `receivePO`.

1. Right-click the binding component **receivePO** and select **Create Initiate Messages**.

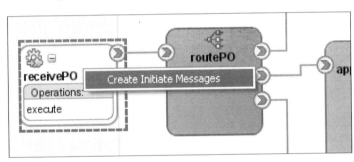

2. In the **Initiate Messages** dialog that appears, insert the following payload (copy from the `c:\po\input\po-unittest.txt` file). This creates an order for a Customer with ID as 1111 and a $1,260 purchase.

```
<PurchaseOrder xmlns="http://xmlns.oracle.com/ns/order">
  <CustID>1111</CustID>
  <ID>2222</ID>
  <productName>TV-LCD</productName>
  <itemType>electronics</itemType>
  <price>1260</price>
  <quantity>1</quantity>
  <status>initial</status>
  <ccType>Mastercard</ccType>
  <ccNumber>8765-8765-8765-8765</ccNumber>
</PurchaseOrder>
```

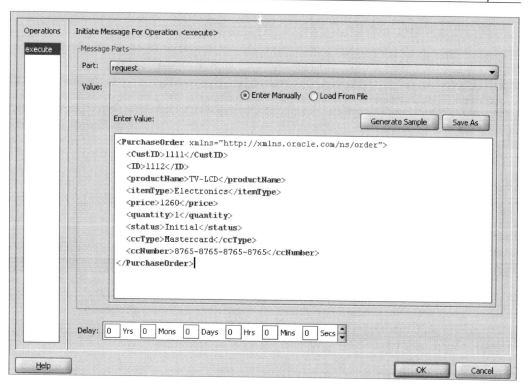

3. Click on **OK**. After closing the dialog, you will see a blue arrow on the inbound component indicating that there is a message set for that service.

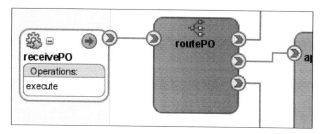

Setting the simulated message

Now simulate the response from the credit card validation service.

1. Double-click on the wire between BPEL process **approveLargeOrder** and the **getCreditCardStatus** web service.

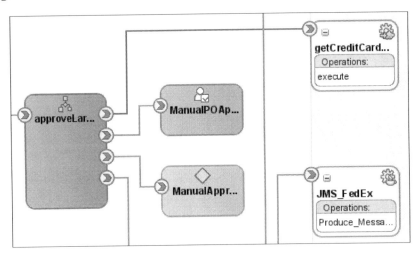

2. Go to the **Emulates** tab and click on the plus sign.

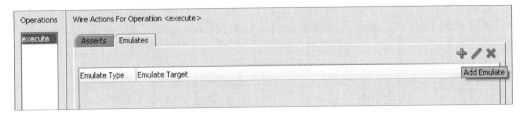

3. Click on **Generate Sample** to have a sample response created automatically for you and edit the XML fragment to change the response value to VALID to simulate what the web service would return in response when the credit card number is valid.

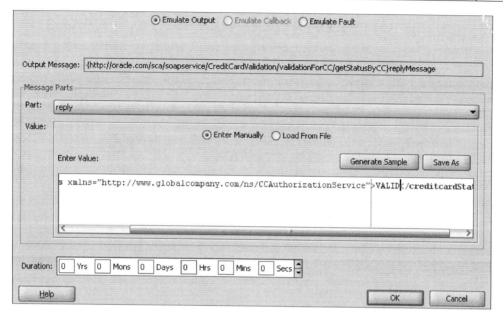

4. Click on **OK** and click on **OK** again. After closing the dialog, notice that the wire has changed to a dashed line and there is an arrow indicating there is a message set for the return value of that service.

Setting the assertion for success

Now perform an assertion to verify the order status.

1. Double-click on the wire between **routePO** and **WriteApprovalResults**.

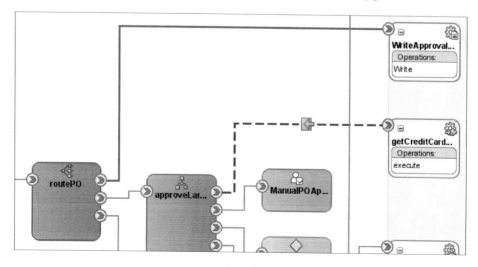

2. Add an assertion by selecting the green plus sign.

3. To check only part of the message click on the **Browse** button to select only one field of the XML structure.

4. Select only **imp1:status**.

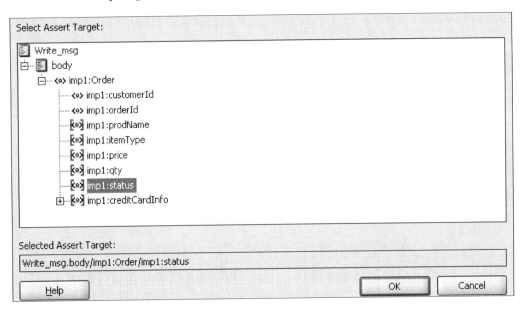

5. Click on **OK**.

6. For assert value, enter **approved** as that is the value you are expecting for the purchase order status.

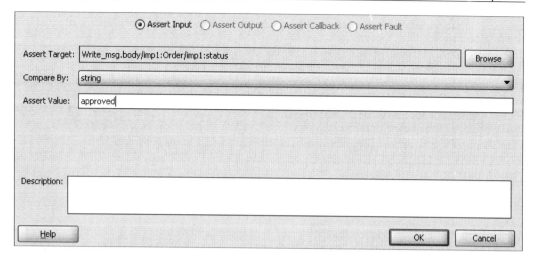

7. Click on **OK** and click on **OK** again. After closing the dialog, notice that the wire has changed to a dashed line and there is an arrow indicating there is an assertion set on data being sent to that service.

Setting the assertion for failure

Now create an assertion that will always fail for the input you provided in this test case.

1. Double-click on the wire between **approveLargeOrder** and **FulfillmentProcess**.

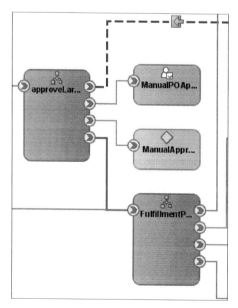

2. Add a new assertion and click again on **Browse** to select only part of the message.

3. Select only **customerId**.

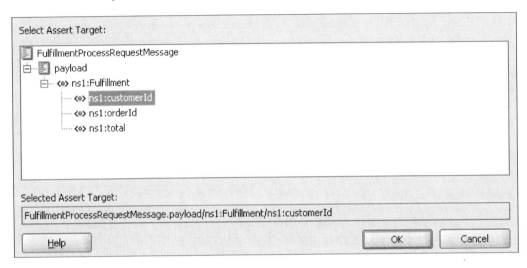

4. Click on **OK**.

5. For **Assert Value** enter **9999**. Normally you set the assert value to what you expect the value to be but this example is to show you what happens when your test fails. You know this assertion will fail because the initial payload that you supply has customer ID as 1111.

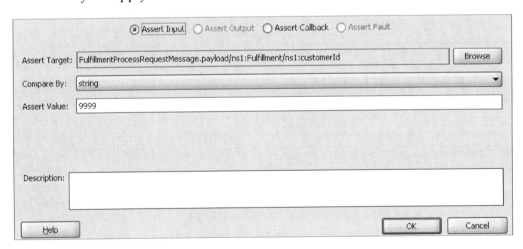

6. Click on **OK** and click on **OK** again.

The whole Test now looks like this:

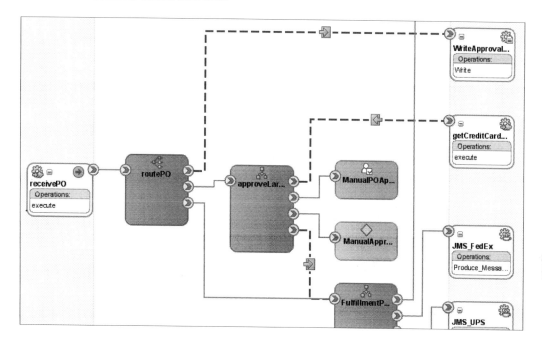

Testing the application

You now execute the unit test using the EM console.

1. Deploy the application by using the **Deploy** command in the **Project** menu.
2. In the EM console, click on the **POProcessing** application and then open the **Unit Test** tab. You see your test suite listed.

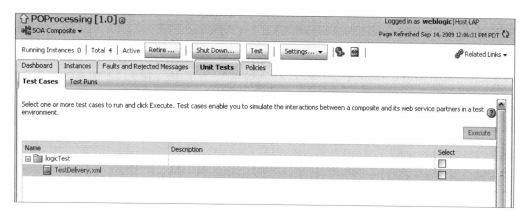

3. Select **TestDelivery.xml** and click on **Execute**.

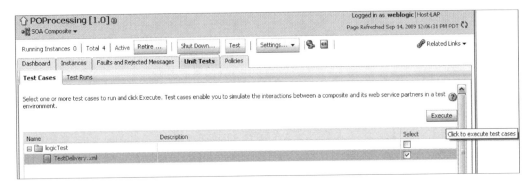

4. Name your test **FirstRun**. You can also set the number of instances to run concurrently and a timeout value. Leave those as defaulted.

5. After the test has completed, the **Test Runs** tab opens. Select **Search** if your test run is not showing. You see that the overall status is marked as **Failed**:

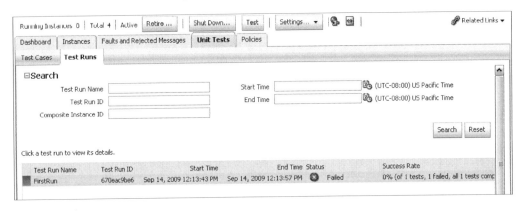

6. Scroll a little down to see the details about the assertions you inserted.

7. Note that the first one has failed as expected because the customer ID is **1111** and not **9999**.

8. The second one has passed as the status sent to **WriteApprovalResult** is **approved** and is equal to the assert value in the test.

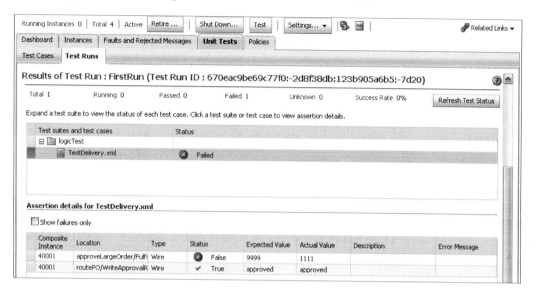

9. Click on the **Composite Instance** ID. You see the complete flow of the process. Note that `getCreditCardStatus` was never called, because of the response emulation you inserted.

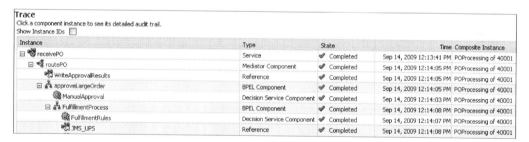

Summary

In this chapter, you learned the capabilities of SOA Suite to enable unit testing. You learned how to define a unit test with an initiating message, emulation of an external reference, and adding both successful and failed assertions. You learned how to execute the unit test in the EM console.

Quick-build instructions

This section gives you all of the operations and names for objects created in this chapter. Experienced users can use this for creating the objects in this chapter quickly. Any questions on details for a particular operation listed here can be found in the preceding sections. The information is divided by the sections in this chapter.

- Create the Unit Test:
    - Test Suite Name: **logicTest**
    - Test Name: **TestDelivery**
- Set the inbound message:

  Set the inbound message to a sample PO
    - Sample file: `c:\po\input\po-unittest.txt`
- Set the simulated message:

  Emulate the credit rating service
    - Response: **VALID**
- Set the assertion for success:

  Assert on input message to **WriteApprovalResults**
    - Status: **approved**
- Set the assertion for failure:

  Assert on input message to **FulfillmentProcess**
    - CustomerID: **9999**

14 Adding Exception Handling

bpelx:bindingFault

The goal of every good programmer is to write unbreakable software programs.
The extent to which this goal is achieved largely depends on how well one is able
to handle and manage expected as well as unexpected exception conditions.
Object-oriented languages such as C++ and Java provide an efficient way for
handling exceptions using constructs such as `try`, `catch`, and `finally`. With
service-oriented applications, most of what is available at the language level is still
valid and usable, but raises different challenges once you start orchestrating services
and creating composite applications.

Introducing exception handling

With service-oriented applications, the need for strong **exception handling** is
even more important as the quality of service becomes a critical factor in service
reusability. Inadequate or faulty exception handling can severely impact the usability
of a service.

How exceptions are handled depends on the type of exceptions that can possibly
occur. Exceptions that occur in a service-oriented composite application can
be broadly classified into two categories—**System Faults** and **Business Faults**.

The terms **Exception** and **Fault** tend to be used interchangeably. For example, the BPEL specification uses the term *Fault*, whereas Java uses the term *Exception* for anticipated and unexpected errors that occur during the execution. Oracle SOA Suite 11*g* uses the term *Fault* for exceptions occurring during execution of a composite.

System faults

System faults are generally thrown by the underlying infrastructure when a *runtime, system-level error* occurs. For example, if a service being invoked is not reachable either because of network issues or due to unavailability of the service provider, the SOA infrastructure will throw a connection exception. Given the nature of these exceptions, you can generalize exception handling across all components as well as composite applications. For example, you may create a single exception handler that notifies system administrators about service unavailability for all connection-related errors.

Business faults

Business faults are thrown when an exception condition occurs during processing of a service operation, *in the business logic of the service*. This exception condition may be due to the violation of certain business rules, to invalid data, or to other non-system related conditions. Generally, business exceptions are handled specifically by the invoker of the service and not as generic exceptions as is done for system faults.

Exception handling in Oracle SOA Suite 11*g*

Oracle SOA Suite 11*g* provides comprehensive exception handling and management features. Some are component specific and some are more general and available at the infrastructure level.

For example, BPEL provides constructs as a part of the specification for catching and handling exceptions, whereas the Mediator doesn't. Using the constructs available in BPEL, one can define exception handlers for handling all types of exceptions. BPEL supports two levels of granularity when it comes to attaching exception handlers—Scope-level and Process-level. BPEL also defines, as part of the specification, a list of runtime exceptions. `runtimeFault` and `bindingFault` are some examples of BPEL runtime exceptions.

The Mediator component also defines a set of exceptions that can occur at runtime. These exceptions are grouped into five different categories—all exceptions (TYPE_ALL), data-related exceptions, such as transformation errors (TYPE_DATA), metadata-related exceptions (TYPE_METADATA), database or infrastructure-related exceptions (TYPE_FATAL) and recoverable or retry-able errors (TYPE_TRANSIENT).

 You can get more information on Mediator exceptions using the online help in JDeveloper. Search for the key words *mediator faults* in the JDeveloper Help window to get relevant topics that discuss Mediator exception handling.

Exception-handling strategies

A BPEL process can become very complex as you start adding exception-handling code to it. It also results in a lot of duplicated code, especially when handling system or runtime exceptions. For example, if you have five service invocations in your process, you will either need five exception handlers or a generic one at the process level that handles all exceptions for all invocations. If you have ten such processes, you will have to duplicate the same code in all these processes.

In the case of Mediator, you don't have any specific constructs to handle exceptions, which means it is difficult to have a consistent way of handling exceptions across different components in a composite.

This is where Oracle SOA Suite 11*g*'s policy-based fault-handling framework helps by externalizing all exception handling.

Policy-based fault-handling framework

Oracle SOA Suite 11*g* provides sophisticated error handling capabilities that enable you to easily define exception handling at various levels in a composite. It allows you to handle both system faults and application-generated business faults.

The fault-handling framework uses exception-handling *policies* described using XML. These exception-handling policies are attached to a composite and are not defined within its code. This allows you to reuse policy definitions across multiple components, composites, and projects.

Defining a policy

Fault-handling policies are defined in a file called `fault-policies.xml`. Policies map namespace-qualified named faults, such as `bpelx:runtimeFault` or `medns:mediatorFault`, to specific actions that should be performed when the fault occurs. The framework provides a number of predefined actions, such as actions for activating human intervention (`humanIntervention`), automatic retries (`retry`), termination (`abort`), and so on. You can also define custom actions using a Java action (`javaAction`).

A fault policy is defined by:

- Fault policy name (`FaultPolicy`)
- A list of faults in a policy (`Fault`)
- A set of fault conditions (`Condition`)
- A set of fault recovery actions corresponding to the fault and the fault condition (`Action`)

The following class diagram shows the relationships between the elements in a fault policy.

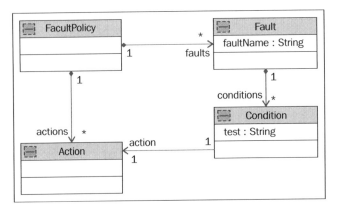

 Actions defined for a named fault in a fault policy override any exception handling defined for a corresponding exception in BPEL.

Binding a policy

Since a fault policy definition is not specific to a composite, you need a way to attach appropriate policies to your composite. This is done by binding a fault policy to a composite or to one or more components within a composite. This binding definition is specified in `fault-bindings.xml`.

Some concrete examples will help understand the policy-based exception handling. Just as before, you will extend the POProcessing project that you have built in the previous chapters to add policy-based exception handling.

Tutorial: Fault handling and fault policies

This tutorial will guide you in implementing very simple exception handling using both the BPEL-specific exception-handling constructs and policy-based exception handling for BPEL and Mediator.

Chapters 11-19 can be done in any order after completing Chapter 10.

In order to follow the tutorial in this chapter you must have either completed the tutorial from Chapter 10 or higher, or set up the environment as described in Chapter 4 and deployed the solution for Chapter 10, which can be found in `c:\po\solutions\ch10`.

Handling remote faults

The first part of the tutorial covers handling an exception caused by a service being unavailable. This type of exception is called a remote fault and you will define a fault policy for handling it. To simulate this condition, you will make the `getStatusByCC` service unavailable and test POProcessing to see how the composite handles the exception without a policy in place. You will then add a fault-handling policy to handle the exception.

Testing service unavailability

Shut the `validationForCC` composite down to simulate that the service is unavailable.

1. Navigate to the **Application Server Navigator** in JDeveloper (**View | Application Server Navigator**).

2. Expand the SOA node under the **MyAppServerConnection** and select **validationForCC**.

3. Right-click and select **Turn Off**.

 You can also turn a composite off from the Enterprise Manager Console

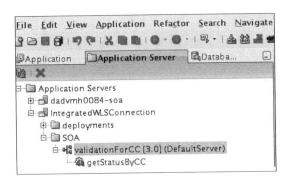

4. From the Enterprise Manager console in your web browser, invoke the **POProcessing** composite. Use the following XML as input while testing the composite—note that you can also find this XML in the following file:
`C:\po\input\po-large-iPodx30.txt`.

```
<soap:Envelope xmlns:soap="http://schemas.xmlsoap.org/soap/
envelope/">
    <soap:Body xmlns:ns1="http://xmlns.oracle.com/ns/order">
        <ns1:PurchaseOrder>
            <ns1:CustID>1111</ns1:CustID>
            <ns1:ID>2222</ns1:ID>
            <ns1:productName>iPod shuffle</ns1:productName>
            <ns1:itemType>Electronics</ns1:itemType>
            <ns1:price>145</ns1:price>
            <ns1:quantity>30</ns1:quantity>
            <ns1:status>Initial</ns1:status>
            <ns1:ccType>Mastercard</ns1:ccType>
            <ns1:ccNumber>1234-1234-1234-1234</ns1:ccNumber>
        </ns1:PurchaseOrder>
    </soap:Body>
</soap:Envelope>
```

5. In the Enterprise Manager console, click on the new instance ID of the **POProcessing** composite to view the flow trace. You should see that the composite has terminated with a remote fault. In addition, there is no way to restart it if you were to make the **getStatusByCC** service operation available.

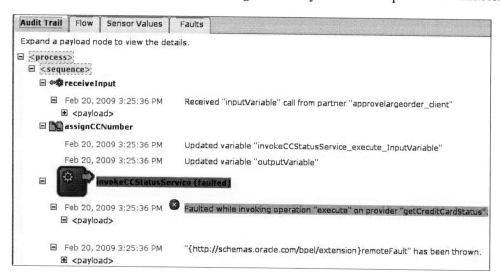

This is the default behavior for this type of exception. Every exception has a default behavior, for example, a binding fault is not automatically retried by default. You will see further in this tutorial how one can change the default behavior by applying appropriate policies.

Creating a fault policy

Now, add a fault-handling policy to catch this exception and make it recoverable after manual intervention.

To begin with, create a skeleton policy and fault-binding definition. Start by creating a fault policy file. Alternatively, you can copy the skeleton policy file from `c:\po\schemas\fault-policies.xml` to `c:\po\POProcessing\POProccsing\fault-policies.xml` and refresh the file list in JDeveloper.

1. In JDeveloper, right-click on the **POProcessing** project and select **New**.

2. Select the **All Technologies** tab.

3. Select **XML** in the **General Categories**.

4. Select **XML Document** in the **Items** pane.

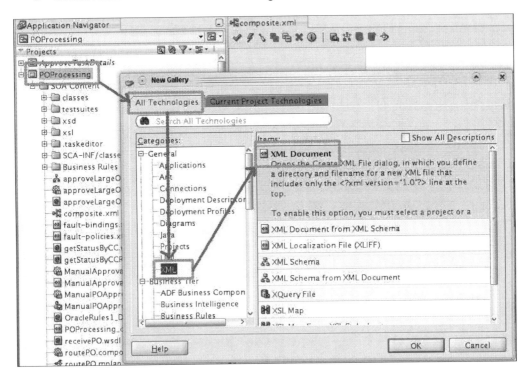

5. Name the new file `fault-policies.xml`.

The names of the policy and the binding definition files can be other than `fault-bindings.xml` and `fault-policies.xml` and they can reside in a location different than the one `composite.xml` resides in. The location can be either within a local directory or remote. If this is the case, you need to specifically define the name and location of these files in `composite.xml` as properties. Here is an example of such a definition in `composite.xml`:

```
<property
name="oracle.composite.faultPolicyFile">/home/oracle/
faultpolicyfiles/my-fault-policies.xml
</property>
<property    name="oracle.composite.faultBindingFile">/
home/oracle/faultpolicyfiles/my-fault-bindings.xml
</property>
```

6. Add the following to the `fault-policies.xml`:

```xml
<?xml version="1.0" encoding="UTF-8" ?>
<faultPolicies xmlns="http://schemas.oracle.com/bpel/faultpolicy">
  <faultPolicy version="2.0.1"
              id="POProcessingFaults"
              xmlns:env="http://schemas.xmlsoap.org/
                          soap/envelope/"
              xmlns:xs="http://www.w3.org/2001/XMLSchema"
              xmlns="http://schemas.oracle.com/bpel/faultpolicy"
              xmlns:xsi="http://www.w3.org/2001/
                          XMLSchema-instance">
    <Conditions>
      <!-- Step #1: Add your fault handler for remote
          fault here: -->

      <!-- Step #2: Add your fault handler for binding
          fault here: -->

      <!-- Step #3: Add your fault handler for mediator
          faults here: -->

    </Conditions>

    <Actions>

      <!-- Step #4: Add the Action definition for handling
          mediator faults using custom java here:-->

      <!-- Custom Java Handler: Logs the fault details
          to a log file -->
      <Action id="my-java-handler">
        <javaAction className="soatraining.faulthandling.
                              MyFaultHandler"
                defaultAction="ora-terminate"
                              propertySet="myProps">
          <returnValue value="OK" ref="ora-rethrow-fault"/>
        </javaAction>
      </Action>

      <!-- Retry -->
      <Action id="ora-retry">
        <retry>
          <retryCount>4</retryCount>
          <retryInterval>2</retryInterval>
          <exponentialBackoff/>
        </retry>
      </Action>
```

```xml
<!-- Rethrow action -->
<Action id="ora-rethrow-fault">
  <rethrowFault/>
</Action>

<!-- Human Intervention -->
<Action id="ora-human-intervention">
  <humanIntervention/>
</Action>

<!-- Terminate -->
<Action id="ora-terminate">
  <abort/>
</Action>
</Actions>
<!-- Property sets used by custom Java actions -->
<Properties>
 <!-- Property set for MyFaultHandler customer java action -->
  <propertySet name="myProps">
    <property name="logFileName">myfaulthandler.log</property>
    <property name="logFileDir">c:\temp</property>
  </propertySet>

  <!-- Step #5: Add new property set for MyFaultHandler
       for logging Mediator faults here:-->

</Properties>
</faultPolicy>
</faultPolicies>
```

7. Save the file.

8. Follow the same steps to create another XML file. This time, name the file as `fault-bindings.xml`. Alternatively, you can copy the bindings file from `c:\ po\schemas\fault-bindings.xml` to `c:\po\POProcessing\POProccsing\fault-bindings.xml` and refresh the file list in JDeveloper.

9. Add the following to this file:

```xml
<?xml version="1.0" encoding="UTF-8" ?>
<faultPolicyBindings version="2.0.1"
                    xmlns="http://schemas.oracle.com/bpel/
                           faultpolicy"
                    xmlns:xsi="http://www.w3.org/2001/XMLSchema-
                               instance">
  <composite faultPolicy="POProcessingFaults"/>
</faultPolicyBindings>
```

10. Save the file.

> The fault-binding definition attaches policies to a composite. In the above code sample, you are binding the policy named **POProcessingFaults** to the **POProcessing** composite. Notice that the name of the composite is not explicitly defined. The binding to the POProcessing composite is implicit. This is because when the project is compiled and packaged, if `fault-bindings.xml` and `fault-policies.xml` exist in the same directory as the `composite.xml`, then the binding is applied to that composite.

11. Open the `fault-policies.xml` file in JDeveloper and add the following XML to handle all remote faults that occur in any component in the POProcessing composite under the comment marked Step #1.

```xml
<faultName xmlns:bpelx="http://schemas.oracle.com/bpel/extension"
                        name="bpelx:remoteFault">
    <condition>
        <action ref="ora-human-intervention"/>
    </condition>
</faultName>
```

> This defines a new policy for handling a fault called **remoteFault**. As mentioned earlier, a policy maps an exception to a set of actions and can specify conditions for which these actions are taken. In this step, you used the action for unconditionally forcing human intervention whenever a `remoteFault` occurs.

12. Click on the **Save All** button and deploy the **POProcessing** composite.

13. Invoke the **POProcessing** composite using the Web Service tester in the Enterprise Manager console.

14. Navigate to the instance ID of the newly invoked **POProcessing** to view the flow trace.

15. In the flow trace window, click on **approveLargeOrder** to view the BPEL
    Audit Trail. You will see that the activity has faulted as before but this time
    it is waiting for a manual recovery. The circled icon shows that the fault
    is recoverable.

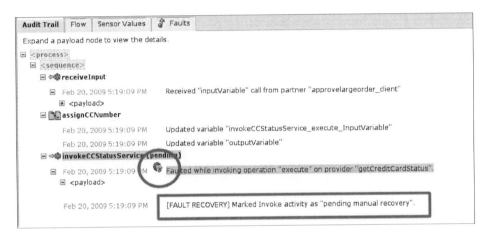

16. Before you attempt a recovery, start the **validationForCC** composite from the
    Application Server Navigator in JDeveloper. In this case, select **Turn On** to
    startup the composite.

17. Back in the **Flow Trace** window, select the **Faults** tab.

18. Click on the row containing the fault. This will show the fault details
    including the contents of the input variable to the invoke activity.

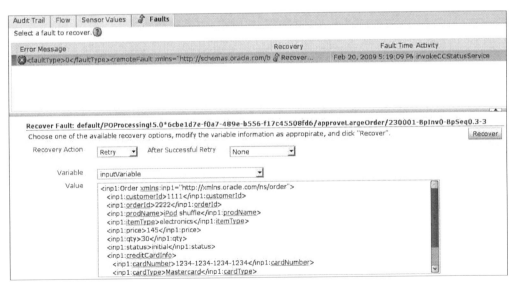

Repairing invalid input payloads in Enterprise Manager
You can repair text-based input payloads directly in Enterprise Manager.
As seen in the above screenshot, you could have edited the payload
before attempting the recovery. This is useful when the cause of the fault
is a malformed message.

19. Select **Retry** as the recovery action and click on **Recover**.

20. You should see the fault clear up from the **Faults** tab. Click on the **Audit
    Trail** tab to view the BPEL flow. You should see that the BPEL has completed
    the execution successfully (you may need to refresh the window to see the
    updated trace).

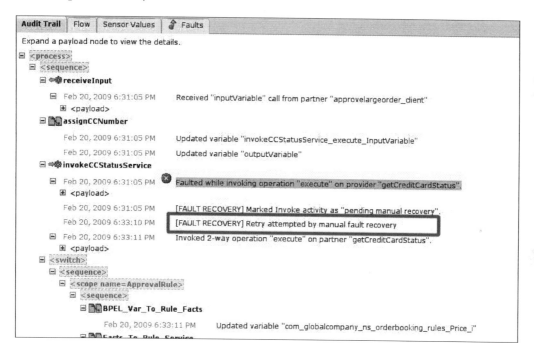

Handling exceptions in BPEL

In the case of BPEL, you can choose to handle exceptions within the process itself
rather than using the fault-handling framework.

For example, in the current implementation of `validateForCC`, while doing the
credit card validation, if a non-existing credit card number is passed to the service, it
just returns an empty response. If the service were to throw a specific exception for
such unknown credit card numbers, you would want to catch that exception and set
the status in the order appropriately.

While system faults are better handled using the policy-based fault-handling framework, handling exceptions in BPEL is the preferred approach for most application-generated exceptions, also called Business faults.

This part of the tutorial illustrates this scenario.

You will modify the `validateForCC` composite to call a database stored function for validating credit cards starting with a specific number. This stored function throws a PL/SQL application exception with an error code of 20001 for credit card numbers not found in the database. You will catch and handle this exception in BPEL.

1. Create the stored function in the SOADEMO schema by running the following SQL script. You can find this script in C:\po\sql\ create_ validate_cc.sql.

```
CREATE OR REPLACE FUNCTION VALIDATECC(cc_number IN VARCHAR2)
RETURN VARCHAR2 AS
    l_status   CREDITCARDINFO.STATUS%TYPE;
BEGIN
    SELECT status
    INTO    l_status
    FROM    creditcardinfo
    WHERE   ccnumber = cc_number;
    RETURN l_status;
EXCEPTION
    WHEN NO_DATA_FOUND THEN
        raise_application_error(-20001, 'UNKNOWN CREDIT CARD');
END VALIDATECC;
/
```

2. Open the `CreditCardValidation` composite and drop a Database adapter into the **External References** swim lane. Step through the wizard to create the reference to the stored function just created using the following values:

   ○ **Service Name:** validateCC

   ○ **Connection:** soademoDatabase

   ○ **Schema:** select SOADEMO

   ○ **JNDI Name:** eis/DB/soademoDatabase

   ○ **Operation Type: Call a Stored Procedure or Function**

   ○ **Procedure:** Browse and select **VALIDATECC**

   Wire the **RouteRequest** mediator component to **validateCC**:

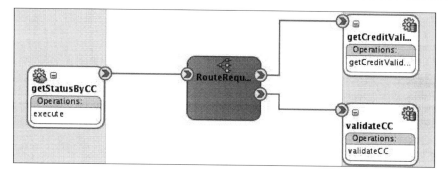

3. Open the **RouteRequest** mediator and add the filter expression for **getCreditValidationSelect** to route all requests for credit card numbers that *don't* start with the number **2**.

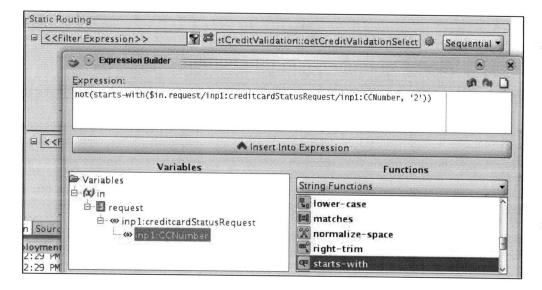

4. Add a filter expression for **validateCC** to route only those requests that have credit card numbers starting with **2** to the database stored function.

5. Create a new transformation for the **validateCC** route, mapping **CCNumber** to **db:CC_NUMBER**. There is no need to put a transformation on the reply since this service never replies but always raises a fault.

6. Save all and deploy the composite.

7. Now make sure that the change is working as expected. Use the web service tester in the Enterprise Manager Console to test the service. Enter credit card number `1234-1234-1234-1234` and you should see a response with status as `VALID`. Try the test again, except this time change the credit card number

to 2234-1234-1234-1234. You should see an error—ORA-20001 UNKNOWN CREDIT CARD.

8. Now, update the **POProcessing** composite to handle this fault in the BPEL component.

9. Open the **POProcessing** composite in JDeveloper.

10. Open the **approveLargeOrder** BPEL process.

11. Add a new Scope activity above the **invokeCCStatusService** activity. Rename it to **checkCC**.

12. Expand the **checkCC** scope and move the **invokeCCStatusService** into the scope.

13. Click on **Add Catch Branch** to add a catch branch and click on **+** to expand it.

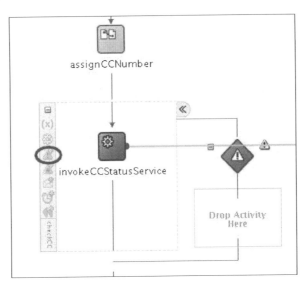

14. Double-click on **Catch** and enter **Fault** details. For **Namespace URI** and **Local** part click on the browse icon and select **System Faults | bindingFault**. Auto create the fault variable and accept the default name.

15. Drop a **Switch** activity in the catch block.

16. Open the expression editor for **<case>** and build an expression checking for **code** in **FaultVar** equal to **'20001'3**.

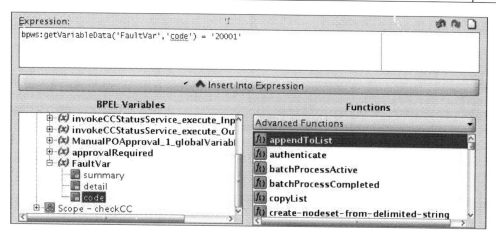

17. Add an **Assign** activity in the **<case>** block to assign the literal string 'UKNOWN CC' to the variable **invokeCCStatusService_execute_ OutputVariable -> reply -> creditcardStatus**.

18. In the **<otherwise>** block, drop a **Throw** activity. Open the **Throw** activity and name it Throw_Binding_Fault. Using the browse button select **System Faults | bindingFault**. For the fault variable, select the fault variable created in the earlier step.

19. The new updated flow should look like the following screenshot:

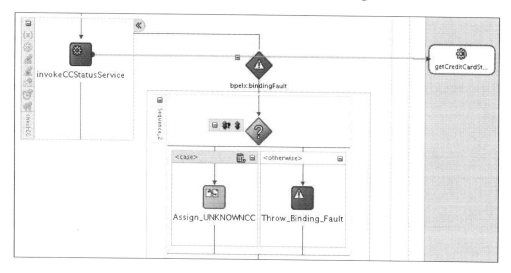

20. Add the following to `fault-policies.xml` after the comment for step 2.

```
<faultName xmlns:bpelx="http://schemas.oracle.com/bpel/extension"
           name="bpelx:bindingFault">
    <condition>
        <!-- Let the component handle this specific
           binding fault -->
        <test>$fault.code="20001"</test>
        <action ref="ora-rethrow-fault"/>
    </condition>
</faultName>
```

 The fault-handling framework takes precedence over the BPEL `catch`, therefore you need to have the fault-handling framework re-throw the fault so that BPEL can process it.

21. Deploy and test the **POProcessing** composite. Use the following XML as input. You can also find this here: `c:\po\input\po-large-iPodx30.txt` but you will change the credit card number as shown below:

```
<soap:Envelope xmlns:soap="http://schemas.xmlsoap.org/soap/
envelope/">
    <soap:Body xmlns:ns1="http://xmlns.oracle.com/ns/order">
        <ns1:PurchaseOrder>
            <ns1:CustID>1111</ns1:CustID>
            <ns1:ID>2222</ns1:ID>
            <ns1:productName>iPod shuffle</ns1:productName>
            <ns1:itemType>Electronics</ns1:itemType>
            <ns1:price>145</ns1:price>
            <ns1:quantity>30</ns1:quantity>
            <ns1:status>Initial</ns1:status>
            <ns1:ccType>Mastercard</ns1:ccType>
            <ns1:ccNumber>2234-1234-1234-1234</ns1:ccNumber>
        </ns1:PurchaseOrder>
    </soap:Body>
</soap:Envelope>
```

22. Note that the `ccNumber` in the above XML starts with a number 2 to force the composite take the path that will create the exception. Once you execute the composite, you should see a fault being re-thrown from the fault-handling framework and being caught and processed in the BPEL process.

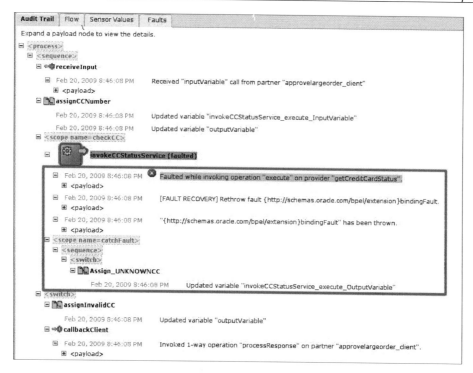

Using a custom Java fault handler

In addition to some of the pre-defined actions like `humanIntervention`, `rethrowFault`, `abort`, and so on, you can also define your own custom exception handler using Java.

In this exercise, you will change the policy for `bindingFault` and, instead of re-throwing the fault, you will use a custom Java class to handle it.

1. Install the custom Java handler by copying the provided `myfaulthandler.jar` available in `c:\po\lib` to the `lib` directory of your Weblogic Server domain home: `c:\Oracle\Middleware\home_11gR1\user_projects\domains\domain1\lib`. If you would like to see the Java source for this handler you will find it in the solutions folder for this chapter.

2. Restart the Weblogic SOA server.

3. Modify the `fault-policies.xml` and change the `bindingFault` handling that you just added from:

```
<faultName xmlns:bpelx="http://schemas.oracle.com/bpel/extension"
                name="bpelx:bindingFault">
        <condition>
                <!-- Let the component handle this specific
```

```
                                binding fault -->
                            <test>$fault.code="20001"</test>
                            <action ref="ora-rethrow-fault"/>
                    </condition>
                </faultName>
```

to

```
<faultName xmlns:bpelx="http://schemas.oracle.com/bpel/extension"
                            name="bpelx:bindingFault">
            <condition>
                    <!-- Let the component handle this specific
                        binding fault -->
                    <test>$fault.code="20001"</test>
                    <action ref="my-java-handler"/>
            </condition>
        </faultName>
```

 With this modification, you changed the exception-handling behavior from re-throwing the fault to running some Java code before re-throwing the fault.

4. This custom Java code will simply write the details of the fault to a log file and return. Once the Java code completes execution, depending on the return value of the Java call, the framework will take appropriate action. In this case, the Java code always returns a status of OK and the exception-handling definition is set to re-throw the fault on receiving an OK. The following code snippet from `fault-policy.xml` shows how you define a Java fault handler. The `defaultAction` attribute defines the action to be taken in case the Java class returns values that are not explicitly handled.

```
<!-- Custom Java Handler: Logs the fault details to a log file -->
        <Action id="my-java-handler">
            <javaAction className="soatraining.faulthandling.
                                    MyFaultHandler"
                        defaultAction="ora-terminate"
                        propertySet="myProps">
                <returnValue value="OK" ref="ora-rethrow-fault"/>
            </javaAction>
        </Action>
```

 This change for handling an exception was done without modifying either the BPEL component or the composite.

5. Ensure that the directory `c:\po\log` exists. If you would like the log file to be created in a different directory, modify the `logFileDir` property in the `fault-policies.xml` file.

6. Deploy the **POProcessing** composite and test using the same XML input as before. You should see a file, `myfaulthandler.log`, in `c:\po\log`. You should also see that **POProcessing** handles the fault when you view the composite process instance in the Enterprise Manager console.

Handling Mediator faults

Since the Mediator doesn't provide any built-in exception-handling mechanism, the policy-based fault handler is the only way to catch and handle exceptions occurring in the Mediator. A variety of exceptions can be caught ranging from adapter exceptions to transformation exceptions.

In this exercise, you define an exception handler for catching all Mediator faults and use the custom Java handler to write a log file. To force the Mediator to throw a fault, simulate a disk write error and have the File adapter throw an exception.

1. Modify `fault-policies.xml` and add the following after the comment that contains the text Step #3. This defines a new fault handler for all mediator faults and refers to a new action called `my-mediator-fault-handler`.

```
<faultName xmlns:medns="http://schemas.oracle.com/mediator/faults"
name="medns:mediatorFault">
    <condition>
        <action ref="my-mediator-fault-handler"/>
</condition>
</faultName>
```

2. Now define the new action by adding the following XML to the fault policy file. Insert the following XML after the comment starting with Step #4. This defines a Java action using the same custom Java class that you used in the earlier exercise but uses a different set of properties and also defines a different action to be performed on return from the custom Java call.

```
<Action id="my-mediator-fault-handler">
    <javaAction className="soatraining.faulthandling.
                          MyFaultHandler"
            defaultAction="ora-terminate"
            propertySet="myMediatorProps">
        <returnValue value="OK" ref="ora-human-intervention">
    </returnValue>
    </javaAction>
</Action>
```

3. Add the following after the comment starting with Step #5. This defines the property set that is to be used by the new `javaAction`.

```
<propertySet name="myMediatorProps">
        <property name="logFileName">
            mediator-faults.log
        </property>
        <property name="logFileDir">c:\po\log</property>
</propertySet>
```

 Property sets allow you to pass information to the Java class that will be handling the exception.

4. Open the **routePO** mediator component and change the route for the filter `price*quantity < 1000` to **Parallel** from **Sequential**.

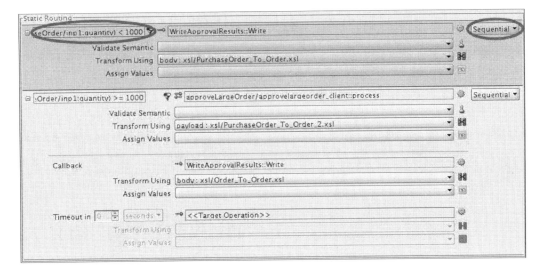

5. Select **Yes** when prompted.

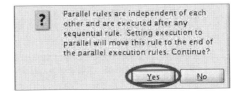

6. You should see the following change when you are done:

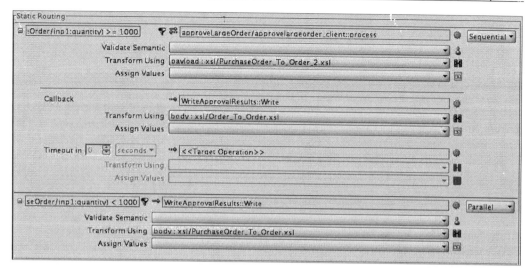

> Without this change, the fault policy handler will not get control when an exception occurs in the Mediator. This is because sequential routes are executed in the same thread and transaction context as the caller of the mediator service. If an exception occurs while executing a sequential route, it is thrown back to the caller and the fault handler is bypassed, otherwise, it could potentially break the transaction. In case of a parallel route, a new thread and new transaction context is created by the Mediator, within which the route is executed. If an exception occurs while executing a parallel route, and a matching fault policy exists, the appropriate fault handler is executed.

7. Deploy the `POProcessing` composite.

8. Change the permission of the directory `c:\temp` to read-only. This will force an error while writing the PO file.

   ○ In Windows, open a command window and enter:

   ```
   > attrib +r c:\temp
   ```

   to make the directory read-only. Once done with this exercise, remove the read-only attribute as follows:

   ```
   > attrib -r c:\temp
   ```

   ○ In Linux, open a command window and enter:

   ```
   $ chmod -w /temp
   ```

   to make the directory read-only. Once done with this exercise, remove the read-only attribute as follows:

   ```
   $ chmod +w /temp
   ```

9. Test the POProcessing composite using an order that is less than $1,000. This time, change the value of the element ccNumber to be 1234-1234-1234-1234, which is a valid credit card so that the process will complete successfully and will try to write the approval to c:\temp and fail. You should see a file, mediator-faults.log, in the c:\po\log directory.

    The SOA Console should show the composite waiting for manual recovery.

Summary

As you have seen in this chapter, you can build high-quality composites without cluttering the implementation with a lot of duplicated code for handling exceptions. Delegating most exception handling to a comprehensive fault-handling framework, like the one available on Oracle SOA Suite 11*g*, not only allows for creating bulletproof composite applications, but also substantially reduces the cost of maintaining these applications. It also reduces the overall time to develop composite applications as exception handling is done declaratively rather than with coding and allows for significant reuse of shared policies.

Quick-build Instructions

Unlike other chapters in this book, this chapter does not have you implement a set of changes to your POProcessing composite but rather shows you how to implement exception handling using policy-based fault handling. As such, instructions summarizing the edits made in this chapter is not applicable.

15
Securing Services

Security tends to be almost an after-thought when it comes to application design. In cases where it is designed into the application, it gets embedded in the code along with business logic. In a service-oriented application, this goes against the concept of separation of concerns and reduces the overall flexibility of the application.

Just as you look for opportunities to externalize business rules-based decision making logic to a rules engine, you should also externalize all security-related, non-functional code. This frees up the developer to concentrate on functional aspects of application development and not worry about security.

Introducing security policy management

Just externalizing security won't address all the issues around implementing comprehensive security in your service-oriented applications. What's needed is a zero-code—a declarative – way of enforcing security using centrally managed policies.

Some of the key challenges that need to be addressed in regards to creating secure service-oriented applications are:

- **Interoperability**: Although one would like to have a single technology stack for security, the reality is that there will be a variety of security products that provide different types of functions. For instance, one product may provide authentication services and another fine-grained authorization services.

- **End-to-end identity propagation**: As you have seen in the previous chapters, a typical SOA composite uses multiple components using different technologies to provide a set of business functions. These composites also use external services as part of their processing. If these different components and services require authentication, you don't want go through the whole process of authentication for every invocation of every component or service. Identity propagation implies establishing the identity at the start of the conversation and then propagating that identity throughout the conversation.

- **Security as a system administration function**: As mentioned earlier, managing and enforcing security should be a system administration function not something that has to be developed and coded.

Before looking at how to address these challenges, first we define the basic requirements for securing an SOA composite:

1. Authenticating the client invoking the composite.

2. Authorizing the client to gain access to the service.

3. Signing the SOAP message to avoid tampering.

4. Encrypting the SOAP message to protect it from prying eyes.

5. If the composite in turn invokes another service or composite, the original identity of the client may need to be propagated securely to the target service.

Securing your composites using Oracle Web Services Manager

Oracle Web Services Manages (OWSM) is an integral component of the SOA Infrastructure in SOA Suite 11*g*. It provides a policy-based, completely declarative way of implementing secure SOA applications. OWSM supports centrally managed policies by providing policy management functions that are available through the **Oracle Enterprise Manager (EM)**. The OWSM runtime is built-in into the service infrastructure and implements an interceptor-based framework for enforcing security policies for web services invocations.

In addition to providing security services, OWSM supports generalized, standards-based policy management, attachment, and enforcement. Policies can be created and attached to composite services, references, and components. Some examples of policies are:

- Authorization policies, to gain access to a composite
- **WS-Security** policy for security
- **WS-Addressing** policy for addressing of SOAP messages
- **Message Transmission Optimization Mechanism (MTOM)**, for optimally handling large binary data
- **WS-ReliableMessaging** for reliability
- Management policies for actions like logging, and so on

Policy management and attachment are integrated seamlessly in the EM console. Policy attachment is also integrated seamlessly in JDeveloper. You can also enable/disable policies or attach new policies during deployment by using a deployment plan. There are a large number of predefined policies that are available for use out of the box. Typically you would use JDeveloper to attach policies in development, and change the policy during deployment into production or change it in the production EM console.

Identity management

For authentication to succeed, users and groups need to be defined in some identity store. There are many options for identity management with SOA Suite. Oracle has identity management solutions that can be used. Alternatively, you can plug in external identity management solutions.

In this chapter, we will only focus on the default capability in WebLogic Server to define users and groups. WebLogic has built-in user management based on the internal LDAP.

Use SSL

An alternative, at least for some aspects of security, to using web services security with OWSM is to use one-way or two-way SSL. The main advantage of SSL is that it is widely used and you do not need a sophisticated web services stack to send and receive messages. However OWSM provides more security capabilities than SSL provides. Examples are **Security Assertion Markup Language (SAML)** for identity propagation and a variety of security authentication tokens like **Kerberos token**, **username token**, and **X509 token**.

A quick look at the policy management UI

To understand the full scope of policy management, including how to author policies, is beyond the scope of this book. In this chapter, we focus on how to attach and enforce policies for composites.

However, you can take a quick look at the policy management console:

1. In the EM console, select **Weblogic Domain** in the lefthand area and right-click on **domain1**.
2. Select **Web Services** and then **Policies**. Look at the policies being managed and the commands to export and import custom policies.

Tutorial: Securing the credit card validation service

Try out a simple OWSM use case by adding policies to the `POProcessing` and `ValidationForCC` composites that you have been building in previous chapters.

You will attach a policy to the service entry point to the `POProcessing` composite to authenticate based on the user ID/password in the SOAP header (**usernameToken**). The identity of the client is securely propagated to the credit card validation composite using a **SAML** token. The invocation of the credit card validation composite passes sensitive data. Hence, you should sign and encrypt the message. This is done by attaching the appropriate policies to the reference in the `POProcessing` composite to invoke `validationForCC` and to the service entry point to `validationForCC` composite.

After testing the secured service, you detach the policies.

Chapters 11-19 can be done in any order after completing Chapter 10.

In order to follow the tutorial in this chapter you must have either completed the tutorial from Chapter 10 or higher, or set up the environment as described in Chapter 4 and deployed the solution for Chapter 10, which can be found in `c:\po\solutions\ch10`.

The state of the JDeveloper application at the end of this chapter is exactly the same as the state at the beginning of this chapter. Consequently there is no solution available for this chapter.

Defining a new user

You use the Weblogic console to define a new user that you use in this exercise.

1. Log into the Weblogic console at `http://localhost:7001/console`.
2. Click on **Security Realms** and then click on **myrealm**.

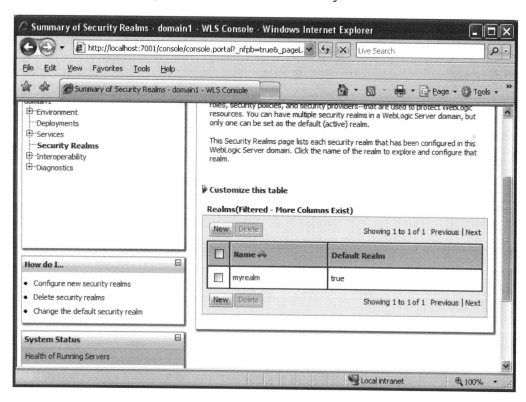

3. Click on the **Users and Groups** tab.

4. Click on **New**.

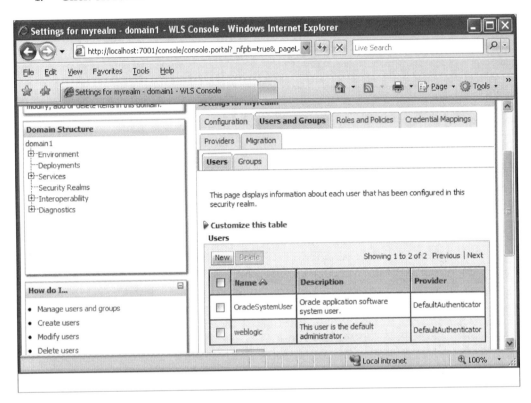

5. Create a new user `weblogic1` with password `welcome1` and click on **OK**.

6. Click on the **weblogic1** user and then click on **Groups** tab.

7. Select **Administrators** as the group and click on **Save**.

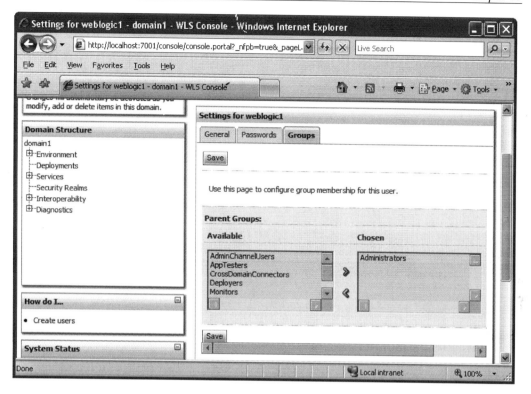

Attaching the policies

1. Log into the EM console at `http://localhost:7001/em`.
2. Click on the **POProcessing** composite link.
3. Click on the **Policies** tab.
4. Select **receivePO** in the **Attach To/Detach From** drop-down.

5. Select **wss_username_token_service_policy**, click on **Attach**, and click on **OK**.

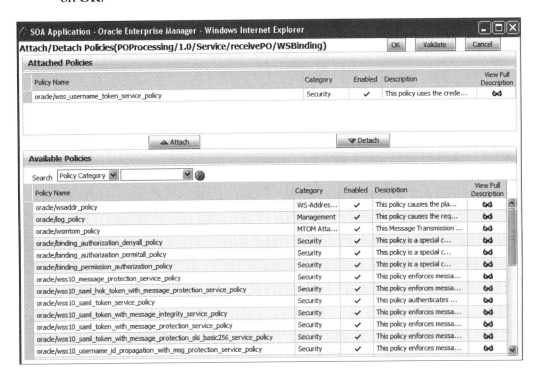

6. Similarly, attach the policy **wss11_saml_token_with_message_protection_ client_policy** to the attach point **getCreditCardStatus**.

7. Similarly, attach the policy **wss11_saml_token_with_message_ protection_service_policy** to the attach point **getStatusByCC** in the **validationForCC** composite.

8. Test using the EM test console.

9. Test **POProcessing** using the EM test console. Be sure to select **WSS Username Token** and specify the user ID/password as `weblogic1/welcome1`.

10. Retest, but specify an invalid password. You will see an authentication failure error.

11. Test **validationForCC**. But this time, do not specify any WSS Username Token. You will see an error because the SAML token is not present and the message is not signed and encrypted.

Detaching policies

1. Click on the **POProcessing** composite link.

2. Click on the **Policies** tab.

3. Select **receivePO** in the **Attach To/Detach From** drop-down.

4. Select the attached **wss_username_token_service_policy**, click on **Detach**, and click on **OK**.

5. Similarly detach the policy **wss11_saml_token_with_message_protection_ client_policy** from the attach point **getCreditCardStatus**.

6. Similarly detach the policy **wss11_saml_token_with_message_ protection_service_policy** from the attach point **getStatusByCC** in the **validationForCC** composite.

Attaching and detaching policies in JDeveloper

To attach/detach policies in JDeveloper, right-click on services, references, and components in the composite view and choose Configure WS Policies. Try to repeat the exercise you did in the EM console by yourself, but this time, use JDeveloper.

Summary

As you have seen in this chapter, a centrally-managed, policy-based security framework like the Oracle Web Services Manager enables you to develop SOA composite applications without worrying about security aspects but still create highly secure applications. This feature highlights how Oracle SOA 11*g* addresses one of the key challenges with service-oriented applications, which is securing applications and at the same time reducing complexity.

Quick-build Instructions

This section gives you all of the operations and names for objects created in this chapter. Experienced users can use this to bypass the step-by-step instructions and complete this chapter more quickly. The complete details for any particular operation listed here can be found in the preceding sections. The information is organized in the same manner that it is introduced in the chapter.

- Define a new user:
  - Username: **weblogic1**
  - Password: **welcome1**
  - Group: **administrators**

- Attach Policies:
  - **POProcessing** composite:
    - Attachpoint receivePO: **wss_username_token_service_policy**
    - Attachpoint getCreditCardStatus: **wss11_saml_token_with_ message_protection_client_policy**
  - **ValidationForCC** composite:
    - Attachpoint getStatusByCC: **wss11_saml_token_with_message_ protection_service_policy**
- Detach Policies: Detach all the previous policies

The application is completed. Deploy and test.

16

Gaining Visibility into Your Process Activities

Business agility is one of the key benefits that are expected to be derived from a successful SOA adoption. Agility requires that an enterprise be able to sense changes in business conditions, either opportunities or threats, and react to them in a timely manner. This requires almost real-time insight into the business process of the enterprise. Traditional **Business Intelligence (BI)** solutions can provide this insight, but it is typically not in real time and often lacks support for taking action in real time when certain events are identified. What's needed is a solution that monitors business activity by analyzing data streams from heterogeneous data sources, identifying and correlating events, and acting on them, all in real time. These actions could range from updating dashboards to reflect the change to activating a new business process to handle the new event.

Introducing Business Activity Monitoring (BAM)

Business Activity Monitoring (BAM) enables process visualization by providing real time visibility into **Key Performance Indicators (KPI)** of the process through real time dashboards and alerts. In Oracle BAM, time-ordered events are received in a continuous stream from various sources. These events are filtered, correlated, and aggregated by using continuous queries that run in memory. The results are evaluated against alert definitions and alerts fired as necessary. The changes are also pushed out to dashboards in real time. Oracle BAM can also provide scrolling time-based window metrics, for example, number of stock trades in the last hour.

Oracle BAM solution comprises two main components:

1. BAM Server: Processes, analyzes, and provides reporting capabilities.

2. BAM web application: Provides a rich user interface for a variety of functions, depending on the user's role and includes dashboards, reports creation, data objects management, and BAM server administration.

The following figure shows the high-level architecture of Oracle BAM:

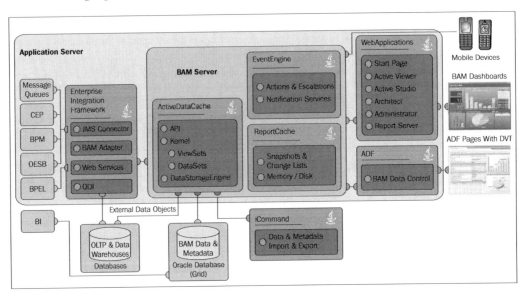

Oracle BAM Server

The Oracle BAM Server is a J2EE application that consists of the following key components:

- **Active Data Cache (ADC)** is a high-performance, persistent, memory-based storage system designed to support active data extracted from various enterprise data sources and provides access to business information for event-based reporting and alerting. Oracle BAM can receive data from a number of data sources, such as:

    ◦ **JMS**

    ◦ **SOA Composites**, including Mediator and BPEL using the BAM adapter as well as using sensors in a BPEL process

    ◦ Web service clients

    ◦ **Oracle Enterprise Manager**

    ◦ **Oracle Service Bus (OSB)** proxy services using the OSB reporting action and a plugin reporting provider

    ◦ **Oracle Data Integrator (ODI)** including change data capture

- **Report Cache** is responsible for assembling and formatting the data for live reports to be displayed in the users' dashboards. This is done by applying report definitions to the data sets retrieved from the ADC. When a user requests a report, the Report Cache obtains a snapshot of the most current data and establishes a change stream. Using the snapshot, it creates an initial display and sends it to the Report Server. After the browser has rendered the initial display, the Report Cache continually processes data as it changes, and forwards those changes to the Report Server.

- **Report Server**, as a stateless engine, is responsible for generating reports and rendering them in a client browser. It maintains an open connection to the user's browser so that it can stream real-time changes as and when it receives deltas from the Report Cache.

- **Event Engine** monitors the information in the ADC for user-defined conditions and rules and executes related actions.

Oracle BAM Web Application

Oracle BAM Web application is an AJAX-based, rich internet application that provides four distinct functions for working with Oracle BAM:

 Oracle BAM Web Application requires Microsoft Internet Explorer 7.

- **Active Viewer** provides dashboards for visualizing reports.
- **Active Studio** is used to create and manage report definitions and layout and provides a rich set of data visualization objects for creating active, real-time reports.
- BAM **Architect** is used to create and manage data objects used for reporting.
- BAM **Administrator** provides administration functions such as creating and managing data source definitions, and managing ownerships of data objects, reports, alerts, and so on. It also provides functions for user and role management.

Tutorial: Monitoring Business Activity in PO Processing

Now let us take a simple BAM use case. You extend the POProcessing application and enable it to send events to BAM so that you can view a report that shows a table of orders and the breakdown of orders by status and item type.

 Chapters 11-19 can be done in any order after completing Chapter 10.

In order to follow the tutorial in this chapter you must have either completed the tutorial from Chapter 10 or higher, or set up the environment as described in Chapter 4 and deployed the solution for Chapter 10, which can be found in `c:\po\solutions\ch10`.

Defining the data object

You first have to define the data object to hold the event data. This has to be done before the dashboard report can be created out of the data object.

1. Before you begin this lab, close any programs that you are not using to free up machine resources.

2. Your BAM server was installed during the installation process but it is not running yet. Start the BAM managed server in a command window as follows and wait for the RUNNING status (see Chapter 4 for more details about starting and stopping servers).

```
cd C:\Oracle\Middleware\home_11gR1\user_projects\domains\domain1

bin\startManagedWebLogic.cmd bam_server1
```

3. Go to `http://localhost:9001/OracleBAM` by using an Internet Explorer 7 browser and log in with the username and password you defined when you created the domain.

4. Open the **Architect** application.

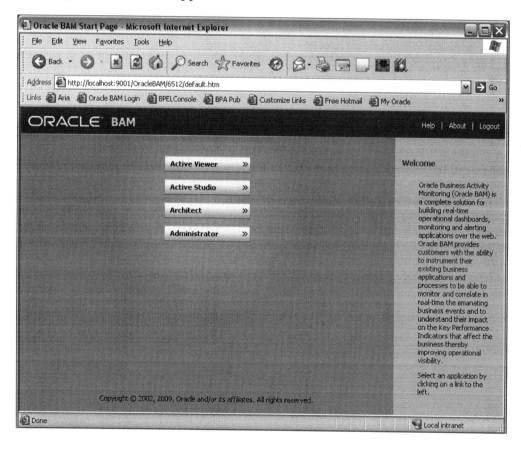

5. Click on the **Data Objects** link in the directory tree on the left pane and then click on the **Create subfolder** link on the top in the right pane. Enter **Training** and click on the **Create folder** button.

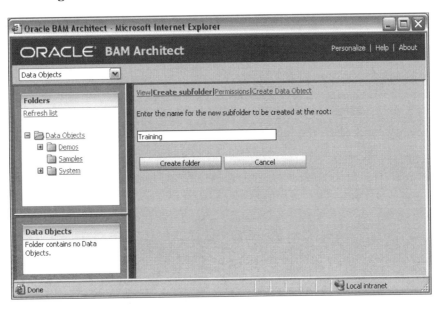

6. Click on **Continue** and **Create subfolder** again. This time, name it **POProcessing** and click on **Create folder** and then click on **Continue**. This creates a subfolder called **POProcessing** inside the **Training** folder.

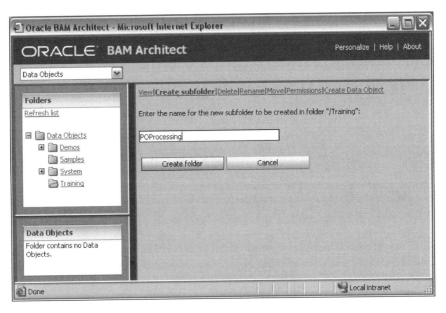

7. Add a new data object by clicking on the **Create Data Object** link.

8. Name the data object `Orders` and click on the **Add a field** link for each of the following data fields, setting the corresponding type and max size or scale:

Name	Type	Max Size or Scale
Order ID	String	30
Customer ID	String	30
Product Name	String	50
Item Type	String	30
Price	Decimal	10
Quantity	Decimal	10
Status	String	50
Total	Calculated	-
Received Date	Timestamp	-

9. When you choose **Calculated** for the type, you get the option to edit the formula. For the field **Total**, click on the **Edit formula** link. In the pop-up box, enter: **Price * Quantity** and click on **OK**.

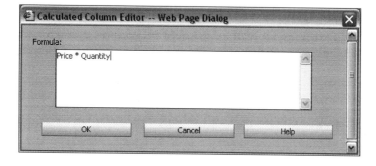

10. When you are ready, click on **Create Data Object**.

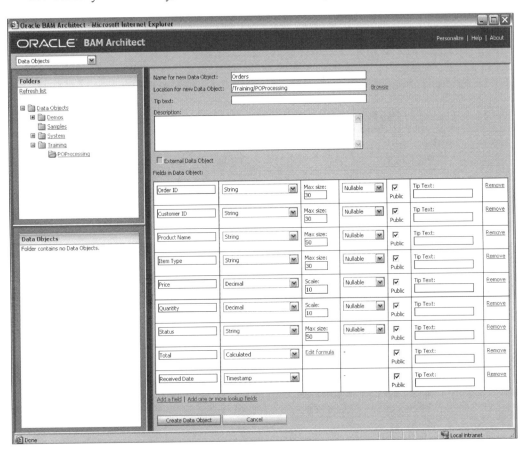

11. You should now see the **Orders** data object listed on the lefthand side. You can click on the **Orders** link and choose the **layout** link from the top righthand side to see the layout.

Defining the BAM dashboard

You now define the dashboard to display the breakdown of orders by status and item type.

1. Go back to the **BAM Start Page** window and choose **Active Studio**.

2. This opens up the report creation environment. You will create a report that everyone can view, so click on the **Shared Reports** tab.

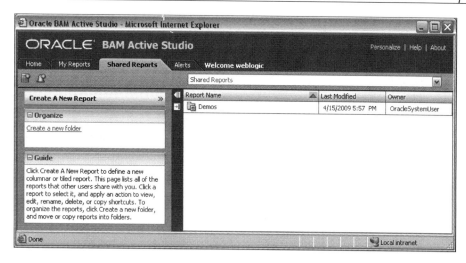

3. To keep reports organized, you create folders to put them in. Choose **Create a new folder** and name the folder **Training**. The **Training** folder shows up in the list in the main window.

4. Double-click on the new **Training** folder to open it. Choose **Create a new folder** and create a subfolder called **POProcessing**.

5. Double-click on **POProcessing** and then click on the **Create A New Report** button. This button is on the left, above the **Actions** section.

6. BAM provides some pre-defined layout templates for your report. Click on the one that gives you a large rectangle area at the top and two small square areas underneath (first column, third row).

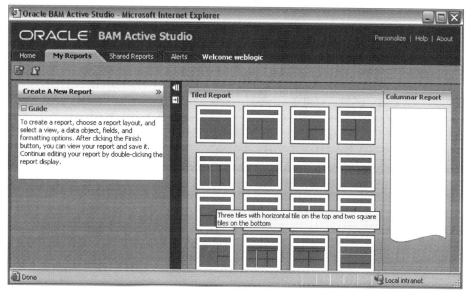

7. Give the report the title **PO Processing Report** by clicking on and typing in the title bar at the top.

Notice that you are provided with many options for types of charts that you can create.

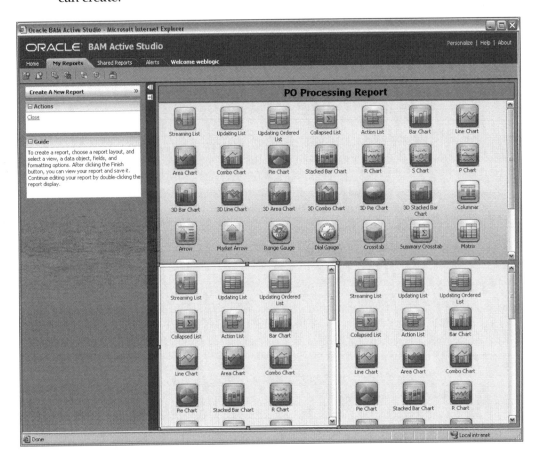

8. For the top, choose **Updating Ordered List** by clicking on that type.

9. You need to specify the data object to assign to this area. At the bottom of the screen, find the data object that you created by double-clicking on the **Training** and then the **POProcessing** folders, and selecting the **Orders** data object; then click on **Next**.

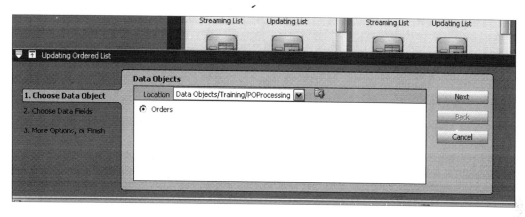

10. Click on **select all** and use the arrows to put the columns in a more user-friendly order, starting with the **Order ID**.

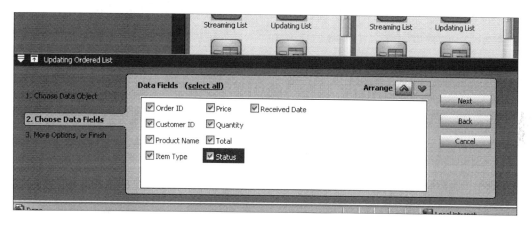

11. Click on **Next**, then click on **Finish**.

12. You need to follow a similar process for the other two views. On the lower lefthand side, click on **3D Pie Chart**.

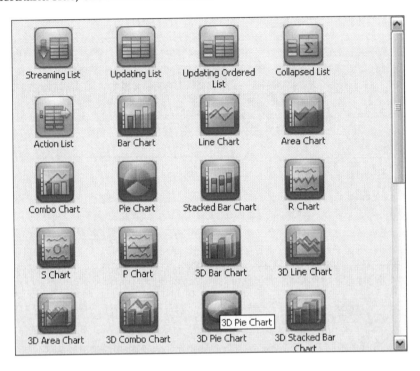

13. Assign the **Orders** data object and click on **Next**.

14. Choose **Item Type** as the **Group By** option, **Total** as the **Chart Values**, and with **Total** still selected, unselect **Sum** and instead choose **Percent of Total** as the **Summary Function**, then click on **Next**.

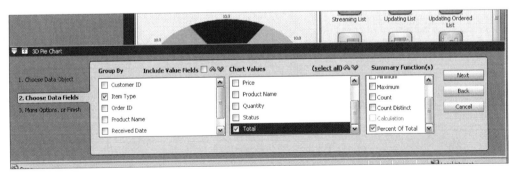

15. Now change some more options by clicking on **Change View Properties**.

16. Change the **View Title** to **Percentage of Total Sales by Item Type** and click on **OK**.

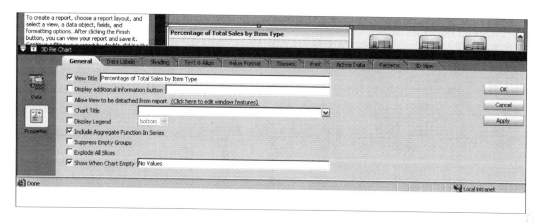

17. Set the final chart to **3D Bar Chart**.

18. Assign the **Orders** data object to it and **Group By Status**. Make the **Chart Values Order ID** and the **Summary Function Count**.

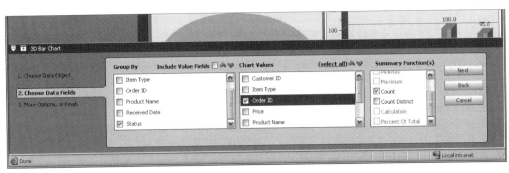

19. Click on **Next** and Choose **Change View Properties** to set the title of the view to **Purchase Orders by Status** and click on **OK**.

20. Click on the **Save Report** link, and then choose the **Shared Reports** button. Drill-down into the **Training/ POProcessing** folder and accept the default report name **PO Processing Report** and click on **OK**.

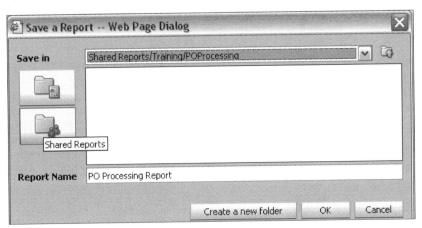

Configuring BAM Adapter on Weblogic Server

You use the BAM Adapter to send events to the data object from the POProcessing composite. Just like you had to configure the database adapter and the JMS adapter, you have to configure the BAM adapter using the Weblogic Server console before it can be used by a composite. In the BAM case, you use a pre-created Connection Pool and configure it for your environment.

1. First, create a BAM Plan directory as follows: `C:\Oracle\Middleware\ home_11gR1\Oracle_SOA1\soa\BAMPlan`.

2. Go to `http://localhost:7001/console` and log in with the username and password that you created for the domain.

3. Click on **Deployments** under the Domain Structure.

4. Locate and click on **OracleBamAdapter** (the name, not the checkbox).

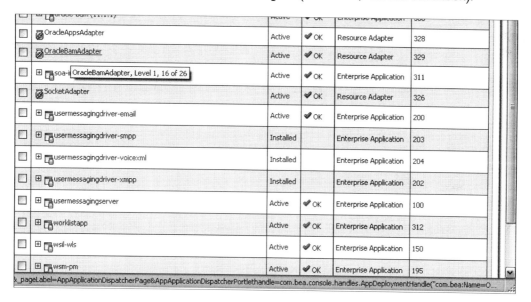

5. Click on **Configuration | Outbound Connection Pools**.

6. Expand **oracle.bam.adapter.adc.RMIConnectionFactory** and click on **eis/bam/rmi**.

7. Enter property values for the host name of the BAM server, username, password, and port 9001. The values can be edited by clicking on the **Property Value** field. Make sure that you press the *Enter* key after setting each value. Click on **Save**.

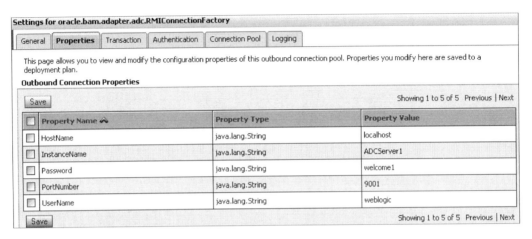

8. Save the plan `Plan.xml` in the new directory you created in step 1 above.

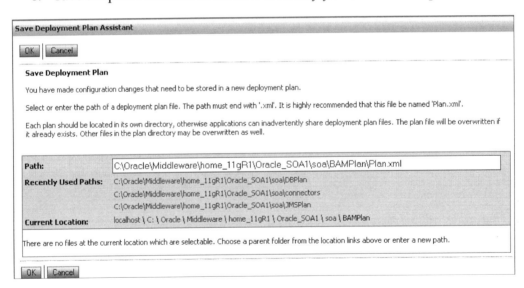

9. Update your deployment to reflect the changes. Go to the **Deployments** screen, select the checkbox for **OracleBamAdapter,** and choose **Update**.

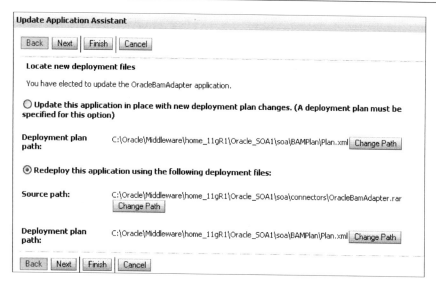

10. Click on **Finish** to finish updating the deployment.

11. Close the browser windows to recover some resources on your machine. You won't need them for a while.

Adding a BAM connection to POProcessing

POProcessing feeds data to the BAM report so it's time to add BAM to the composite.

First, you need a JDeveloper connection to the BAM server to view the data objects that are available so JDeveloper can generate appropriate WSDL files automatically.

1. Open JDeveloper and open the **POProcessing** application.

2. Create a connection to the BAM server by right-clicking on **Connections** in **Application Resources** and choosing **New Connection | BAM**.

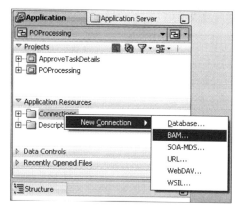

3. In step 1 (the **Name** screen), select **Application Resources**, accept the default name **BAMServerConnection1**, and click on **Next**.

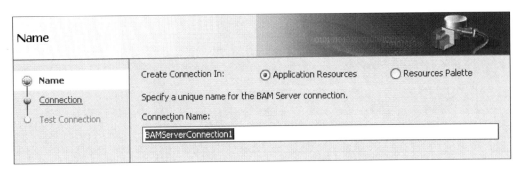

4. Enter the host name of your server for **BAM Web Host** and **BAM Server Host**.

5. Enter the HTTP port for BAM in the **HTTP Port** field. The HTTP port for BAM is in the URL for the Oracle BAM start page; for example, `http://localhost:9001/OracleBAM/`. It is the port number that was defined for the managed server `bam_server1` when you ran the configuration wizard.

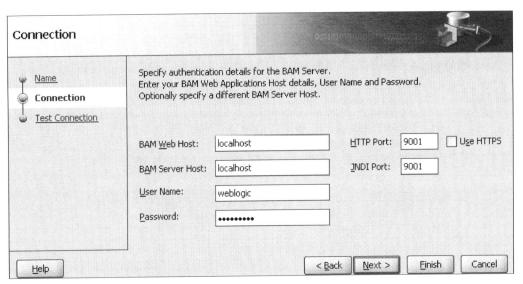

6. Enter the username and password.

7. Click on **Next**.

8. On the Test Connection page, click on the **Test Connection** button and confirm the connection is successful.

9. Click on the **Finish** button.

In the Application Navigator, **Application Resources** pane, the new BAM Server connection is listed in the **Connections** folder under the BAM node.

Adding a BAM Adapter to POProcessing

You now add a BAM adapter to the composite to send events to BAM.

1. Drag the **BAM Adapter** icon, which is located under **Service Adapters** into the **External References** column in composite.xml. The configuration wizard for the BAM Adapter opens.

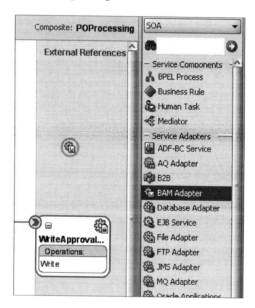

2. Give the service the name **OrdersBAMAdapter** and click on **Next**.

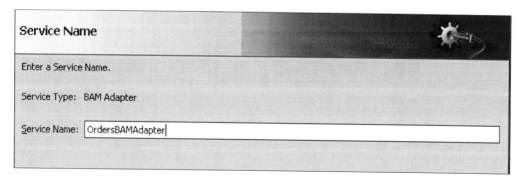

3. Use the **Browse** button to select the **Orders** data object under **BAMServerConnection1 | Training | POProcessing** and click on the **OK** button.

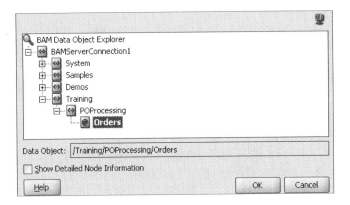

4. Change the **Operation** to **Upsert**, leave the default **Operation Name** as **writetoBAM**, and select **_Order_ID** as the key for the **Upsert** operation. The **Upsert** operation inserts the row if doesn't exist or updates it based upon the specified key.

5. Select the **Enable Batching** checkbox. This allows messages to be captured even when the BAM server is not available. When the BAM server is available again, messages that were generated while the server was down are sent.

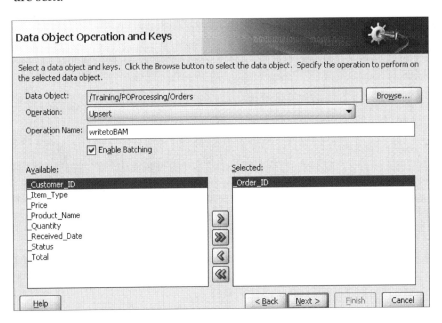

6. Click on the **Next** button.

7. Change the **JNDI name** to **eis/bam/rmi** to use the connection pool you configured for BAM.

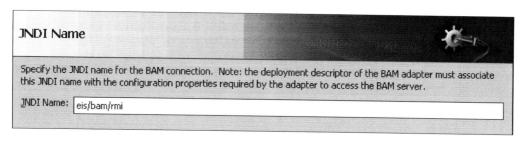

10. In the final step, click on the **Finish** button.

Modifying the Mediator component

You now modify the mediator to send events to BAM with the BAM adapter.

1. Drag a link from the **Route PO** Mediator component to the **OrdersBAMAdapter** reference that you just created. This creates a link between the mediator and the BAM Adapter.

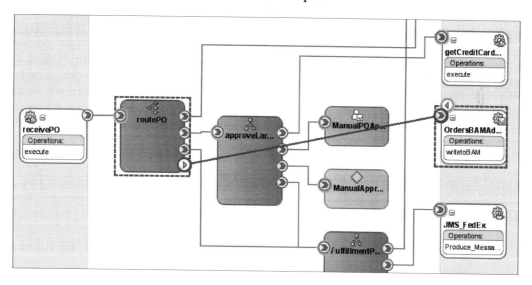

2. Double-click on the **routePO** mediator, to modify the configuration.

3. Find the **OrdersBAMAdapter::writetoBAM** operation and click on the icon next to **Transform Using** to create a transformation map.

4. Choose **Create New Mapper File**, accept the default name, and click on **OK**.

5. This opens the new mapper file. Drag from each field in the Purchase Order request to the corresponding field in the **OrdersBAMAdapter** WSDL. You do not need to drag anything for the **_Total** and **_Received_Date** fields as these are populated automatically for you in BAM.

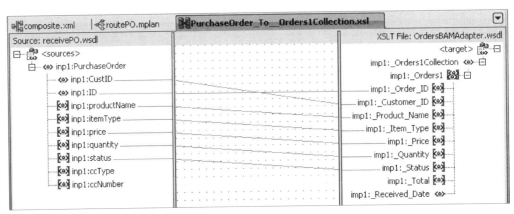

6. When you have finished the mapping, choose **Save All** from the **File** menu to save all files that were created or modified.

Testing the adapter connection

Test that the mediator routes the data to the BAM data object.

1. Deploy the composite.

2. Test in the EM console with `c:\po\input\small_validCC.txt` as the sample payload.

3. Log in to BAM Architect and verify that the data was received in the data object by selecting the **Orders Data Object** and the **Contents** link. This verifies that the adapter changes were made correctly and everything is working properly.

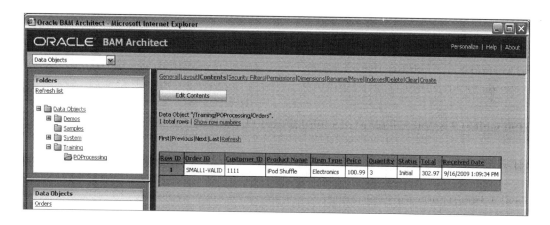

Adding BAM sensors to the BPEL process

In this step, you add BPEL sensors to the existing BPEL process to detect changes in status and update the BAM data object. In the previous section, the row was inserted by calling the BAM adapter from the Mediator. This section shows you another way that you can integrate BAM with the composite using BPEL.

1. Open the BPEL Process by double-clicking on **approveLargeOrder**.

2. Double-click on the **assignCCNumber** activity to start to modify it.

3. Select the **Copy Operation** tab and click on the plus button to add a new copy operation.

4. Use the **Expression 'Pending Approval'** and map it to the **status** field of the **Order** output Variable.

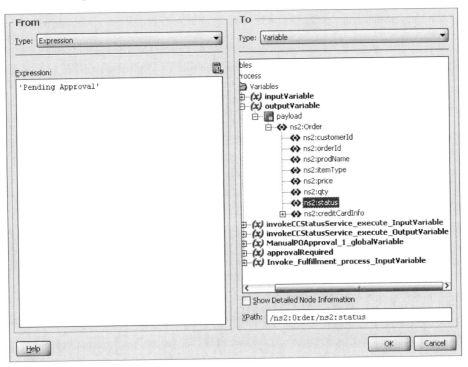

5. Click on **OK**.

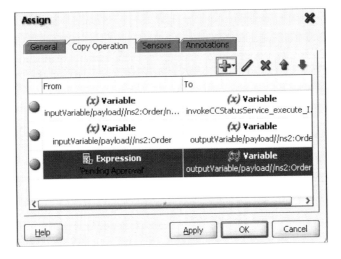

6. Click on the **Sensors** tab to start the process of adding a new sensor.

7. Use the plus button to create a new activity sensor.

8. Set the name of the sensor to **PendingApprovalActivitySensor** and set the **Evaluation Time** to **Completion**.

9. Use the plus button in the **Activity Variable Sensors** box to add a variable.

10. Click the pencil icon to open the XPath builder and set the **Variable XPath** to **outputVariable | payload | Order**.

11. Click on **OK**.

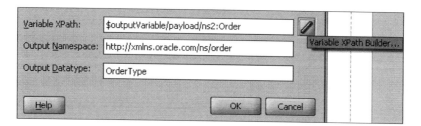

12. Click on **OK** to close the **Create Activity Variable Sensor** dialog.

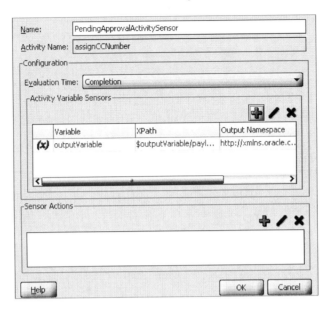

13. Click on **OK** to create the activity sensor and click on **OK** again to close the **Assign** dialog.

14. There is no sensor action assigned to this activity sensor yet. With the **approveLargeOrder** BPEL process open, navigate to the **Sensor Actions** folder in the Structure panel. If the **Structure** panel is not open, select if from the **View** menu.

15. Right-click on **Sensor Actions** and select **Create | BAM Sensor Action**.

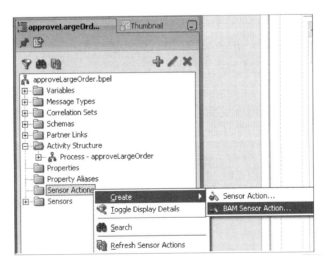

16. The **Create Sensor Action** dialog opens:

   ○ Enter the **Name** as **PendingApprovalSensorAction**.

   ○ Choose **PendingApprovalActivitySensor**.

   ○ Use the magnifying glass next to **Data Object** to select the **Orders** data object.

   ○ Select **Upsert** as the BAM **Operation**.

   ○ Select **_Order_ID** as the key.

   ○ Modify the name of the map file to: bam\xsl\
     PendingApprovalSensorAction.xsl.

   ○ Change the JNDI setting to **eis/bam/rmi** for the **BAM Connection Factory JND**.

   ○ Keep the **Enable Batching** checkbox selected.

   ○ If the plus symbol is disabled, select the magnifying glass, enter the file name and select Open then accept error message and Cancel the dialog. The plus symbol will now be enabled.

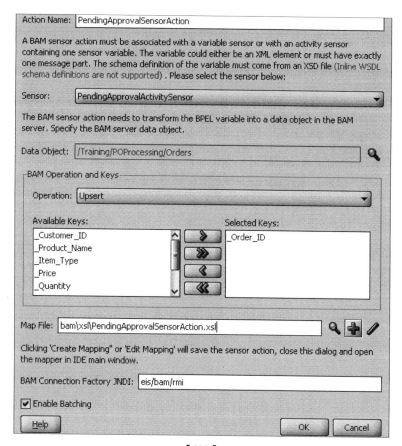

x. Map fields from the source side under **tns:actionData | tns:payload | tns:variableData | tns:Data | sensor:Order** to the corresponding fields on the target side in **tns:_Orders1**.

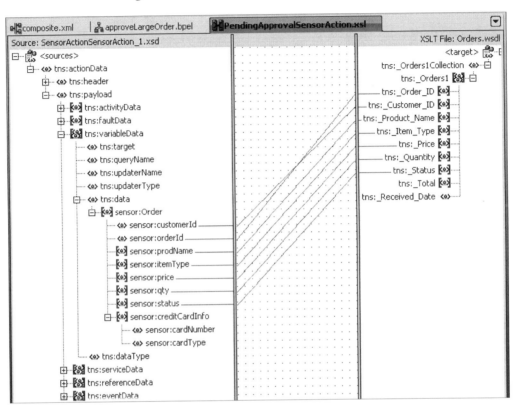

17. By following the same process that you used to create a **PendingApprovalActivitySensor** and a **PendingApprovalSensorAction**, create a **CallbackActivitySensor** and a **CallbackSensorAction**. Add this sensor to the **callbackClient** activity at the end of the process. This time, set the **Evaluation Time** to **Activation**. Make sure you add the activity variable and perform the mapping.

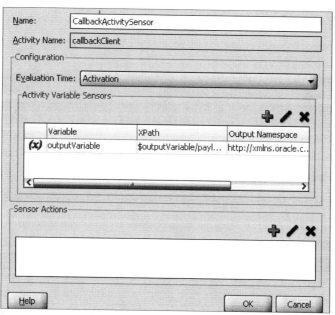

Remember you can only create a BAM Sensor Action from the structure panel while the BPEL process is open.

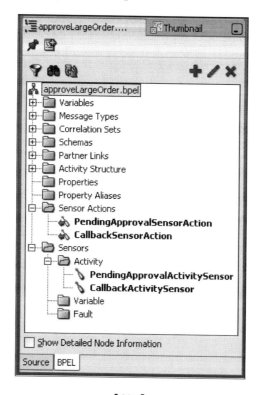

18. When you are done, go back to the **Sensors** tab of the activity. Double-click on the sensor that you want to edit (or use the pencil icon) and you see the **CallbackSensorAction** associated with the **CallbackActivitySensor**.

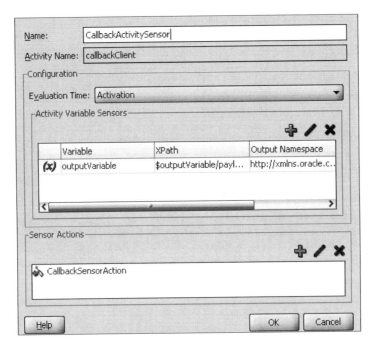

Deploying and running the composite

In this step, you re-deploy the new composite from JDeveloper and test it using the Enterprise Manager testing function.

1. In JDeveloper, re-deploy the composite. Then, close JDeveloper to free up machine resources. You won't use JDeveloper again in this lab.

2. In the EM console, test the composite using `c:\po\input\large_invalidCC.xml` as the test data.

3. Open the report using **Active Viewer** to see the data. It updates in real time as new purchase orders are received.

4. Test again with a large purchase order over $5,000 with a valid credit card. Check that the status of that purchase order in BAM is **"Pending Approval"**.

5. Use the BPM Worklist application to approve the order. Notice that the status is updated to **"approved"**.

6. Submit another order and change the Item Type and Order Id to something new to see the pie chart updated.

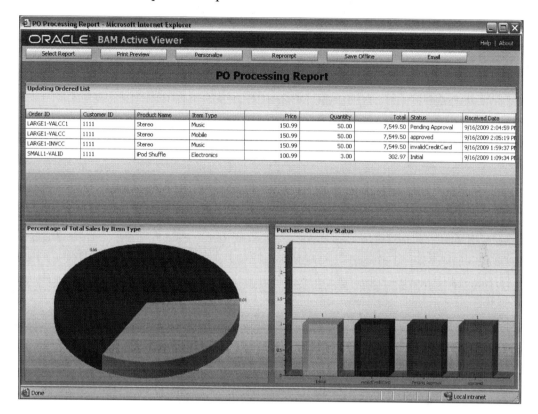

Summary

In this chapter, you learned how BAM events can be generated from Mediator and BPEL and how the events can populate a BAM data object. You also learned how to create a dashboard report that aggregates and correlates the events and updates the dashboard in real time.

Quick-build Instructions

This section gives you all of the operations and names for objects created in this chapter. Experienced users can use this to bypass the step-by-step instructions and complete this chapter more quickly. The complete details for any particular operation listed here can be found in the preceding sections. The information is organized in the same manner that it is introduced in the chapter.

- Create the Data Object — BAM Architect:
    - Folder: **Training**
    - Sub-Folder: **POProcessing**
    - Data Object Name: **Orders**
    - Data Object Fields:

Name	Type	Max Size or Scale
Order ID	String	30
Customer ID	String	30
Product Name	String	50
Item Type	String	30
Price	Decimal	10
Quantity	Decimal	10
Status	String	50
Total	Calculated	-
Received Date	Timestamp	-

    - Formula for Total : **Price * Quantity**
- Define the BAM dashboard — BAM Active Studio:
    - Define report areas and title:
        - Type: **Shared Reports**
        - Folder: **Training**
        - Sub-Folder: **POProcessing**
        - Choose long area on top and two small areas at bottom
        - Title: **PO Processing Report**
    - Define long area on top:
        - Type: **Updating Ordered List**

- ○ Data Object: **Orders**
- ○ Define lower left area:
  - ○ Type: **3D Pie Chart**
  - ○ Data Object: **Orders**
  - ○ Group By: **Item Type**
  - ○ Chart Values: **Total**
  - ○ Summary Function: **Percent Of Total**
  - ○ Title: **Percentage of Total Sales by Item Type**
- ○ Define lower right area:
  - ○ Type: **3D Bar Chart**
  - ○ Data Object: **Orders**
  - ○ Group By: **Status**
  - ○ Chart Values: **Order ID**
  - ○ Summary Function: **Count**
  - ○ Title: **Purchase Orders by Status**
- ○ Save Report:
  - ○ Name: **PO Processing Report**
- Configure BAM Adapter on Weblogic Server:

  Define Outbound Connection Pool:
  - ○ **oracle.bam.adapter.adc.RMIConnectionFactory**
  - ○ JNDI Name: **eis/bam/rmi**
  - ○ Enter property values for the host name of the BAM server, username, password, and port 9001
  - ○ Plan Directory: `C:\Oracle\Middleware\home_11gR1\Oracle_SOA1\soa\BAMPlan`
  - ○ Plan Name: `Plan.xml`
  - ○ Deployments: Update **OracleBAMAdapter**
- Creating a BAM connection:

  Add BAM connection in JDeveloper:
  - ○ Name: **BAMServerConnection1**

- Adding a BAM Adapter to composite:

  Add BAM reference:

  - Name: **OracleBAMAdapter**
  - Data Object: **Orders**
  - Operation: **Upsert**
  - Operation Name: **writeToBAM**
  - Key: **_Order_ID**
  - Enable Batching: checked
  - JNDI Name: **eis/bam/rmi**

- Modifying the Mediator component:

  - Wire Mediator to BAM Adapter
  - Create a transformation map. Don't map **_Total** and **_Received_Date**.

- Add BAM sensors to the BPEL process:

  - Add sensors to **ApproveLargeOrder**
  - Modify **assignCCNumber** activity:
    - Add copy operation
    - Expression: **'Pending Approval'**
    - Variable: **outputvariable | Order | status**
  - Add sensor:
    - Name: **PendingApprovalActivitySensor**
    - Evaluation Time: **Completion**
    - Variable: **outputvariable | Order**
  - Add sensor action for **PendingApprovalActivitySensor**:
    - Action Name: **PendingApprovalSensorAction**
    - Data Object: **Orders**
    - Operation: **Upsert**
    - Key: **_Order_ID**
    - JNDI Name: **eis/bam/rmi**
    - Enable Batching: Checked

- ° Create transformation map. Don't map **_Total** and **_Received_Date**:
  - ° Map file name: `bam/xsl/PendingApprovalSensorAction.xsl`
  - ° Mapping source: **actionData | payload | variableData | data**
  - ° Mapping target: **OrdersCollection | Orders**
- ° Add sensor and sensor action for **CallbackClient** activity:
  - ° Sensor Name: **CallbackActivitySensor**
  - ° Evaluation Time: **activation**
  - ° Variable: **outputvariable | Order**
  - ° Sensor Action Name: **CallbackSensorAction**
  - ° Sensor: **CallbackActivitySensor**
  - ° Data Object: **Orders**
  - ° Operation: **Upsert**
  - ° Key: **_Order_ID**
  - ° JNDI Name: **eis/bam/rmi**
  - ° Enable Batching: Checked
- ° Create transformation map. Don't map Total and Received_Date.
  - ° Map file name: `bam/xsl/CallbackSensorAction.xsl`
  - ° Mapping source: **actionData | payload | variableData | data**
  - ° Mapping target: **OrdersCollection | Orders**

The application is completed. Deploy and test.

17

Event Delivery Network

Creating truly decoupled composite SOA applications requires a complete separation of the service consumer and the service provider. This is typically achieved through the use of asynchronous messaging. In an asynchronous messaging pattern, applications can perform in a "fire and forget" mode. This removes the need of an application to know details of the application on the other side. Additionally, it also improves resource utilization as applications are not holding onto resources until the interaction is complete. On the other hand, this introduces complexities of creating and managing message queues and topics. It requires that both the publisher of the message and the consumer use the same messaging technology. Each messaging system also has its own constraints on the types of programming languages and environments that can use the service.

In a service-oriented world, this tight coupling to the implementation of the underlying messaging system is at odds with the fundamental requirement of implementation independence. What's needed is a level of abstraction that allows applications to generate an event using business terms and associate a business object in an implementation-independent form.

Oracle SOA Suite 11g addresses this with the introduction of a new feature in the form of the Event Delivery Network.

Creating and managing event definitions

Events are defined using an Event Definition Language (EDL), an XML schema used to build business event definitions. An EDL consists of the following:

- A global name.

- Custom headers: These can be used for content-based routing without having to parse the XML payload and apply XPath queries to get at the value to be used for the routing decisions. For instance, one can put the purchase order type in the custom header. This easily accessible custom header could then be used to efficiently decide how to process delivered events.

- Payload definition: Typically this is an XML schema for the business data that needs to accompany the event. For example, a "NewPO" event's payload definition will be a schema for a purchase order.

Event definitions can be created declaratively in JDeveloper in a couple of different ways depending on triggering conditions.

To publish events from a SOA composite, one would create new event definitions and register them with the SOA Infrastructure. It is this option that you will be able to try out later in this chapter during the hands-on exercise.

If you want to raise events on one or more database operations such as insertion of a new row or update of an existing one, you can use **ADF-BC** to define these events. **Application Development Framework (ADF)**, a model-view-controller pattern based UI development framework for creating **Rich Internet Applications (RIAs)** and **Business Components (BC)**, an object-relational mapping tool, provide an easy way to define events. ADF-BC has built-in support for associating these events with database actions like insert, delete, and modify. For example, an event called "NewCustomerAdded" could be generated every time a new customer record is inserted into the database.

Registered events, their subscribers, and any faulted deliveries can all be tracked and monitored using the Oracle Enterprise Manager, in the same fashion that you would be managing and monitoring other aspects of your SOA infrastructure.

Defining the event

1. Open the POProcessing application in JDeveloper and open `composite.xml`, and click on the **Event Definition Creation** icon:

2. In the **Event Definition Creation** window, enter **POEvents** as the name of the event definition. Accept the namespace value generated.

 Event names are fully qualified names, which means the combination of a namespace and the event name together identify a unique event. For instance, the event called `NewCustomerAdded` with name space `http://schemas.oracle.com/events/edl/POEvents` is different than the event with the same name but under a different namespace, for example, event `NewCustomerAdded` with namespace `http://schemas.oracle.com/event/edl/CRMEvents`.

3. Add a new event by clicking on the + icon.
4. Select the `PuchaseOrder` element from the `po.xsd` file using the chooser.
5. Enter **NewPO** as the name of the event and click on **OK** to close the **Add an Event** window.

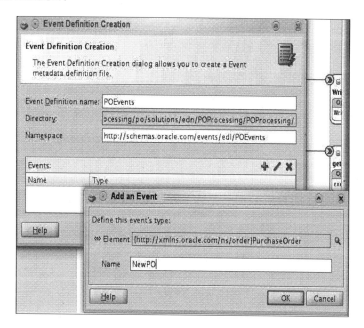

6. Click on **OK** to complete the event definition.

7. Close the **POEvents.edl** panel.

8. Save all.

> You have just created a new event called POEvent.
> It is now available to this and other composites
> to subscribe to or publish. Whenever this event is delivered,
> it will also carry with it a document for the new purchase order.

Subscribing to the NewPO event

1. Drag-and-drop a **Mediator component** onto the composite.

2. Name the mediator **receiveNewPO**.

3. Select **Subscribe to Events** for the **Template**.

4. Click on the **+** to add an event. Select the **NewPO** event from the **Event Chooser** window.

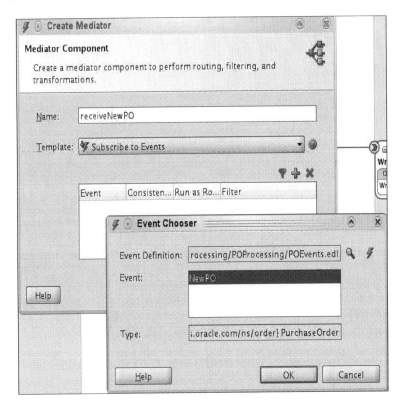

5.   Click on **OK** to accept and create the mediator.

6.   Save all.

7.   Connect the **receiveNewPO** mediator to the **routePO** mediator:

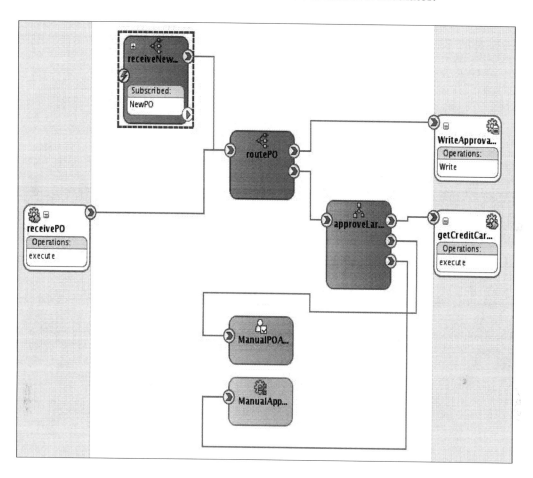

8.   Double-click on the **receiveNewPO** mediator and define a new transformation map. In the transformation-map, map the all the fields from the source to the target.

9.   Close the mediator and save all.

Deploying and testing

1.   Deploy the POProcessing composite to the server.

2.   Browse to the EM console at http://localhost:7001/em.

3. Right-click on folder **soa-infra (soa_server1)** under folder **SOA**:

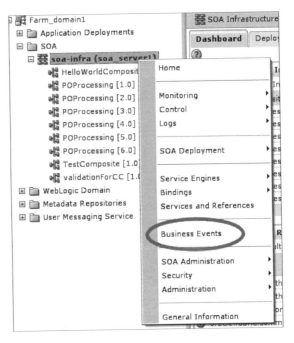

4. Click on item **Business Events**.

5. You should see the Business Events management page with the **NewPO** event listed in the **Events** tab.

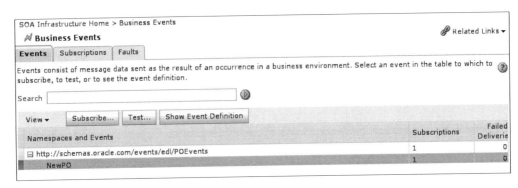

6. Select the event and click on the **Test...** button to publish the event.

7. In the pop-up window, enter the following XML and click on **Publish**:

```
<PurchaseOrder xmlns="http://xmlns.oracle.com/ns/order">
        <CustID>1111</CustID>
        <ID>33412</ID>
        <productName>Sony Bluray DVD Player</productName>
        <itemType>Electronics</itemType>
        <price>350</price>
        <quantity>5</quantity>
        <status>Initial</status>
        <ccType>Mastercard</ccType>
        <ccNumber>1234-1234-1234-1234</ccNumber>
</PurchaseOrder>
```

8. You should get a "The Event published successfully" message.

9. Click on **soa-infra** in the navigation panel on the left to get the soa-infra dashboard.

10. Click on the **POProcessing** composite to view new instances. You should see an instance created for processing the event you just published. Click on the instance ID to view the flow trace.

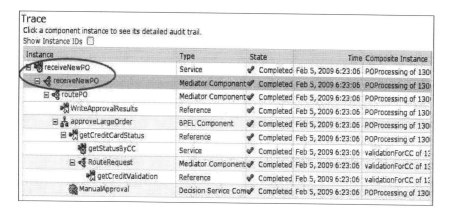

This was just one way of publishing an event and will typically be used as a way to test the composite. In most cases, the events will be published from a number of sources—from a Mediator, from PL/SQL by calling the EDN_PUBLISH_EVENT stored function or from a Java class using the EDN API. An ADF-BC application can also publish events based on database insert, update, and delete operations.

Summary

You cannot really build comprehensive SOA applications without business events. Traditionally, this requirement has been fulfilled by **message-oriented-middleware (MOM)**. However, MOM-based solutions don't necessarily fit very well within a service-oriented architecture. They are low-level technical solutions that provide no business semantics, whereas one of the main objectives of creating services is to provide business functions using semantics that are better understood by business analysts.

With EDN, Oracle SOA Suite 11*g* fills this gap by providing an event-handling solution that allows creation and use of events using business semantics, without the publisher or subscriber of the event ever having to worry about the mechanics of messaging.

As you have seen in this short lab, events are created in a way that directly maps to actual business events, in this case creation of a new purchase order. The process of subscribing to this event was done declaratively without having to configure any messaging queues or topics.

Quick-build Instructions

This section gives you all of the operations and names for objects created in this chapter. Experienced users can use this to bypass the step-by-step instructions and complete this chapter more quickly. The complete details for any particular operation listed here can be found in the preceding sections. The information is organized in the same manner that it is introduced in the chapter:

- Define an event:
    - Event Definition Name: **POEvents**
    - Namespace: `http://schemas.oracle.com/events/edl/POEvents`
- Subscribe to the **NewPO** event:
    - Mediator name: **receiveNewPO**
    - Mediator template: **Subscribe to Events**
    - Choose event: **NewPO**
- Connect **receiveNewPO** to **routePO**:
    - Create a new transformation map, to map data received from the event to data to be sent to the **routePO** mediator

The application is completed. Deploy and test.

18

Data Handling with Service Data Objects (SDO)

A **Service Data Object**, or an **SDO**, is a standard defined by the Open Service Oriented Architecture consortium for providing access to business data, regardless of how it is physically accessed.

Introduction to Service Data Objects

The **SDO** specification, to which Oracle is one of the contributors, is intended to create an abstraction layer for accessing data from heterogeneous data sources in a uniform way. Although the current data access abstraction solutions, such as JDBC, do allow you to access and operate on data without depending on a specific database server, they still do not provide access to non-SQL data sources and they are tied to a specific programming language. The SDO specification adds a programming language-agnostic abstraction layer on top of technologies such as JDBC and is not meant to replace it.

The SDO specification addresses the following key requirements for building a flexible composite application:

- Unified access to heterogeneous data sources.
- Unified support for both static and dynamic data APIs. Object-relational solutions like Oracle TopLink and entity EJBs are two examples of static or strongly typed interfaces. For example, you would access the Amount data in a purchase order object by traversing it (for example, `purchaseOrder.getAmount()`). Whereas, JDBC's `ResultSet` provides only an un-typed, or dynamic, data API (for example, `resultSet.getDouble("AMOUNT")`).
- Support for disconnected programming models, which is essential in multi-layered application architecture such as composite service-oriented applications.
- Decoupling application code from data access code.
- Support for tools and frameworks.

Key components

The SDO architecture is based on disconnected **Data Graphs**. Data graphs are tree structures of **Data Objects** retrieved from data sources, which are then accessed and modified by the client as part of its data processing logic. These changes are then persisted to the underlying data source in a consistent manner ensuring that data in the data source that is being updated is not stale. These changes are detected and automatically applied by the SDO without the client having to invoke an update operation explicitly.

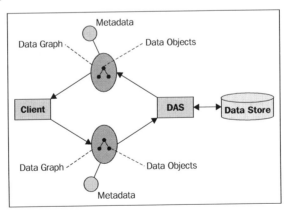

SDOs by themselves do not provide a mechanism to access a data store. This functionality is provided by a **DAS**, or **Data Access Service**. A Data Access Service queries data from data sources, builds the data graphs of the data objects retrieved, and applies the changes to the data back to the data source.

A key requirement addressed by SDO is the ability to do simple introspections so that tools and frameworks can query the shape of the data. **Metadata** (which is data about the data objects) makes this possible. Metadata describes the shape, that is, it describes the data objects, their types, their relationships, and constraints.

 You can get more information on the SDO specification at the OSOA web site: `http://www.osoa.org`.

Oracle SOA Suite 11*g* SDO Support

Oracle SOA Suite 11*g* supports SDOs via a new feature in the BPEL component called **Entity Variables**. This feature allows developers to work with remote data as if it were local, without having to be too concerned about flushing and synchronizing the data it is operating on with the remote copy. For instance, the infrastructure will take care of updating the remote data before dehydrating the BPEL process to database (as it could happen if the process was entering a `wait()` or placing an asynchronous call). Indeed, one never knows how long it will take before the process is resumed and holding onto the data would result in a significant risk of stale data. The following figure illustrates the behavior:

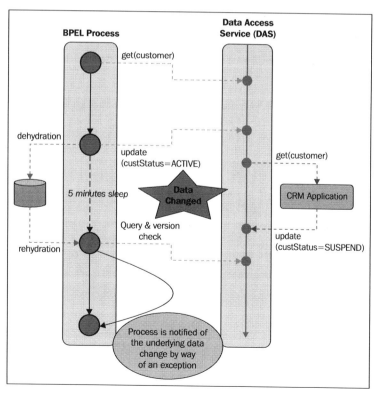

The Entity Variable feature leverages Oracle **ADF-BC** (**Advanced Developer Framework, Business Component**) for data access services and tooling for creating SDOs.

Let's dig a little deeper, using a hands-on tutorial and understand what ADF-BC is and how Entity Variables work and use SDOs.

Tutorial: Using a Service Data Object

This lab exercise gives you a brief introduction to using Service Data Objects in an SOA Composite for accessing and manipulating data.

To illustrate the usage of SDOs, you first use ADF-BC to create view objects that are made available as SDOs through an ADF-BC service. You then use this service to retrieve data from the database using the primary key of the table and then subsequently update the retrieved row.

You add a new step in the `approveLargeOrder` BPEL process to enrich the purchase order data with the name of the customer using the customer identifier in the purchase order. At the end of the processing, you update the customer data about the last purchase order processed.

Chapters 11-19 can be done in any order after completing Chapter 10.

In order to follow the tutorial in this chapter you must have either completed the tutorial from Chapter 10 or higher, or set up the environment as described in Chapter 4 and deployed the solution for Chapter 10, which can be found in `c:\po\solutions\ch10`.

Preparing for the lab

Before you start with this tutorial, you need to create a new table in the database. In the SOADEMO schema, create a new table called CUSTOMERS, which contains customer information.

1. Start SQL*Plus from the command line.

2. Using the soademo user, run the following SQL script to create a new table called CUSTOMERS and populate it with sample data. This script is also available in the `c:\po\sql` directory:

```
CREATE TABLE CUSTOMERS
(
    CUSTOMER_ID        VARCHAR2(10) NOT NULL PRIMARY KEY,
```

```
    CUSTOMER_NAME       VARCHAR2(255) NOT NULL,
    LAST_ORDER_NUMBER VARCHAR2(4000),
    LAST_ORDER_AMOUNT NUMBER(10,2)
);

INSERT INTO CUSTOMERS VALUES ('1111', 'Test Customer', NULL,
NULL);

COMMIT;
```

Creating the ADF Business Component service

As a first step, you create a service that exposes data objects as SDOs. This feature is provided by ADF Business Components (ADF-BC).

ADF Business Components, a quick primer

Oracle Application Development Framework for Java is an end-to-end, standards-based, application development framework that allows rapid development of high-quality web-based, as well as desktop applications using standard Java, Java EE (Enterprise Edition), and web services models.

Oracle ADF uses the Model-View-Controller pattern, where:

- The model layer represents the data to be used for presentation and update
- The view layer contains the user interface for viewing and modifying the data
- The controller layer handles user input and manages page navigation

ADF also introduces another layer, the business service layer, which handles data access and encapsulates business logic.

ADF Business Components provides a simple, wizard-based approach to create these database-centric business services easily. You will see how this is done when you create one for accessing and updating the CUSTOMER table in the database.

ADF-BC can be broken down into three key components:

- An **Entity Object (EO)** represents a row in a database and is responsible for all data manipulation.

- A **View Object (VO)** represents a SQL query and is the component used in user interfaces for providing data. View objects use underlying Entity Objects to validate and save modifications to the data.

- An **Application Module (AM)** represents an updateable data model and associated functions that clients interface with.

Each of these components will be described in a bit more detail as you start using them in the hands-on tutorial.

 You can get more information on Oracle ADF using the online help available in JDeveloper. From JDeveloper, start the Help Center by clicking on **Help | Table of Contents**. This opens the **Help Center** window. In the **Contents** tab, expand the **Designing and Developing Applications** folder. Click on **Developing Oracle ADF Applications**.

Creating an ADF-BC application

You start by creating a new application and project for the ADF-BC service.

1. Create a new application by using the **File | New** menu, the **New Application** command from the application menu, or by selecting **New Application** from the **Application Navigator** drop-down list.

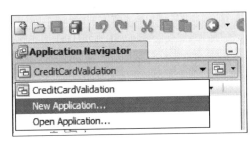

2. Name your application **CustomerSDOApp** and make its location in `c:\po` or your preferred root folder of your lab.

3. Select Generic Application from the Application Template list.

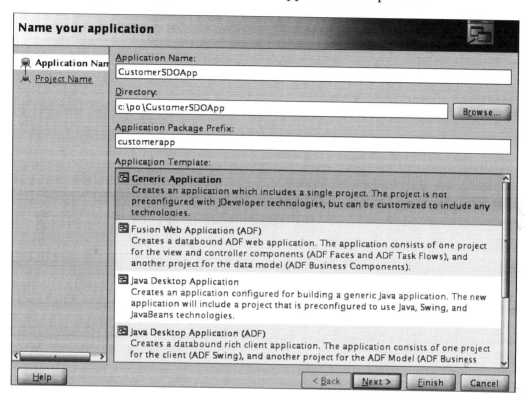

4. Click on **Next**.

5. Use the name **CustomerSDO** for the project and select **ADF Business Components** for the **Project Technologies**.

6. Click on **Next** and then click on **Finish** to create the empty project.

Creating the Business Components

Now that you have the right type of project created, you add the Entity and View objects:

1. Right-click on the **CustomerSDO** project in the **Application Navigator** and click on **New**.

2. In the **New Gallery** window, select **ADF Business Components** in the Categories list and **Business Components from Tables** in the **Items** list.

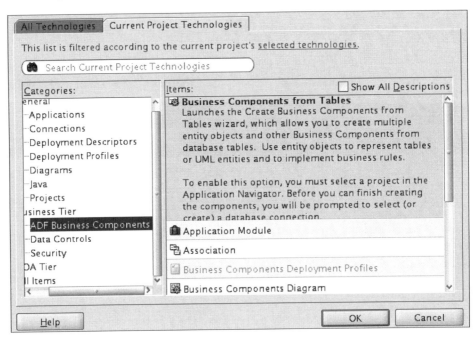

3. Click on **OK**.

4. In the **Initialize Business Components Project** window, create a new connection to the database with the SOADEMO schema.

5. Test the connection to ensure that the user ID and password are correct.

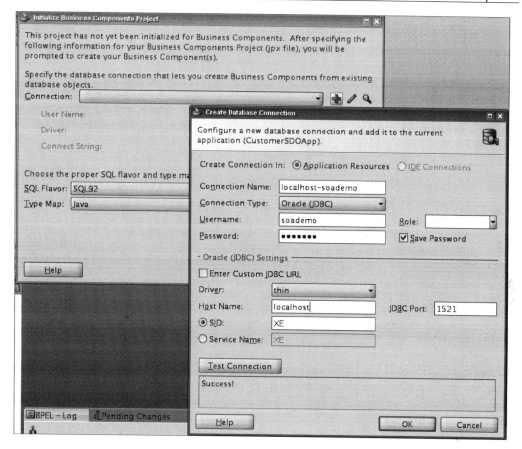

6. Accept the default **SQL Flavor** and **Type Map** settings and click on **OK** to continue.

7. In the **Entity Objects** window, click on **Query** to retrieve tables. Select **CUSTOMERS** from the **Available** list and move it to the **Selected** list.

8. Click on **Next**.

9. In the **Updatable View Objects** window, select **Customers** (SOADEMO. CUSTOMERS) from the **Available** list and move it to the **Selected** list and click on **Next**.

10. Accept defaults in the **Read-Only View Objects** window and click on **Next**.

11. In the **Application Module** window, enter the name of the module as **CustomerSDOAppModule** and click on **Next**.

12. Click on **Finish** in the Diagram window.

13. Click on **Save All** to save the project.

Testing the application module

Test the application module created in the previous step to ensure everything is in order for the next steps.

1. To test it, right-click on the **CustomerSDOAppModule.xml** file in the navigator (not the project name) and select **Run**. This will start a Java application window called **Oracle Business Component Browser**.

2. Double-click on **CustomersView1** in the lefthand pane. This opens up a form based on the view object called `CustomerView1` that you created in the earlier step. You should see the row that was populated when you created the CUSTOMERS table.

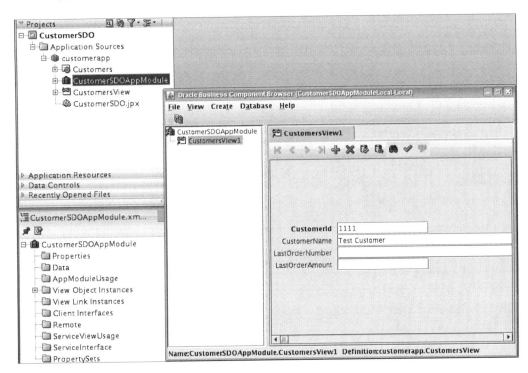

3. Close the Java application by selecting **File | Exit** in its toolbar.

Creating the service interface

Now create a service interface for your **CustomersView1** view object:

1. Double-click on the **CustomerSDOAppModule** in the Application Navigator. This opens the application module configuration panel.

2. Click on **Service Interface**.

3. Click on the **+** sign in the top-right corner to add a new interface. This starts a wizard for defining the new service.

4. In the **Service Interface** window, change the name of the web service to **CustomerSDOService**.

5. Use the default target name space and click on **Next**.

6. Click on **OK**

7. Click on **Next** on the **Service Custom Methods** page.

8. In the **Service View Instances**, select **CustomersView1** and add it to the **Selected** list.

9. Select the **CustomersView1** in the **Selected** list. This populates the **Basic Operations** tab. Select all the operations listed (don't forget to scroll) and click on **Next**.

10. Click on **Finish**.

 You just created a **DAS**, or a **data access service**, and an SDO. In this case, SDO definitions for the Customer data object were automatically created by JDeveloper based on the `CustomerView1` view-object.

Deploying the service

At this point, you now have a new service interface created for the `CustomersView1` view-object. Before you can deploy this service, you need to ensure that service can participate in a distributed transaction. To do that, you need to configure it to use the JDBC data source, `jdbc/soademoDatabase` that was created for the `soademo` schema in the earlier labs.

1. Click on **Configurations** in **CustomerSDOAppModule**.

2. Edit the **CustomerSDOService** configuration.

3. Change the **JDBC DataSource** name to **jdbc/soademoDatabase**.

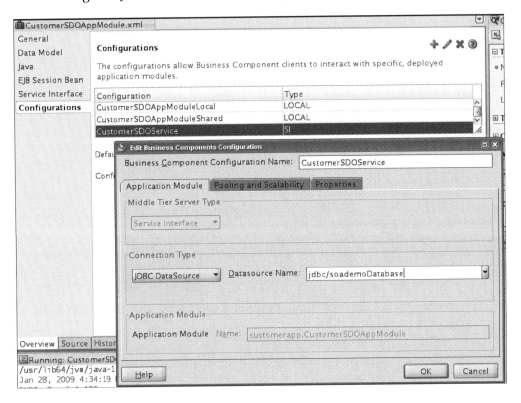

4. Click on **OK**.

5. Back on the **Configurations** page, select **CustomerSDOService** as the default configuration.

6. Click on **Save All** to save the project.

7. You now need to create a deployment profile. Right-click on the CustomerSDO project in the application navigator and select **Project Properties**.

8. Select **Java EE Application** in the lefthand panel.

9. Change the **Java EE Web Application Name** to CustomerSDO-webapp.

10. Change the **Java EE Web Context Root** to customer-app.

11. Click on **OK**

12. Right-click on the CustomerSDO project in the application navigator and select Project Properties again.

13. Click on **Deployment** in the lefthand panel.

14. Click on **New** to create a new deployment profile.

15. Select **Business Components Service Interface** as the Archive Type.

16. Change the Name to **customerSDOProfile**.

17. Click on **OK**.

18. Expand the **customerSDOProfile** and select **Middle Tier** and click on **Edit....**

19. Change the **Enterprise Application Name** to CustomerSDO.

20. Change the name of the EAR file to customer-app.ear.

21. Click on **OK**.

22. Click on **OK** to close the **Project Properties** window.

23. Click on **Save All** to save the project.

 With the above steps, you have configured the deployment properties for deploying the CustomerSDO as a J2EE application. The following steps set it up to be accessible as an SDO service to any SOA Composite.

24. Click on **Application Menu** in the toolbar and select **Application Properties...**.

25. Select **Deployment** in the lefthand panel.

26. In the **Application Properties** window, edit the selected deployment profile by clicking on the **Edit...** button.

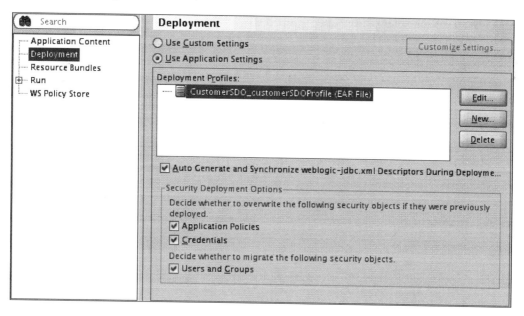

27. In the **Edit EAR Deployment Properties** window, enter **CustomerApp** as the **Application name**.

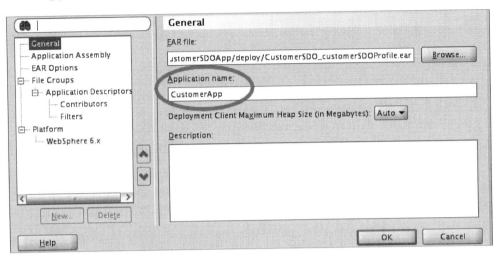

28. Click on **OK** on both the open windows.

29. Save all.

> The SDO service is published as web service using SOAP over HTTP, which is not transactional. For it to participate in a transaction, it needs to be invoked using a protocol, like RMI, that can join the composite's global transaction. The following steps set up a WebLogic application life cycle listener, which will register the service with the SOA Infrastructure when the **CustomerSDO** application starts up. When you use this service in a composite, you need to provide a registry key at design time. At runtime, the SOA Infrastructure looks up this service using the registry key and invokes it using RMI.

30. Browse to **Descriptors** in **Application Resources** in the **Application Navigator** pane. Open the **weblogic-application.xml** file under the **META-INF** folder.

31. In the editor window, add the following lines to the file as shown in the following figure:

```
<listener>
    <listener-class>
        oracle.jbo.client.svc.ADFApplicationLifecycleListener
    </listener-class>
</listener>
```

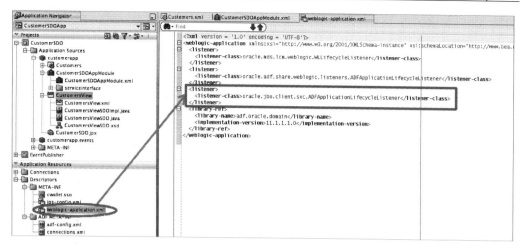

32. Save all.

33. In the **Application Menu** in the toolbar, select **Deploy**.

34. Select **CustomerSDO_customerSDOProfile | MyAppServerConnection**.

35. Select the **soa_server1** managed server as the target.

Testing the Customer SDO service

To test the service, start your browser and navigate to: `http://localhost:8001/customer-app/CustomerSDOService`.

> You can also use EM to test the service by selecting the **Test** icon in the **Web Services** pane of the **CustomerSDOApp** application page.

1. On the Web Service testing page, select **getCustomersView1** in the **Operation** drop-down list.

2. The page will re-render to show only **customerId** text input. Enter **1111** and click on **Invoke**. You should see the response with the customer name as **Test Customer**.

Notice the different data manipulation and retrieval operations that were automatically created for the data access service (DAS).

```
Test Result

View: Formatted XML | Raw XML

Return to Test Page


<env:Envelope
  xmlns:env="http://schemas.xmlsoap.org/soap/envelope/">
<env:Header/>
<env:Body>
 <ns0:getCustomersView1Response
   xmlns:ns0="/customerapp/common/types/">
  <ns0:result
    xmlns:ns0="/customerapp/common/types/"
    xmlns:ns1="/customerapp/common/"
    xmlns:xsi="http://www.w3.org/2001/XMLSchema-instance"
    xsi:type="ns1:CustomersViewSDO">
   <ns1:CustomerId>1111</ns1:CustomerId>
   <ns1:CustomerName>Test Customer</ns1:CustomerName>
   <ns1:LastOrderNumber
     xsi:nil="true"/>
   <ns1:LastOrderAmount
     xsi:nil="true"/>
  </ns0:result>
 </ns0:getCustomersView1Response>
</env:Body>
</env:Envelope>
```

Using the new ADF-BC Service in the POProcessing composite

In this step, you modify the POProcessing composite to use the customer as an SDO through the ADF-BC service created in the last step. The approveLargeOrder BPEL process is modified to retrieve the customer information using the customerId in the input order and replace the ID in the input with the name from the SDO. You also update the customer information in the database with the information of the last approved order ID and the value of the purchase order.

Adding the CustomerSDOService as a reference

1. Open the POProcessing application and open the composite.xml and add a new **ADF-BC Service** component, from **External Adapters** section in the component palette, to the **External References** swim lane on the composite diagram.

2. In the **Create ADF-BC Service** window, enter the name of the service as **CustomerSDOService**.

3. Browse to the service test page as mentioned in the **Testing the Customer SDO Service** section and copy the WSDL URL referenced by the **Service Description** hyperlink.

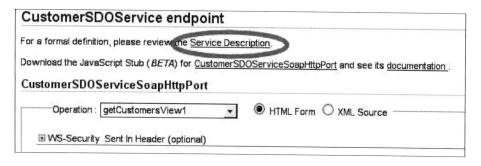

4. Paste the URL into the **WSDL URL** field in the **Create ADF-BC Service** window and press the *Tab* key to process the URL. The wizard will load the WSDL and populate the Port Type appropriately.

5. Enter `CustomerApp_JBOServiceRegistry` in the **Registry** field.

6. Press **OK** to complete the definition.

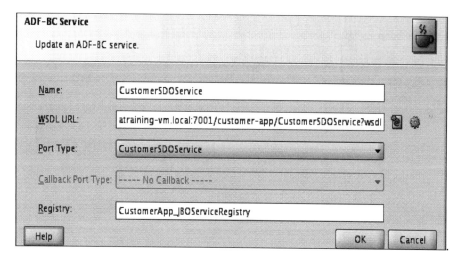

The service registry key is used to look up the appropriate ADF-BC service for executing the service operation. Recollect the change made to the `weblogic-application.xml` file earlier to enable registration of the service with the SOA Infrastructure on CustomerSDO application startup.

7. Connect the **approveLargeOrder** BPEL process to the **CustomerSDOService** ADFBC service:

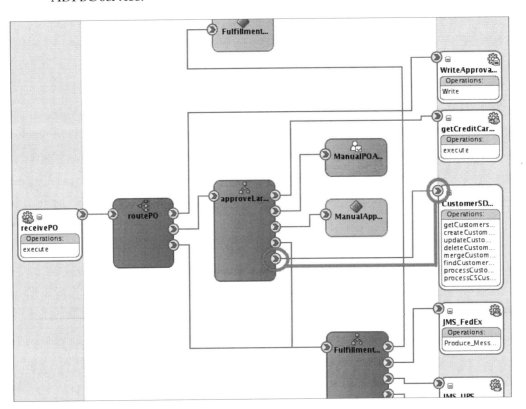

8. Save all.

Using the SDO in BPEL

Now that you have a service that provides data manipulation operations, you use it in BPEL to get the customer name from the database. Generally, you would invoke the service by passing it the appropriate data and expect the customer details in the response.

In Oracle SOA Suite 11*g*, a new feature has been introduced called **Entity Variables**. An entity variable is a special type of variable that can be used in a BPEL process for accessing and manipulating data. It is used like the standard BPEL variables, except for the following key differences:

- The underlying data form for an Entity Variable is an SDO, which is an in-memory data structure rather than an XML DOM as is used for regular BPEL variables.

- Entity variables are data-aware and detect changes to underlying data in the data source that are then reflected in the entity variable. This is because, unlike regular variables, only a reference to the actual data is held and not the data itself. The data is held by the underlying data service provider in its native form. Changes to the entity variables are also pushed to the underlying data source in a transactional manner.

- Due to the nature of SDO, you are restricted in the type of XPath queries that can be used on entity variables.

In this step, you use an Entity Variable that represents the customer data.

1. Open the `approveLargeOrder` BPEL process.

2. Create a new *Entity Variable* by clicking on the **Variables** icon **(x)** in the main scope for `approveLargeOrder`.

3. In the **Structure** pane, click on the **Variables | Process | Variables folder** and then click on + to add a new variable.

4. Name the variable `CustomerInfoEV`.

5. Select **Element** and click on the browse icon to select an element. In the **Type Chooser**, traverse down the **Project WSDL Files** tree and select the **customersViewSDO** element as shown in the following image:

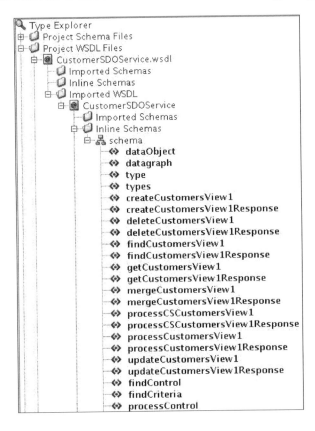

6. Back in the **Create Variable** window, select **Entity Variable** and choose the **CustomerSDOService** for the partner link.

7. Click on **OK**.

You have now associated an entity variable with the CustomerSDOService. As mentioned earlier, this variable only holds the reference to the data. The underlying data provider takes care of retrieving and holding the data. To retrieve a row from the database, you need to assign a value for the primary key. The action of assigning the value, called *binding*, initiates the retrieval of the corresponding row. This row becomes the current row represented by the entity variable. The act of changing the contents of this variable is the same as changing the column values of the row. These changes to the entity variable are automatically applied to the database in a consistent manner.

8. To bind the primary key, drag a **Bind Entity** activity and drop it just after the **receiveInput** activity.

9. Rename the activity to `BindCustomerId`.

10. Double-click on the activity to open its properties. Select **CustmerInfoEV** as the entity variable and add a unique key by clicking on the **+** icon. For the **Key Local Part**, click on the browse variables icon **(x)** and select **ns7:CustomerId** from the **CustomerInfoEV** variable. Note that you may have a different namespace prefix other than **ns7**.

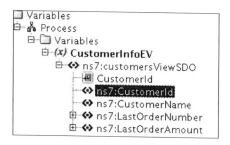

11. For the **Key Value**, click on the express builder icon and select the customer ID from the input variable.

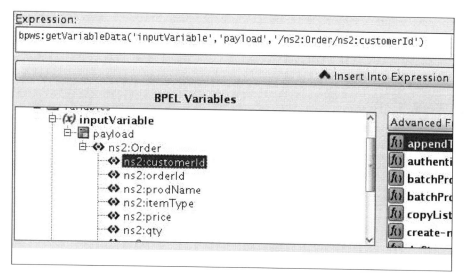

12. Click on **OK** in the **Bind Entity** window to complete the activity definition.

13. Drop an **Assign** activity directly below the **BindCustomerId** activity and assign the customer name from the `CustomerInfoEV` variable to the `customerId` in the input variable.

14. Click on **OK**. You can ignore the **Variable is not initialized** warning on this assign activity.

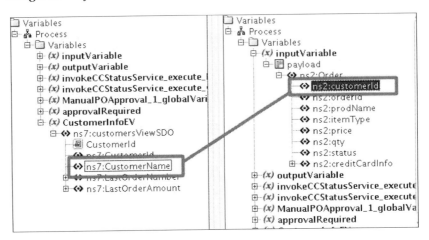

 Now that you have retrieved the customer data corresponding to the value in the customer ID, you now update this customer information with the current purchase order information. This demonstrates how changing values in an entity variable using the standard BPEL Assign activity automatically updates the underlying row in the database table.

15. Create an **Assign** activity in the case branch that has the **ApprovalRule** rules activity as shown in the following image:

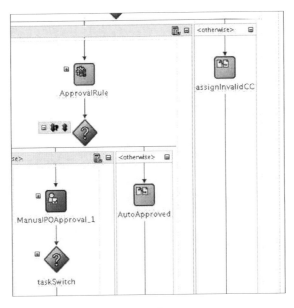

16. In the assign activity, create two copy operations. One is for copying the **orderId** from the **outputVariable** to **LastOrderNumber** in **CustomerInfoEV**.

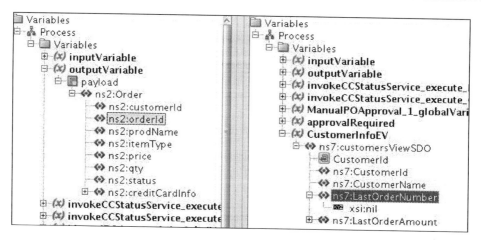

The second copy operation is to copy the value (**price * qty**) from the **outputVariable** to **LastOrderAmount** in the entity variable.

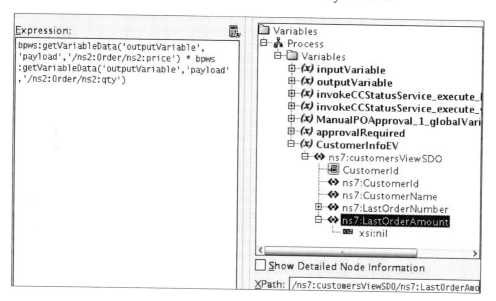

16. Save all to save the project.

Deploying and Testing

1. Deploy the `POProcessing` composite using the **Deploy** command in the **Project** menu.

2. Run it using an order between $1,000 and $5,000.

3. View the instance using the SOA console.

4. In the **Flow Trace** window, click on **approveLargeOrder** to open the BPEL audit trail.

5. Expand the **<payload>** node at the end under the **callbackClient** node. You should see the `customerId` element value is now the name of the customer that was retrieved from the database as a result of the Bind activity you added to the flow.

6. Query the CUSTOMER table in the database using SQL*Plus or your web browser using Application Express (http://localhost:8080/apex), if you are using Oracle XE database. You can also do this using the **Database Connections** tab in JDeveloper (**View** menu).

7. If using Application Express, log in as soademo/soademo and click on **Object Browser**. In the Tables list select **CUSTOMERS** and click on **Data**. You should see the **LAST_ORDER_NUMBER** and **LAST_ORDER_VALUE** set to the corresponding order ID and the value.

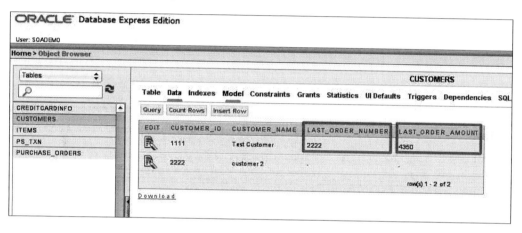

8. Try creating a new customer in the database and submit a new PO, but this time, change the customer ID to reflect the ID of the new customer created.

Summary

SDOs, with their corresponding data access services, provide service-oriented applications a standard way of accessing and manipulating data without knowing anything about the underlying data store, its access methods, and technology. Oracle Fusion Middleware 11*g* provides support for creating SDOs and data access services declaratively using ADF-BC. With the introduction of Entity Variables in BPEL, it is now easy to operate on data that needs to be persisted to the database, in a transaction, from within a BPEL process. Entity variables can be especially useful in cases where there is a requirement for a "chatty" interaction with the database.

Quick-build Instructions

This section gives you all of the operations and names for objects created in this chapter. Experienced users can use this to bypass the step-by-step instructions and complete this chapter more quickly. The complete details for any particular operation listed here can be found in the preceding sections. The information is organized in the same manner that it is introduced in the chapter.

- Create CUSTOMERS table in SOADEMO and populate it.
- Add the ADF-BC application:
  - Application Name: **CustomerSDOApp**
  - Project Name: **CustomerSDO**
  - Project Technologies: **ADF Business Components**

- Create Business Components:
  - Item Type: Business **Components from Table**
  - Entity Objects: **CUSTOMERS**
  - Updateable View Objects: **CUSTOMERS**
  - Application Modules: **CustomerSDOAppModule**
  - View Object name: **CustomersView1**

- Create service:
  - Service Name: **CustomerSDOService**
  - Service View Instances: **CustomersView1**
  - Select all operations
  - JDBC Data Source Name: **jdbc/soademoDatabase**

- Update Java EE in Project Properties
  - Java EE Web Application Name: **CustomerSDO-webapp**
  - Java EE Web Context Root: **customer-app**
  - Save properties and open properties again

- Create Deployment Profile in Project Properties
  - Archive Type: **Business Components Service Interface**
  - Name: **customerSDOProfile**

- Edit Middle Tier (EJB JAR File) Properties:
  - ° EAR File: **customer-app.ear**
  - ° Enterprise Application Name: **CustomerSDO**
- Test the ADF-BC service:
  - ° Test URL: `http://localhost:8001/customer-app/ CustomerSDOService`
- Modify the POProcessing composite:
  - ° Add New Reference: **ADF-BC Service**
  - ° Service Name: **CustomerSDOService**
  - ° WSDL URL: `http://localhost:8001/customer-app/ CustomerSDOService?wsdl`
  - ° Registry: **CustomerApp_JBOServiceRegistry**
- Modify the approveLargeOrder BPEL Process:
  - ° New Entity Variable: **CustomerInfoEV**
  - ° Element: **customerViewSDO**
  - ° Partner Link: **CustomerSDOService**
  - ° Add new Bind Entity activity:
    - ° Position: After `receiveInput`
    - ° Entity Variable: **CustomerInfoEV**
    - ° Key Local Part: `ns:CustomerId`
    - ° Key Value: `bpws:getVariableData('inputVariable', 'payload', '/ns2:Order/ns2:customerId')`
  - ° Add new Assign activity:
    - ° Position: After Bind Entity
    - ° Name: **AssignCustomerName**
    - ° From: `CustomerInfoEV | customersViewSDO | CustomerName`
    - ° To: `inputVariable payload/Order/customerId`

- ○ Add new Assign activity:
    - ○ Position: In Case activity (creditStatus=VALID), at the end
    - ○ Name: **AssignOrderInfo**
    - ○ From: `outputVariable/payload/Order/orderId`
    - ○ To: `CustomerInfoEV/customersViewSDO/ LastOrderNumber`
- Deploy and test using order with value between $1,000 and $5,000.

The application is completed. Deploy and test.

19

Connecting to Trading Partners (B2B)

OracleServices   PurchaseOrder_def   MarketInc

So far we have been dealing with processes that were entirely contained within the enterprise. Often times, you need to extend these processes beyond the boundaries of your enterprise to reach out to customers, suppliers, and partners. Traditionally, inter-enterprise interactions have been handled quite differently from the typical intra-enterprise processes. The inter-enterprise processes were focused around the electronic exchange of business documents between trading partners. **Electronic Data Interchange (EDI)** came into being decades ago to address this **business-to-business (B2B)** interaction problem. More recently, standards like **RosettaNet** and **ebXML** have gained popularity in handling and managing these types of document exchanges between trading partners. But regardless of the technology, there has always been a gap between the technology used for document exchanges and the internal processing systems, making the creation of a seamless end-to-end process a challenge. **B2B** solutions have been mainly concerned with the mechanics of sending and receiving documents electronically from the edges of one enterprise to another. For instance, in an order-to-cash process, a B2B solution would receive a purchase order document from a customer and just drop it into a file system or a message queue for further processing. All that was exchanged between the B2B solution and the business process was a single file or a message on a queue, without any context information about the B2B process itself.

Introducing B2B integration

Before we discuss how Oracle SOA Suite 11*g* addresses these challenges, let's take a quick look at some basic B2B characteristics.

B2B characteristics

- B2B processes are primarily concerned with sending and receiving business documents electronically.

- B2B interactions use electronic representations of business documents using standards like EDI **X12**, RosettaNet, **OAGIS**, **HL7**, **EDIFACT**, and so on. They may also use custom formats like fixed-length or variable-length text files and comma-separated files.

- These business documents are exchanged using message exchange standards like **ebMS**, **AS1**, **AS2**, **RNIF**, **HTTP**, **FTP**, and email.

- Given the wide variety of document standards and message exchange protocol standards, it becomes necessary to define precise and enforceable, agreements between trading partners that specify how a particular document will be exchanged between the two businesses.

- Messages in an exchange may need to be correlated and batched, if necessary, and multiple levels of acknowledgements might have to be issued.

- **Security (signature, encryption, and so on) and non-repudiation** are fundamental requirements. B2B deals with the exchange of business documents, often involving large sums of money. In case of any dispute, a company has to be able to prove the authenticity and origin of the transactions. Without a comprehensive security infrastructure for digital signatures, encryption, and message tracking, a B2B solution is incomplete.

Oracle B2B

Oracle B2B is an **eCommerce** gateway that enables the secure and reliable exchange of documents with trading partners and addresses all of the above requirements. It not only tackles all the B2B functions, but can also be connected into a composite as a **binding component**. This feature allows true end-to-end tracking of business exchanges, from the receipt of a document to the end of its processing, as well as from the start of a creation process to the sending of the resulting business document to the trading partner.

 Refer to Chapter 2 for more information on "Binding Component".

Oracle B2B is one of the core components in the Oracle SOA Suite 11*g* and is installed as part of the SOA Suite. It provides a simple-to-use, web-based interface for managing trading partner profiles, partner agreements, and document definitions.

Composites and B2B

Although B2B can be directly connected to internal enterprise applications using **JMS, AQ,** or file exchange, as a good design practice, you should have B2B go through an intermediate layer such as a SOA composite. This approach reduces tight coupling between B2B and the internal systems, therefore resulting in more flexible solutions that are not tied to any specific applications. This is where Oracle B2B 11*g* makes it easy by providing the ability to wire a B2B interaction into a SOA composite.

To have B2B be part of the composite application, you connect a B2B interaction defined by an agreement, as a service (for inbound documents) or a reference (for outbound documents). Both the service and the reference use an optimized, B2B-specific binding. For inbound documents, B2B will instantiate the composite for processing the document using this binding information. For documents to be sent using the B2B, a component like the **Mediator** or a **BPEL** process can invoke the B2B via the reference.

Document management

Business documents are what B2B is all about. As mentioned earlier, there are a number of document standards currently in use. The majority of businesses still use EDI standards for their B2B document exchange. EDI is a broad term and covers different standards like **X12, EDIFACT,** and **EANCOM.**

Challenges due to evolving standards

Each of these standards has evolved over time and has gone through numerous revisions. Quite a number of these revisions are still in use, resulting in interoperability issues between trading partners that might be using different revisions of the same standard. For instance, one business may be using X12 revision 4010 and its supplier may be using 4040. To add to this complexity, the standards provide for extending the document formats to cater to business-specific data. What this means is that for any given document, say a Purchase Order using X12 4020 revision, there is no guarantee that two trading partners can exchange a document without having to perform some transformation.

This is why document management becomes a key function in a B2B solution. Document management involves cataloging all the different formats and versions that the business will be supporting as part of its electronic data exchange. This also covers registering machine-readable document specifications that can be used to validate inbound and outbound documents to ensure they meet specific trading partner agreements.

Oracle B2B provides document management as part of the web-based B2B console. It also provides a Windows-based specification builder that comes with complete dictionaries of all published X12, EDIFACT, HL7, and other widely used standards. These dictionaries are used to generate document specifications for registering with the B2B.

EDI is not XML

Most of the widely used B2B document formats are not XML based. For instance, all the different EDI formats are text based with their own definition of document and record structures. But for B2B to seamlessly integrate into a composite application, it needs to exchange data with components like Mediator or BPEL using XML. To address this, the document validation engine within B2B generates an XML representation of non-XML documents as part of the validation process. This generated XML is what gets sent to or from the composite.

Trading partner profiles and agreement

All the trading partners are registered along with their capabilities, contact information and identifiers. This set of information makes up the **trading partner profile**.

The trading partner reaches an agreement with the B2B host enterprise (called the **host trading partner**) on what documents are exchanged and what messaging service and transport is used. This is captured in a **trading partner agreement** and plays a fundamental role in determining where to route a document and what transport and messaging service should be used.

The mechanism to send messages to a trading partner is called the partner delivery channel and is captured in the agreement. The mechanism for the host to receive messages from a trading partner is called the host delivery channel and is also captured in the agreement.

In addition, B2B also provides **Listening Channels**. A listening channel allows the B2B server to receive documents from any trading partner. Messages received via a listening channel are analyzed to identify the type of document received and the identity of the trading partner that sent it. If both the document type and revision and the trading partner are registered in the B2B, then an agreement is selected and the processing continues.

Tutorial: Triggering POProcessing using B2B transactions

It is time to try out a simple B2B use case to illustrate all of the previously mentioned B2B features. To keep it simple, you use a file transport that is defined as a listening channel to receive messages from the trading partners. You use a custom XML document representing the purchase order document that your POProcessing composite uses. You define a single trading partner who sends the message, which is then routed to a composite according to the agreement. The composite consists of a mediator that routes the purchase order to the PO Processing composite.

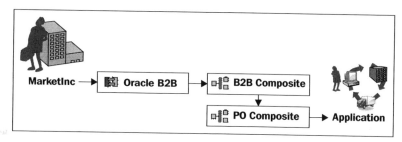

Chapters 11-19 can be done in any order after completing Chapter 10.

In order to follow the tutorial in this chapter you must have either completed the tutorial from Chapter 10 or higher, or set up the environment as described in Chapter 4 and deployed the solution for Chapter 10, which can be found in `c:\po\solutions\ch10`.

Defining the B2B configuration

Log into the Oracle B2B console at `http://localhost:8001/b2b` and perform the following steps. The user name is `weblogic` and the password is the same one you've been using for this tutorial, probably, `welcome1`.

Creating a document definition

You will start by defining the Purchase Order that you have been using as input to the POProcessing composite. Using `po.xsd`, you create a B2B document definition.

1. Select **Administration** at the top right of the screen.
2. Select **Custom** under **Document protocols** in the left navigation bar.
3. Create a new version by selecting the **New Version** button on the top right.
4. Enter **Version Name: 1.0**.
5. Click on **Save**.
6. Create a new type by selecting the **New Type** button on the top right.
7. Name the document type: **PurchaseOrder**.
8. Click on **Save**.
9. Create a new definition by selecting the **New Definition** button on the top right.
10. Name the Document Definition: **PurchaseOrder_def**.

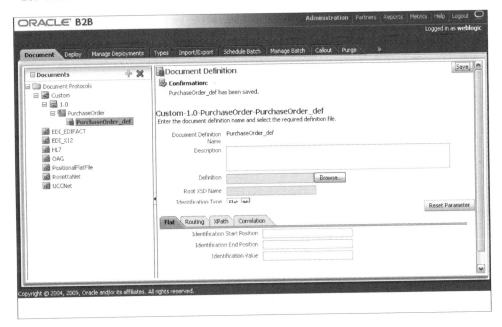

11. Click on **Save**.

12. Select **Browse** next to the **Definition** field and choose **po.xsd**.

13. Select identification type: **xml**.

14. On the **XML** tab, set the **Identification Expression**:

```
//*[local-name()='PurchaseOrder']
```

 The **Identification Expression** is how the document is identified. The XPath notation indicates what to look for the in the document coming in to match up with the document definitions defined in B2B.

15. Select the **Routing** tab, and set the **Routing ID**: PurchaseOrder10. The **Routing ID** can be used to route the document to the right composite. Here you are giving it a name composed of the type and version number.

16. Click on **Save**.

Defining the trading partners

The company that is running or hosting the B2B server is called the host trading partner. Oracle B2B has a predefined default host trading partner. You first update the default host trading partner to give it a meaningful name and after that you define a second trading partner that will be sending documents to the host.

1. Select **Partners** on the top right.

2. In the left navigation bar, you see the default host trading partner, **My Company**, selected. Select the **Edit** icon and change the name to **OracleServices**.

3. Create a new trading partner **MarketInc** using the **Add New Trading Partner** icon.

4. Now select the document this trading partner will send. Select **MarketInc** and select the **Documents** tab:

    i. Select the green plus sign to **Add Document Definition**.

    ii. Navigate through the documents to select **Custom | 1.0 | PurchaseOrder | PurchaseOrder_def**.

      iii. This trading partner is sending the document so select the
          Sender checkbox.

      iv. Deselect the **Receiver** checkbox.

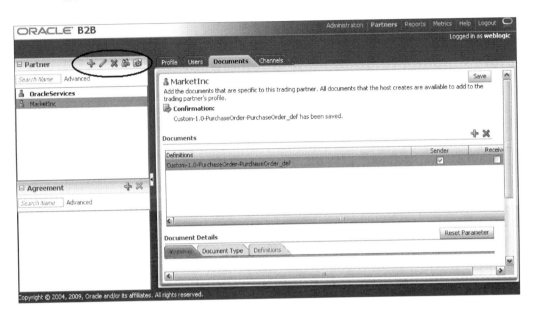

  5.   Click on **Save**.

Creating a listening channel

As we mentioned earlier, a listening channel allows any trading partner to send a
message to the host. In this part of the lab, you define a file listening channel.

  1.   Select **Administration**.

  2.   Select the **Listening Channel** tab.

      If the browser window is too narrow to show all of the tabs, you can use the
      expansion arrow to see the Listening Channel tab

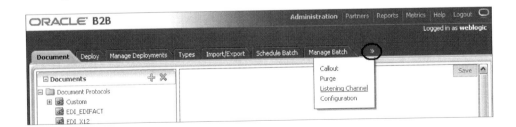

3. Select the green plus sign to **Add Channel to Trading Partner**:
   - ○ **Name: File_ListeningChannel**
   - ○ **Protocol: Generic File-1.0**

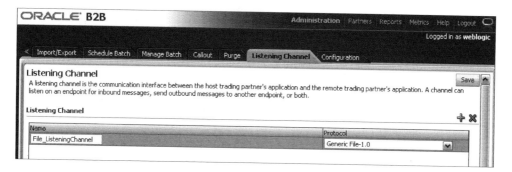

4. Click on the **Transport Protocol Parameters** tab in the **Channel Details** section of the **Listening Channel** page and set the following:
   - ○ **Polling interval: 5**
   - ○ **Folder name: c:\orclsrvs_in**

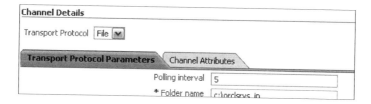

5. Click on the **Channel Attributes** tab:
   - i.   Select the **Enable Channel** radio button
   - ii. Uncheck the **Internal** checkbox

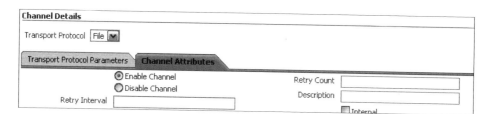

6. Click on **Save**.

Creating an agreement

Now create a new agreement between the MarketInc trading partner and the OracleServices host:

1. Select **Partners** on the top right.

2. Select the green plus sign at the lower left to **Create New Agreement**.

3. Click on the **Select Partner** link in the image at the top of the screen:

   i. Select the Partner **MarketInc**.

4. Click the **Select Document Definition** icon:

   i. Select the document **Custom-1.0-PurchaseOrder-PurchaseOrder_def**.

5. Enter **Agreement Id**: OS_MI_1000

   This gives the agreement you are creating this identifier, composed of the initials of the two trading partners and the version number.

6. Enter **Name: OracleService_MarketInc_Agr**.

7. This is a more human-readable name for this agreement.

8. Click on **Save**.

9. Saving the agreement automatically validates it but you can also click **Validate** to verify manually.

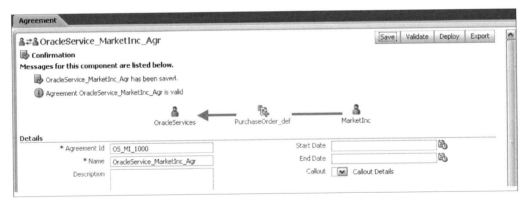

10. Click on **Validate**—you see the validation message below the agreement name on the top left of the Agreement window.

11. Click on **Deploy** to make the agreement available for runtime processing.

Creating the composite: B2Bprocessing

Create the composite that uses this agreement. When completed, it looks like the following figure:

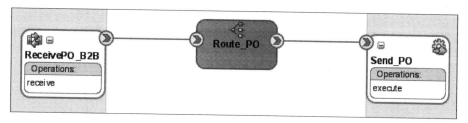

In JDeveloper, create a new SOA application called B2Bprocessing with a project called B2Bprocsesing starting with an empty composite.

First create a B2B service called receivePO_B2B.

1. Drag-and-drop a **B2B Service** to the left swim lane and enter the following values:
    - **Service Name**: ReceivePO_B2B
    - **B2B Integration Type**: Default
    - Pick server connection and set port to the SOA Server at port 8001 and click on the **Test B2B** button
    - **Operation**: Receive
    - **Document Definition Handling**: Basic
    - **Document Definition**: **Custom**, select (navigate tree): **PurchaseOrder_def**

2. Define a Web Service reference called **Send_PO**.

3. Drag-and-drop a Web Service reference to the right swim lane. Name the service Send_PO.

4. Click on the icon next to the **WSDL URL**. Select **Resource Palette**, and select **receivePO**. This puts the URL of the **receivePO** WSDL in the **WSDL URL** field.

5. Create and configure a Mediator called **Route_PO**. Drag-and-drop a mediator component. Call it **Route_PO**. Select **define the interface later**.

6. Wire the mediator to the B2B service on the left, and the PO service on the right.

7. Define a simple one-to-one transformation to map the input to the output.

Testing the process

1. Deploy the process.

2. Drop one of the sample input files supplied in `c:\po\input` (any of the files starting with MarketInc) into the input directory (`c:\orclsrvs_in`).

3. The input file is picked up and the B2B adapter calls POProcessing. View the new instance of POProcessing in Enterprise Manager.

4. Go to the Oracle B2B console to view the metrics using the **Reports** and **Metrics** links on the top right.

   - Review **Reports**—click on **message Details** link to see details:

     ○ **Wire Message**: Review details and URL. The wire message is the message received by the host from the trading partner.

     ○ **Business Message**: Review detail and data. This is the message after translation.

     ○ **Application Message**: Review details, Application Name, Composite Name / Version, Reference, Service, etc. This is the message delivered to the composite.

   - Review **Metrics**.

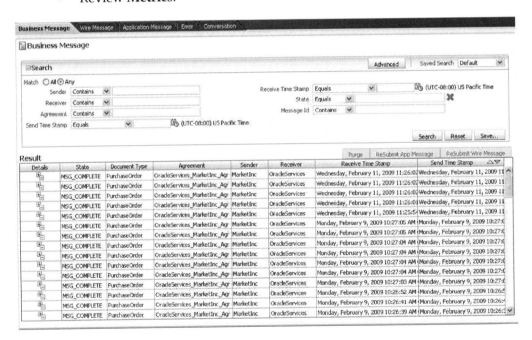

Summary

The B2B component of Oracle SOA Suite 11*g* provides you with the ability to extend your processes beyond your enterprise and reach out to your trading partners. In this chapter, you have learned how to use the B2B console to define documents, create trading partners profiles and agreements, as well as listening channels. You have also seen how the new B2B binding in 11*g* greatly simplifies the interconnection of SOA processes to the B2B server. With this knowledge, you should now feel comfortable about diving in the world of business-to-business integration to extend your business processes.

Quick-build Instructions

This section gives you all of the operations and names for objects created in this chapter. Experienced users can use this to bypass the step-by-step instructions and complete this chapter more quickly. The complete details for any particular operation listed here can be found in the preceding sections. The information is organized in the same manner that it is introduced in the chapter.

- Create a document definition:
    - **Document protocol**: custom
    - **Version Name**: 1.0
    - **Document Type**: PurchaseOrder
    - **Document definition**: PurchaseOrder_def
    - **Schema**: po.xsd
    - **Identification Expression**: //*[local-name()='PurchaseOrder']
    - **Routing ID**: PurchaseOrder10
- Define the trading partners:
- Change host trading partner name.
    - **Name**: OracleServices
- Define the MarketInc trading partner:
    - **Name**: MarketInc
    - **Document**: PurchaseOrder_def
    - **Sender**: Check
    - **Receiver**: Uncheck

- Create a listening channel:
  - ◦ **Name**: File_ListeningChannel
  - ◦ **Protocol**: Generic File-1.0
  - ◦ **Polling Interval**: 5
  - ◦ **Folder Name**: c:\orclsrvs_in
  - ◦ **Enable Channel**: Selected
  - ◦ **Internal**: Uncheck
- Create agreement:
  - ◦ **Partner**: MarketInc
  - ◦ **Document**: Custom-1.0-PurchaseOrder-PurchaseOrder_
    def
  - ◦ **Agreement ID**: OS_MI_1000
  - ◦ **Name**: OracleService_MarketInc_Agr
- Validate and deploy:
- Create Composite: B2BProcessing.
- Create B2B service binding:
  - ◦ **Name**: ReceivePO_B2B
  - ◦ **B2B Integration Type**: default
  - ◦ **Operation**: Receive
  - ◦ **Document Definition Handling**: basic
  - ◦ **Document Definition**: PurchaseOrder_def
- Define Web Service Reference:
  - ◦ **Name**: Send_PO
  - ◦ **WSDL URL**: WSDL URL of **receivePO**
- Define Mediator component:
  - ◦ **Name**: Route_PO
  - ◦ Define interface later
  - ◦ Wire mediator to B2B service and Web Service reference.
- Define simple one to one transformation.

The application is completed. Deploy and test.

20
Concluding Remarks

Congratulations! If you did most or all of the exercises in this book, you will have gained a lot of useful experience towards building SOA composites. The tutorial covered many of the key features of SOA Suite 11gR1 including the foundational infrastructure, mediator, database and file adapters, BPEL, human workflow, rules and decision tables, and JMS. The tutorial also provided you an introductory exposure to the related topics like service life cycle management, unit testing, fault handling, security, events handling, SDO, BAM, B2B, service bus, and registry/repository. You also experienced how Oracle, leveraging SCA concepts and a user-friendly product architecture that is well integrated and spans the full life cycle of development to deployment to management, has made the task of working with complex SOA composites relatively easy.

With SOA Suite 11gR1, you can *compose* your solution either in a *top-down* fashion or in a *bottom-up* fashion. In a top-down approach, you would start with a layout of all the necessary components inside the composite, while in a bottom-up approach, you would start with already available services and the composite will orchestrate those services. Of course, most real-life problems will require a combination of these two approaches. The composites that you would create can be useful in a variety of situations. When looking for patterns of composite usage, often it is convenient to consider potential consumers of these composites. As we alluded to in Chapter 1, consumers of composite services could range from purely machine applications to those requiring a lot of human interactions. For example, web sites or portal frameworks may invoke web service interfaces of composites via SOAP over HTTP. The use cases cover both fetching data for presentation in portal pages and initiation of actions in backend applications, for example, kick-off processes, record data items entered on the portal pages, and so on.

In an integrated business environment, a typical **commercial-off-the-shelf** (COTS) application needs to interact with other applications and processes. It (the COTS application) may do so by many possible means: by invoking web services, through message queues, through custom code such as Java programming hooks, or by using adapters. Composites built with SOA Suite 11g can expose their functionalities via web services, communicate through message queues like JMS, and interact through Java APIs or via a wide variety of adapters that are available to work alongside the SOA Suite infrastructure, and thus help in application integration.

Organizational efficiency is closely tied to process management, where the processes may facilitate one or a combination of automated system-to-system interactions, document processing, or human workflow type activities. Composites can be very useful in supporting process management platforms—in some cases, they could encapsulate the whole process, and in others, they may represent the activities that are sequenced or orchestrated in order to realize the process.

A business transaction that may be supported by a composite can either generate events or be impacted by events. For example, external events could initiate, suspend, roll-back, or terminate a transaction. Similarly, events originating from the transaction can provide valuable insight. As we showed you in an earlier chapter, SOA 11g has made the handling of events within its infrastructure as easy as handling services.

We would also like to remind you that **operational features** of SOA composites, such as reliability, availability, scalability, performance (or RASP), and security of SOA composites are just as important as basic functional features. In addition, the use of properly designed service contracts is one of the key strategies for achieving change resilience. In the past, it has been quite common for project owners to dismiss the potential use of SOA assets by concern around operational features and change resilience. So, our advice for you is to consider these aspects sufficiently early during the implementation of SOA composites and review how Oracle SOA Suite 11g is handling the RASP aspects.

So, what's next? The first thing we would suggest is that you **repeat the exercises** (or some variants of them) sometime soon—this will further enforce the learning that you have just acquired. Of course you can always use the step-by-step instructions; however, what about taking a less directed path this time around and instead use the functional and design sections of the chapters, along with the quick-build instructions, and try to implement the necessary features on your own? You will probably end up implementing the assignment in half or less the amount of time than the first attempt, and you will come away with a much better overall understanding.

The next thing would be to further explore SOA Suite 11*g*. SOA Suite is a general-purpose tool-set that can easily handle problems of much wider variety and greater complexity than covered in the tutorial exercises. This product has been designed in a way that it is suitable both for creating solutions of departmental and for enterprise-level problems. Select some actual problems and apply your knowledge of SOA Suite to solve them. If you have the option, start with simpler projects and progressively take on more difficult and mission-critical ones as your SOA 11*g* skills and confidence increase.

Finally, it is worth noting that SOA Suite is a key component of the larger **Oracle Fusion Middleware (FMW)** offering, which provides a complete set of tools for the creation, integration, and management of modern business applications: development environment, portals, and so on. We invite you to leverage more of SOA Suite and Fusion Middleware as you strive to deliver higher business value.

Index

Thank you for buying
Getting Started with Oracle SOA Suite
11*g* R1 – A Hands-On Tutorial

About Packt Publishing

Packt, pronounced 'packed', published its first book "*Mastering phpMyAdmin for Effective MySQL Management*" in April 2004 and subsequently continued to specialize in publishing highly focused books on specific technologies and solutions.

Our books and publications share the experiences of your fellow IT professionals in adapting and customizing today's systems, applications, and frameworks. Our solution based books give you the knowledge and power to customize the software and technologies you're using to get the job done. Packt books are more specific and less general than the IT books you have seen in the past. Our unique business model allows us to bring you more focused information, giving you more of what you need to know, and less of what you don't.

Packt is a modern, yet unique publishing company, which focuses on producing quality, cutting-edge books for communities of developers, administrators, and newbies alike. For more information, please visit our web site: www.packtpub.com.

Writing for Packt

We welcome all inquiries from people who are interested in authoring. Book proposals should be sent to author@packtpub.com. If your book idea is still at an early stage and you would like to discuss it first before writing a formal book proposal, contact us; one of our commissioning editors will get in touch with you.

We're not just looking for published authors; if you have strong technical skills but no writing experience, our experienced editors can help you develop a writing career, or simply get some additional reward for your expertise.

BPEL Cookbook: Best Practices for SOA-based integration and composite applications development

ISBN: 978-1-904811-33-6   Paperback: 188 pages

Ten practical real-world case studies combining business process management and web services orchestration

1. Real-world BPEL recipes for SOA integration and Composite Application development

2. Combining business process management and web services orchestration

3. Techniques and best practices with downloadable code samples from ten real-world case studies

Business Process Driven SOA using BPMN and BPEL

ISBN: 978-1-847191-46-5   Paperback: 328 pages

From Business Process Modeling to Orchestration and Service Oriented Architecture

1. Understand business process management and how it relates to SOA

2. Understand advanced business process modeling and management with BPMN and BPEL

3. Work with tools that support BPMN and BPEL (Oracle BPA Suite)

4. Transform BPMN to BPEL and execute business processes on the SOA platform

Please check **www.PacktPub.com** for information on our titles